12   Mid-Century World

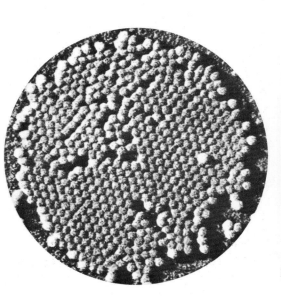

1950

1953

1953

Newsweek Books New York

Editor Roger Morgan

1956   1956   1957   1958

Milestones of History

12 Mid-Century World

1962

1962

1964

1967

ISBN: Clothbound edition 0-88225-080-9
        Deluxe edition 0-88225-081-7
Library of Congress Catalog Card No. 73-86878

© George Weidenfeld and Nicolson Ltd, 1970 and 1975
First published 1970.   Revised and expanded edition 1975
Printed and bound in Italy by
Arnoldo Mondadori Editore—Verona

1967   **1969**   **1971**   **1973**

1973

1973

1974

1974

Contents

Introduction

One of the main features of world history during the third quarter of the twentieth century was the phenomenon of interdependence. Events in one part of the globe set off a chain reaction whose effects would be felt acutely far away: at the beginning of this period the Korean War had an immediate and profound impact on the course of East-West relations in Europe, and at the end of the period, in 1973–74, the quadrupling of world oil prices in the aftermath of the Yom Kippur War affected economic and political relationships in every part of the world.

The Korean War marked the most acute phase of the Cold War between the Soviet bloc and the Western world. With major military forces engaged on both sides, the international struggle was clearly more than a battle of ideas. Even when an uneasy peace came to Korea in 1953, bloody fighting was still going on in Indochina, where the French Fourth Republic saw its struggle to maintain French influence as a part of the worldwide contest against Communism lead to disaster.

Only with the achievement of a provisional peace settlement in Indochina in the summer of 1954, after the humiliating French defeat of Dien Bien Phu, could the statesmen of East and West really explore the possibilities of replacing the Cold War by some form of coexistence or even cooperation. In 1953, when the death of Stalin had opened up new hopes of a better world, the British Prime Minister Winston Churchill had spoken of the need to strive for "a new Locarno"—a new version of the 1925 reconciliation between France and Germany—but the Cold War was not to be overcome so easily. The East German rising of June, 1953, was brutally suppressed by the Red Army, and the West German state, thanks partly to the impact of the war in Korea, was rearmed and firmly embedded in the Western alliance. This meant that although the leaders of the two sides met in a long series of conferences—at Geneva in 1955 and 1959, at Camp David in 1960, at Vienna in 1961—the Cold War was far from giving way to real peace.

All that happened was that in a halting dialog interrupted by new crises—Suez and Hungary in 1956, Berlin in 1958 and 1961, Cuba in 1962—the major powers groped their way toward a less tense relationship.

One result of the relaxation of tension between the two blocs was a greater freedom of maneuver for the individual states within them. In the Communist world the process began soon after the death of Stalin, when the Chinese People's Republic challenged the Soviet Union's predominant position, and the smaller states of Eastern Europe began to explore the possibilities of greater independence. The Italian Communist leader Palmiro Togliatti coined the term "polycentrism" to describe this new decentralization of power in the once monolithic Soviet bloc. The Russians were determined to set limits to the process—as the East Germans discovered in 1953, the Hungarians in 1956, and the Czechs in 1968—but the Communist world was quite clearly, by the 1960s, divided in a way that Stalin would not have recognized.

The West had its "polycentrism" too, of which the leading spokesman was President Charles de Gaulle of France. After extricating France in 1962 from the Algerian deadlock (which had in fact destroyed the Fourth Republic in 1968, bringing de Gaulle back to power at the head of the Fifth), he turned his attention to building up France's independent position in world affairs. De Gaulle defied both the idea of an Atlantic Community preached by President John F. Kennedy and the reality of the European Community of six nations, to which France had belonged since 1958. Although no other state in the West carried the pursuit of national independence to the same lengths as France, and both the Atlantic alliance and the European Community survived into the 1970s, there was no doubt that the world was returning to a period of nation-state independence very different from the tense confrontation of the two Cold War blocs.

This independence, however, was in many ways

more apparent than real. Even though in political and strategic terms the governments of the world seemed freer to explore new diplomatic relationships, to exchange visits and to develop new contacts between their peoples, the underlying reality was one of interdependence rather than independence. This remained true partly for economic reasons, as national economies became increasingly interwoven through the growth of cross-frontier investment, mergers and technological cooperation, but it was also important that the fundamental conflict of interests in power politics remained the one between the Western alliance and the Soviet-led Warsaw Pact.

By the early 1970s, the states of East and West were engaging in many-sided diplomatic negotiations in the pursuit of détente: the two superpowers were conducting the Strategic Arms Limitation Talks (known as "SALT" for short); most of the member states of NATO and the Warsaw Pact were discussing Mutual and Balanced Force Reductions ("MBFR"); and an assembly of more than thirty states with an interest in European affairs was engaged in the Conference on Security and Cooperation in Europe ("CSCE"), an attempt to break down the barriers between the two alliances.

Despite all these East-West negotiations, and despite even the spectacular diplomatic breakthroughs that had brought Communist China back into the international community and the two German states into the United Nations, the world in the mid-1970s remained divided between the Communist and non-Communist systems. The cohesion of the former continued to be strained by the underlying rivalry between Moscow and Peking; the cohesion of the latter by a series of economic pressures, of which the most acute was the energy crisis, and the unprecedented accompanying inflation, arising out of the Middle East war of October, 1973, and its aftermath.

The Yom Kippur War itself hardly interrupted the dialog between East and West, at least at the level of the two superpowers. Like the Vietnam war that had dragged on with increasing violence throughout the later 1960s and early 1970s, it provided a striking example of how local wars could be prevented from escalating and affecting the broader process of international relations. Political-crisis management between the superpowers, however, could not prevent the economic strains within the non-Communist world that resulted from a quadrupling of oil prices between 1973 and 1974. By the mid-1970s the Western world faced the prospect of uncontrollable inflation, grave economic recession and the consequences of political conflicts both within and between states.

We should remember that this new threat of economic turbulence came on top of a decade of radical changes within society, whose effects had been felt in varying degrees throughout the world. The claims of underprivileged racial groups, the student revolt, the movement for women's liberation, were all aspects of a challenge to the established order of things that expressed the spirit of the 1960s and 1970s.

The combination of these economic, social and international pressures posed an unprecedented challenge to the political leaders of the world as it entered the last quarter of the twentieth century.

ROGER MORGAN

The Korean War

The ancient kingdom of Korea, a Japanese colony from 1910 until 1945, was divided after World War II into a Communist North and an anti-Communist South. In 1950, Northern forces invaded the South. The United Nations approved an American request to condemn the aggression, and a U.N. force was sent in. Despite intervention from China and bitter fighting up and down the peninsula, the Northern troops were forced back. At war's end, North and South remained divided along roughly the same lines as before, U.S. relations with China were further exacerbated, but the West had shown—as it had not at Munich—its resolve to stand firm.

The United Nations Security Council's decision on June 27, 1950, to defend South Korea against a North Korean attack, inaugurated the first war fought by an international body dedicated to collective security. When Robert Schuman, the French Foreign Minister, was told that President Truman intended to defend South Korea, his eyes filled with tears; "Thank God," he said, "this will not be a repetition of the past." He was thinking of the failure of the democracies to act in time against Hitler.

After the defeat of the Axis powers in 1945, Southeast Asia became rapidly involved in the world ideological struggle. China was soon conquered by Mao Tse-tung's Communist forces, and until the early 1960s Communist China remained a satellite of the Soviet Union. The defeated Nationalist leader, Chiang Kai-shek, fled to Formosa.

The United States attempted to band together the leading anti-Communist powers in Southeast Asia into a Southeast Asia defense organization, a Far Eastern equivalent of NATO. In 1949, Truman, who had refused to allow the Soviet Union a zone of occupation in Japan similar to its zone in Germany, was preparing to sign a peace treaty with Japan, which might well lead to Japan being incorporated into the anti-Communist defense arrangements.

The ancient kingdom of Korea could not remain unaffected by the onset of the Cold War, lying as it did adjacent to both the Soviet Union and China, and having been a Japanese colony from 1910 to 1945. During the wartime conferences at Cairo, Teheran and Yalta, the Allies promised ". . . that in due course Korea shall become free and independent" after the defeat of Japan. Roosevelt and Stalin had agreed at Yalta in February, 1945, that until Korea was ready for independence it should be governed by a four-power trusteeship.

When Japan surrendered, the 38th Parallel became the line to the north of which Japanese troops surrendered to Soviet forces, and to the south to American forces. In the American view, the Parallel was a military convenience until the trusteeship arrangements could be put into effect; certainly there was no economic rationale behind the demarcation, which cut off the industrial North from the agricultural South.

The Soviet Union, however, proceeded to treat the 38th Parallel as a permanent border between two different zones of Korea, and gradually they became separate states. North Korea became dominated by the Communist Korean National Democratic Front, which in November, 1946, obtained ninety-seven percent of the votes in a general election; the leader of the Front, Kim Il Sung, who had returned to Korea in 1945 as a major in the Soviet army, became Prime Minister of North Korea in 1948. Thus North Korea, which by 1949 comprised 9 million out of the total Korean population of 30 million, became part of the Communist bloc.

South Korea was dominated by the authoritarian, strongly anti-Communist Syngman Rhee. In 1948, South Korean elections, described by the United Nations Temporary Commission on Korea as "a valid expression of the freewill of the electorate in those parts of Korea which were accessible to the Commission," led to Rhee becoming President of the newly proclaimed Republic of Korea.

The two states lived in a state of uneasy tension for the next twenty-two months, with sporadic Communist guerrilla activity in the South being firmly and ruthlessly repressed by Rhee. Then, on June 25, 1950, in a surprise move, North Korean troops moved south of the 38th Parallel. The next day, Kim Il Sung argued that North Korea must

. . . liquidate the unpatriotic fascist puppet regime of Syngman Rhee which has been established in the southern part of the republic; they must liberate the southern part of our motherland from the domination of the Syngman Rhee clique.

Kim Il Sung, Prime Minister of North Korea which, unprovoked, invaded South Korea in June, 1950.

Opposite U.N. patrol manning a .05-caliber machine gun at an ambush point on the Han River. Acting through the U.N., the West's response to North Korea's aggression was immediate.

The Korean People's Navy. In the first phase of the war North Korea captured the Southern ports of Inchon, Kunsan and Yangdok.

Top Australian troops riding on a Centurion tank. The U.N. force comprised contingents from fifteen countries.

claimed that the invasion was originally Kim Il Sung's idea. Kim consulted Stalin who, after conferring with Mao Tse-tung, gave his approval.

Stalin, who had done his best to secure a zone of occupation in Japan, as he had done in Germany and Korea, was clearly perturbed at the build-up of American power in Japan. With the peace treaty ready for signature, he no doubt wished to show the Japanese that American protection was worth little. Misled by Communist ideology, Stalin felt that South Korea, being an "exploited" country, would welcome Communism with open arms: guerrilla activity in the South reinforced this belief.

Moreover, South Korea appeared to offer excellent possibilities for a swift takeover. For by the middle of 1949, all U.S. occupation forces had been withdrawn, and in March, 1949, the U.S. Far East Command had publicly excluded Korea and Formosa from the American defense perimeter. This was reiterated by the U.S. Secretary of State, Dean Acheson, in January, 1950. It must then have seemed to Stalin that South Korea could rapidly be overrun—the North Korean army gave itself a two-month deadline—without any serious risk either of American intervention or of a general war. Upon hearing of the North Korean invasion, Truman was confronted with what he described as "... the toughest decision I had to make as President." John Foster Dulles, at that time the U.S. special ambassador negotiating the Japanese peace treaty, cabled from Tokyo: "To sit back now while Korea is overrun by unprovoked armed attack would probably start a disastrous chain of events leading most probably to world war."

Truman did not hesitate. On the day of the invasion, he called a meeting of the U.N. Security Council which proceeded to condemn North Korea by a vote of nine to one, with Yugoslavia abstaining. Fortunately for the West, the Soviet Union was at this time boycotting the Security Council because of its refusal to seat Communist China in the place of the exiled Nationalists. Had the Soviet representative been present, he could, of course, have prevented U.N. action by using the veto.

When North Korea ignored the U.N. call to cease the invasion, Truman informed the Security Council on June 27, 1950, that he had "ordered United States sea and air forces to give the Korean government troops, cover and support. The attack upon Korea makes it plain beyond all doubt that Communism has passed beyond the use of subversion to conquer independent nations and will now use armed invasion and war." The Security Council endorsed the American action and, following a British initiative, recommended member-states of the U.N. to "furnish such assistance to the Republic of Korea as may be necessary to repel the armed attack and to restore the international peace and security in the area." Fifteen countries, including Britain, Australia, New Zealand and Canada, responded to this request by offering troops, and thirty more countries provided nonmilitary aid.

The United Nations Commission on Korea informed the U.N. Secretary General, Trygve Lie, that

... judging from actual progress of operations the Northern regime is carrying out a well planned, concerted and full scale invasion of South Korea, second, that the South Korean forces were deployed on a wholly defensive basis in all sectors of the Parallel, and third, that they were taken completely by surprise as they had no reason to believe from intelligence sources that invasion was imminent.

The Korean War had begun.

Why the North Koreans attacked at this particular time is not known. With her Soviet-trained army, North Korea would be unlikely to attack without Soviet approval. Khrushchev, in his memoirs,

On July 8, 1950, Truman designated General Douglas MacArthur, the hero of the Japanese war, as Commander in Chief of the United Nations forces. The struggle was to last for more than three years.

In the first phase of the war, North Korean forces surged into the South, overwhelming such opposition as they met. On June 28, Seoul, the South Korean capital, was captured, and by the middle of September U.N. and South Korean forces had been forced to retreat into the southeast corner of Korea, to the Pusan perimeter behind the Naktong River. "When it struck, it struck like a cobra," said MacArthur of the North Korean army.

To save the situation, MacArthur planned a daring naval raid on the captured South Korean port of Inchon, eighteen miles west of Seoul. Landing to the rear of North Korean forces, he succeeded in disrupting the Communist army, forcing it to fight a two-front war. Seoul was recaptured by the United Nations at the end of September: "Few people can have suffered so terrible a liberation," wrote R. W. Thompson, the war correspondent of the London *Daily Telegraph*. But, with South Korea freed, and the North Korean troops retreating and destroyed, the U.N. and particularly the United States faced a terrible dilemma. Were they to remain content with preventing aggression and liberating South Korea? Or should they advance beyond the 38th Parallel to reunite Korea in accordance with U.N. policy?

In July, 1950, Syngman Rhee had written to Truman, "for anything less than reunification to come out of these great sacrifices of Koreans and their powerful allies would be unthinkable." But the danger in attempting to reunify Korea by force was that it might bring China, and perhaps also the Soviet Union, into the battle.

Truman, however, convinced himself that China would be unlikely to intervene, and on September 15, 1950, told General MacArthur, "If there were no indication of threat of entry of Soviet or Chinese Communist elements in force ... [he] was to extend his operations north of the Parallel and to make plans for the occupation of North Korea." The following month Truman asked MacArthur, "What are the chances for Chinese or Soviet intervention?" MacArthur replied, "Very little. ... We are no longer fearful of their intervention." The General Assembly of the U.N. agreed by forty-seven votes to five with seven abstentions to work for "the establishing of a united, independent and democratic government in the sovereign state of Korea."

MacArthur crossed the 38th Parallel, and captured Pyongyang, the North Korean capital, on October 19. MacArthur then advanced rapidly toward the Yalu, the river between China and North Korea. "The war is very definitely coming to an end shortly," he declared, promising his troops that they would be home in time for Christmas.

But from this point, the tide of war began to turn against the United Nations forces. For, contrary to

U.S. Air Force B-29 bombers destroy two important railroad bridges north of Pyongyang in North Korea, July 27, 1950.

Left American troops patrolling No Man's Land along the 38th Parallel, the 1945 frontier between North and South Korea.

15

A South Korean officer briefing new arrivals to an outpost overlooking the Chorwon Valley in the demilitarized zone.

British and American expectations, Chinese "volunteers" began to attack MacArthur's forces. Chinese Premier Chou En-lai had made it clear that China would not allow the U.N. forces to conquer North Korea or approach the Yalu. "The South Koreans did not matter, but American intrusion into North Korea would encounter Chinese resistance," he had told the Indian Ambassador to Peking, K. M. Pannikar. But his warning had been ignored.

MacArthur continued to underestimate the threat from China. Within a week of the capture of the first Chinese volunteer on October 25, there were 180,000 Chinese troops in North Korea. MacArthur, however, refused to retreat, and continued the march to the Yalu in sub-zero temperatures.

The Chinese counteroffensive when it began was swift and sure. "Lo, and behold, the whole mountainside turned out to be Chinese," exclaimed one American commander. On December 5, 1950, Pyongyang had to be evacuated; by the end of 1950, the whole of North Korea was again under Communist control. "We face an entirely new war," claimed MacArthur.

At this point, public opinion reflected panic in the United States and Britain. Many thought that Korea would have to be evacuated. In the United States, over fifty percent of the population polled thought that a general war with China was imminent. Congress, which had previously called for strong measures against China, now claimed that the commitment to defend South Korea had been a mistake. In a press conference on November 30,

President Truman indicated that the use of the atom bomb had always been under "active consideration." An alarmed Prime Minister Attlee flew to Washington in an attempt to moderate American policy.

But, in fact, Truman realized that the attempt to unify Korea had failed, and that to wage all-out war against China ran the risk of breaking up the United Nations coalition, and of encouraging Soviet intervention either in Korea or in Western Europe. The British Prime Minister did not find it difficult, therefore, to convince Truman that the aim of the United Nations should be to limit Communist forces to the 38th Parallel, to preserve South Korea, rather than to unify Korea by force. Thus, after a brief attempt to liberate Communist territory, the United States was again fighting a strictly limited war.

The Korean War now entered its decisive phase. In the United States, Truman declared a state of emergency, while in Korea the Chinese advance continued relentlessly, and it did not stop at the 38th Parallel. The Chinese were attempting to secure by force a Communist Korea, just as MacArthur's forces had previously tried to secure a unified, anti-Communist Korea. On the last day of 1950, the Chinese army launched an offensive "to liberate Korea, . . . crush the imperialist aggression, . . . drive warmonger MacArthur into the sea." For the second time in the war, the Communists captured Seoul and the United Nations forces were in full retreat. Not until January 20 was the front stabilized to the south of Seoul, by General Matthew B. Ridgway's Eighth Army. Ridgway raised the morale of United Nations troops, and resisted a further Chinese offensive in February, 1951. His aim was to fight a war of containment, pushing the Chinese forces back to the 38th Parallel.

MacArthur, however, believed that a limited war of this kind could never succeed. He began to criticize the policy of the Truman administration publicly, and, allying himself to the Republican opposition in Congress, demanded the air bombardment of China, together with an economic blockade. The climax of this campaign came in April, 1951, when MacArthur addressed an open letter to a Republican congressman:

It seems strangely difficult for some to realize that here in Asia is where the Communist conspirators have elected to make their play for global conquest. . . . As you have pointed out, we must win. There is no substitute for victory.

Truman was left with no alternative but to replace MacArthur if he wished to retain civilian control of foreign policy and maintain the unity of the United Nations in Korea. But MacArthur's dismissal brought to the surface all the suppressed resentment of American opinion, astonished to find that America was involved in a war that she could not win. "We are trying to prevent a world war," Truman said, "not to start one," but his popularity sank to a miserable twenty-nine percent, while there was a surge of emotional support for MacArthur. In Britain, Aneurin Bevan and Harold Wilson resigned from Attlee's government in protest at the rearmament program imposed by the necessities of war in Korea, and the left began to attack the Anglo-American alliance. The U.N. coalition seemed to be disintegrating.

What held it together was the military skill of MacArthur's successor as leader of the U.N. forces in Korea, General Ridgway. He was able to recapture Seoul in March, and to repulse a third Chinese offensive aimed at retaking Seoul by May Day as a present for Stalin. A final Chinese assault in May was repulsed with heavy losses, and, by the end of May, most of South Korea was held by U.N. forces.

It was now clear that neither side could hope to unify Korea by force, and neither Communists nor the U.N. were willing to risk an extension of the war. At the United Nations, Dean Acheson, the U.S. Secretary of State, said of Korean reunification, "I do not understand it to be a war aim," and the stage was set for armistice negotiations to begin on July 8, 1951, first at Kaesong, and then at Panmunjom, just south of the 38th Parallel.

These armistice negotiations lasted more than two years before a cease-fire could be signed to go into effect July 27, 1953. The main problem at issue turned out to be the question of repatriation of prisoners, North Korea demanding that all captured prisoners on either side be returned, the United States, fearing for the fate of anti-Com-

American soldiers who have been hiding in a cave are taken prisoner by Chinese "volunteers."

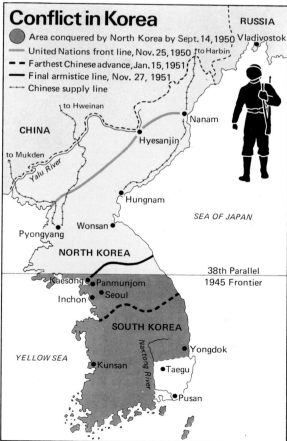

Conflict in Korea

- Area conquered by North Korea by Sept. 14, 1950
- United Nations front line, Nov. 25, 1950
- Farthest Chinese advance, Jan. 15, 1951
- Final armistice line, Nov. 27, 1951
- Chinese supply line

RUSSIA
Vladivostok
to Harbin
to Hweinan
CHINA
to Mukden
Yalu River
Hyesanjin
Nanam
Hungnam
SEA OF JAPAN
Wonsan
Pyongyang
NORTH KOREA
38th Parallel
1945 Frontier
Kaesong
Panmunjom
Inchon
Seoul
SOUTH KOREA
Naktong River
YELLOW SEA
Yongdok
Kunsan
Taegu
Pusan

U.N. troops firing their weapons as they advance up a hill.

Opposite above Keeping watch, through camouflage netting, on North Korean activity across the Imjin River.

Opposite below A South Korean policeman mans a 30-caliber machine gun in a turret at the easternmost checkpoint of the demilitarized zone.

munists forcibly returned to the North, insisting that repatriation be voluntary. By May, 1953, the new Republican administration of General Dwight Eisenhower in the United States had finally lost patience and, in Eisenhower's words, declared that if a truce was not signed, "We could not hold it to a limited war any longer. . . ." This was interpreted as meaning that the United States was willing to carry the war to China and to use the threat of the atomic bomb. This threat, together with the liberalization in the Soviet Union that followed the death of Stalin on March 5, 1953, persuaded China to end the war. Syngman Rhee solved the problem of repatriation by simply releasing any prisoners of war who were unwilling to return to Communist territory.

The armistice agreement reflected the military stalemate. A new border between North and South in Korea paid more attention to the facts of geography than the 38th Parallel had done, and South Korea gained a marginal amount of territory in the process. Other articles of the agreement proved ineffective: a call for the limitation of armaments by North and South was ignored, as was the pro-

posal for a political conference to unify Korea. North and South Korea became integrated more closely into their respective military blocs.

In the United States, resentment at fighting a war that could not be won led to Eisenhower's election as President in 1952, and the end of the Democratic Party's twenty-year rule. In their frustration, many Americans found comfort in the anti-Communist hysteria of Senator Joseph McCarthy. Korea dented the "illusion of American omnipotence," even if it was to require a further war in Southeast Asia finally to shatter it.

Communist China first emerged as a world power during the Korean War, for it was the military protection that Mao's China gave to North Korea that frustrated the original United Nations aim of unifying Korea. The Korean War widened the rift between China and the United States. Eisenhower determined to treat China as an outlaw in world affairs by refusing to recognize the regime of Mao Tse-tung and clinging to the illusion that Chiang Kai-shek spoke for the Chinese people. Formosa and South Korea became part of the American defense perimeter, and the Southeast

Asia Treaty Organization (SEATO) became a Far Eastern NATO, part of a global policy of containing Communism.

The United Nations decision to aid South Korea was not, however, entirely futile. Its success in halting North Korean aggression deterred further aggression from the Communist bloc. The Communist powers concentrated their efforts upon the newly independent, ex-colonial states, and military warfare was replaced by political and economic offensives.

It would be mistaken, however, to see the effective response to aggression as a success for the United Nations. For the U.N. could only act because Russia was boycotting it. As the United Nations grew in size, and came to be dominated by the "Third World" states, the disparity of views was to make rapid action even more difficult. But what made the decision to intervene in Korea a milestone was that it demonstrated the determination of the West not to repeat the mistakes of the 1930s, when appeasement coupled with disunity had led to disaster on a world scale.

VERNON BOGDANOR

Indochina

While the world's attention was concentrated on Korea, elsewhere in the Far East a struggle was beginning that was eventually to involve the United States in the longest and costliest foreign war of her history. Initially, however, the battle for Vietnam did not involve America. France's hold over the different regions of Indochina had been threatened since before World War II by both nationalist and Communist opponents. In Vietnam, in particular, the Communist Party, formed in 1930 by Ho Chi Minh, became the most effective opponent of the French reoccupation after World War II.

Although by 1947 the Communists were strong enough to start an armed struggle and to "liberate" many rural areas, they could not compete in military strength with the French colonial forces. The Communists instead adopted guerrilla tactics, while the French—unsuccessfully—sought to force the rebels into the open. Despite substantial reinforcements from France—there were eventually nearly 200,000 French troops in Vietnam—the French found their power increasingly restricted to the larger towns.

The success of the Communists in China made it increasingly unlikely that the French could ever hope for outright military victory in Vietnam; the Chinese could supply pro-Communist troops without difficulty while the French were dependent on an unwieldy supply situation. The French military command, however, believing

that decisive victory was near, failed—as the Americans were later to do—to recognize the grim reality of the strategic situation. Also, as was to happen later in the United States, French public opinion, which at first had favored the war, began to swing against the continuation of *la sale guerre* (the dirty war).

In Vietnam itself the French tried to build up an effective army and in the fall of 1953 a major Franco-Vietnamese operation under General Henri Navarre was launched against the Communists. The operation led merely to the isolation of numerous small French garrisons in villages in southern Annam. This was to prove serious enough in itself, but its consequences were even worse. A large French garrison—twelve battalions—had been gathered at the strategically important village of Dien Bien Phu in the northwestern corner of the country, near the Laotian and Chinese borders.

It was around Dien Bien Phu that the decisive battle of the war was to be fought. The Communists brought in 40,000 men, supported by heavy artillery, to besiege the village. The French reinforced their garrison with six more battalions before the airstrip was destroyed. On March 13, 1954, the Communists under General Vo Nguyen Giap launched a major offensive and after fifty-five days the massive French defenses collapsed to the unconcealed amazement of the French high command.

The loss of Dien Bien Phu forced the French to conclude a hasty settlement with the Vietminh at the Geneva peace talks, which led to the partitioning of Vietnam. The North became a Communist

state with its capital at Hanoi, while the South, governed from Saigon rather than the old imperial capital of Hue, was recognized as an independent and sovereign state, and Ngo Dinh Diem (1901–63) formed a government which deposed the last Emperor, Bao Dai. The formation of South Vietnam was to the enormous pleasure of American Secretary of State John Foster Dulles, who said, "We have a clear base there now without taint of colonialism . . . . Dien Bien Phu was a blessing in disguise." As the French withdrew, a new era of peace seemed about to begin, but neither the Communist North nor the nationalist South was serious in wanting peace. As a result the peace was little more than a truce, acceptable to none of the participants. The French had gone, but the Americans were now in danger of being drawn into the struggle.

Tibet

The determination of the Americans to protect Vietnam from Communist attack was in large measure due to fears that the fall of Vietnam would have a "domino effect" throughout Southeast Asia. The aggressiveness of the new Communist government of China was the main reason for this fear. The war in Korea had in part been a nationalist struggle, but the Chinese had invaded another country—Tibet—where they had found almost no local support for their territorial claims.

China had often claimed sovereignty over Tibet in the past, and had sometimes succeeded in exercising it. Mao Tse-tung had made clear his belief that Tibet was an

The Dalai Lama escaping from Tibet disguised as a servant.

integral part of China within a few months of his final conquest of the mainland. In 1950, the Chinese forced the Dalai Lama to acknowledge Chinese sovereignty, and early in 1951, 20,000 Chinese troops were stationed in Tibet. The Tibetan government fell increasingly under Chinese control over the next few years, and rumors from the Himalayan state suggested that forced reforms were taking place. In 1959 there was a rising against the Chinese, which was put down with great brutality after the flight of the Dalai Lama to India, and Tibet was formally absorbed into China.

Although the inward-looking nature of Tibetan society meant that events there aroused relatively little interest in the West, the United States saw the Chinese annexation of Tibet as another example of Communist aggression. This was only partly due to Cold War attitudes, as the Chinese claim to Tibet had at least some grounding in history.

Espionage and the bomb

The Cold War between East and West, Communist and non-Communist, had many other effects too. Russian anger at having been kept in the dark by the Western Allies about the existence of the atomic bomb during World War II, led the U.S.S.R. to undertake a massive nuclear-research program. During the postwar years, the military inferiority of Russia and her allies led to a deep-seated fear of the intentions of the Western Allies, who in 1949 had formed a military alliance, the North Atlantic Treaty Organization (NATO); but the result of the Russian armaments program of the Communist countries was to create Western fears and suspicions that were no less deep-seated.

The evacuation of wounded French soldiers after the fall of Dien Bien Phu.

Cold War rages between Russia and the West

In its search for atomic weapons the Soviet Union found espionage most valuable. Many of the Europeans who had emigrated from fascist countries in the 1930s were drawn by their hatred of fascism into sympathy for Communism. Many had been Communists and many more were "fellow travelers." Scientists such as Klaus Fuchs, arrested in 1950, and Bruno Pontecorvo, who defected in 1951, provided Moscow with valuable information about atomic weaponry. In the United States, Julius and Ethel Rosenberg were convicted of espionage and treason in 1951 and executed in 1953 in a case that would have reverberations years later. The Russians, who had not been expected to produce an atomic bomb until 1952 at the earliest, were able to do so in 1949 and it was widely believed that the stolen secrets significantly advanced their timetable. In a real sense, Russian possession of nuclear weapons marked the beginning of the end of the Cold War; military stale-

Harold Philby, a British Foreign Office official who spied for Russia.

mate had been reached and other considerations became more important. But it was not until after Stalin's death that the great thaw really began to get under way.

Military-scientific espionage was only one part of the postwar Russian intelligence network; political, diplomatic and industrial information was also assiduously sought. In 1951, for example, two British Foreign Office officials, Guy Burgess and Donald Maclean, defected to Russia in order to avoid questioning in connection with leakages of information. It was only twelve years later, when another

Foreign Office official, H. A. R. Philby, who was subsequently shown to have been a Communist agent for many years, defected to Russia, that the Foreign Office was able to clear up the mystery of how Burgess and Maclean had found out that they were under suspicion.

The West's espionage efforts in Communist countries were less widely publicized, but there is no reason to believe that they were any less extensive. The chief aim was, however, political subversion and propaganda, and as a result Western methods were rather different. The widespread use of high-powered transmitters, operated with funds largely provided by the Central Intelligence Agency (CIA), backed up the work of agents in the field.

McCarthyism

The Cold War attitudes engendered by fear and suspicion of the enemy without were directed also to the detection of the enemy within by the knowledge that espionage was so widespread. In most West European countries and to an even greater extent in the United States there was a deep distrust of nonconformists. Those who felt that possession of nuclear power created dangers for the world, those who spoke or wrote against the harsh rhetoric of the Cold Warriors, those who professed sympathy with socialist or sometimes even mildly liberal ideas, found that they were subject to persecution.

In the United States the role of chief witch-hunter was taken by Joseph McCarthy, the junior senator from Wisconsin. On February 9, 1950, in Wheeling, West Virginia, he accused the State Department of having Communist infiltrators among its staff. Only weeks later, he denounced the Democratic administration as being riddled with Communists. It was a charge that he was to repeat four years later when he described the previous two decades of Democrat power as "twenty years of treason."

None of the charges had any real meaning; there probably were a few Communists in the State Department, but there certainly were not enough to justify the outcry that followed, and it was obviously untrue to suggest that the Democrats had been helped by Communist support. But McCarthy's demagoguery had struck

Senator Joseph McCarthy, instigator of anti-Communist hysteria.

a deep chord in American society and he became a political idol almost overnight. For the next four years, he was a major influence in American domestic and foreign politics and had a decisive part in shaping American attitudes to the world. At home his denunciations of academics, civil servants and politicians were no less influential. Both Truman and Eisenhower found their attempts to produce a workable foreign policy and to attract worthwhile talent into the administration frustrated by McCarthy's obsessions.

The basis of McCarthy's power was enormously expanded in 1953, when he became chairman of the Senate Permanent Investigations Subcommittee, and used the committee to attack his enemies and to root out "Communists" from any office of responsibility. His crusade extended far beyond the confines of government. Eventually McCarthy overreached himself by a lengthy attack on Army Secretary Robert T. Stevens and on Brigadier General Ralph W. Zwicker, and the might of the U.S. Army proved stronger than that of the senator and in December, 1954, the Senate voted to "condemn" him for his activities. Thereafter his influence steadily declined. By that time, however, enormous damage had been done. One among the many who suffered from the atmosphere of hysteria had been Dr. J. Robert Oppenheimer, chairman of the advisers to the U.S. Atomic Energy Commission, whose security clearance was revoked; although Oppenheimer was often referred to as "the father of the bomb," he was by that time working on the peaceful application of atomic power.

While McCarthy remained an influence, popular hysteria prevented any kind of American détente with the Soviet Union. After his censure, however, the State Department was free to follow a more constructive foreign policy. It was perhaps no accident that censure of McCarthy followed close on the heels of the death of Joseph Stalin. Symptomatic of the thaw in East-West relations that this made possible was Russia's cooperation in medical research.

J. Robert Oppenheimer answering questions before a joint Congressional committee.

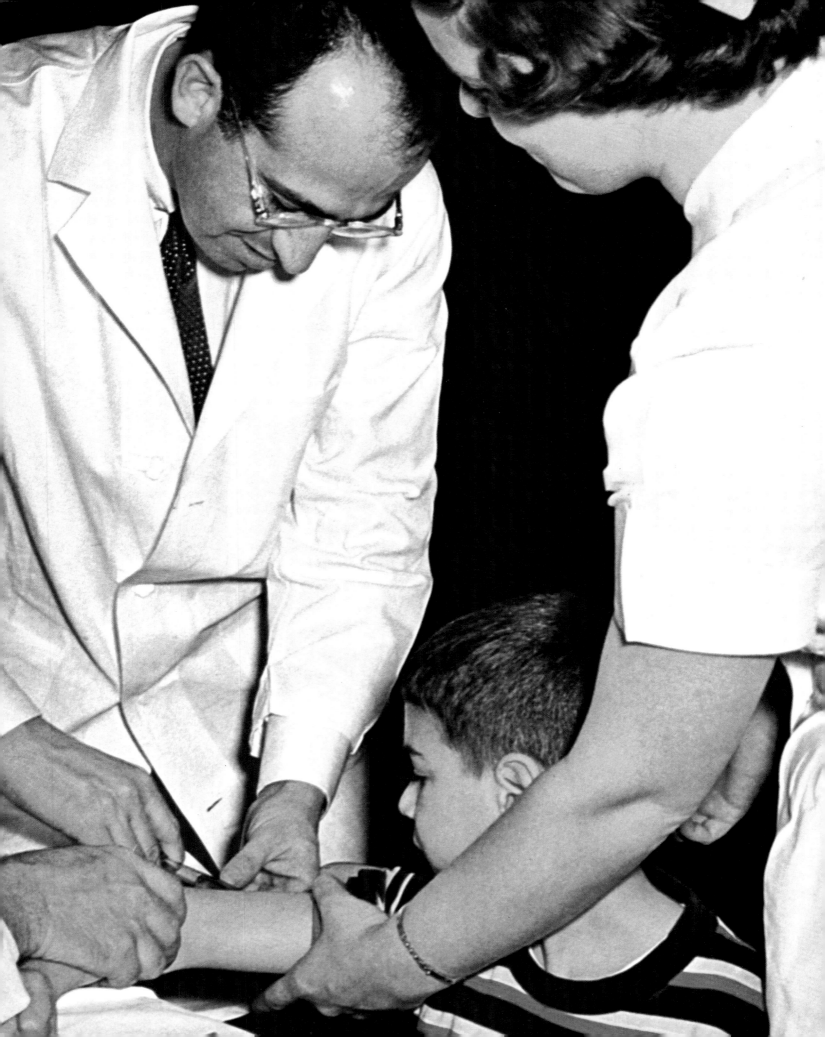

The Conquest of Polio 1953

One of the scourges of the twentieth century is polio—a disease that afflicts mostly children, leaving them crippled or even paralyzed. Although it had long been known to be of viral origin— meaning that immunization against it was at least theoretically possible—the disease proved intractable during the first half of the century. Finally, in 1953, Jonas Salk developed his killed virus vaccine. Tested the following year, it proved safe and effective. In 1961, Albert Sabin was to introduce his even more effective live virus vaccine. At long last, it was possible to wipe out a major disease by means of mass medication.

Even though man's fight against disease extends back to prehistoric times, no strong scientific basis for medicine developed until the nineteenth century. Even then, the advance of scientific medicine was slow. Mass medication is essentially a twentieth-century idea. With it came the concept not only of fighting disease, but of making particular diseases extinct. To plan the extermination of a disease, provision had to be made for testing therapeutic agents on a grand scale and for their subsequent administration in a way that would effectively blanket the population. Such large-scale planning is another twentieth-century phenomenon, reliant as it is on high-speed, effective communications. The earliest example of this modern approach to health-care delivery was the mass trial of Salk polio vaccine in the United States.

Poliomyelitis has been known since ancient times. On an Egyptian stele (engraved slab) of the Eighteenth Dynasty (1567–1320 B.C.) is depicted a youth with a withered leg, which is a characteristic feature of the disease. The fifth-century B.C. Greek physician Hippocrates mentions the disease, and, during archeological investigations in South Greenland earlier in this century, fifteenth-century skeletons showing bone deformations characteristic of polio were discovered. And yet, polio attracted little attention until modern times. The first recorded epidemic was in Stockholm in 1887.

There are two reasons for the neglect of polio in historical medical records. First, while polio may leave its victims permanently paralyzed, it does not always kill. Second, its rise to epidemic proportions only followed the growth of personal hygiene.

Polio is caused by an enteric virus, that is, one whose usual habitat is the intestines. Generally, if a child catches the virus before the age of three, the disease runs a mild and harmless course. At the same time it produces immunity. Consequently, in underdeveloped communities, with low standards of hygiene, it is probable that almost the entire populace had caught polio at an early age and become immune to it. With the growth of public-health standards, the incidence of early polio declined. Ironically this gave the disease an opportunity to reach epidemic proportions in unprotected communities, attacking people at an age when they were less able to resist the crippling side effects which arise when the virus attacks the nervous system.

During the first half of the twentieth century, polio—then called infantile paralysis, because it was children who most frequently contracted it— reached epidemic proportions almost every year in the United States, the most severe period being 1942–50.

The first major U.S. epidemic occurred in 1916, when more than 27,000 people were affected, and more than 6,000 deaths occurred. It was particularly lethal in New York City, where one in three of the victims died. A few years before this, the German doctor, Karl Landsteiner, who was responsible for discovering blood grouping, had shown that the causative agent for polio was a transmissible virus. This meant, in principle, that the disease could be combated by developing a vaccine; however, it was to be several decades before Jonas Salk produced the first effective vaccine.

Vaccines had been known since the end of the eighteenth century, when Edward Jenner in England developed the technique of inoculating people with the mild disease cowpox in order to protect them against the more severe smallpox. (The name vaccination reveals the origins of the technique—*vacca* is the Latin word for cow.) Jenner's procedure resulted from observation rather than scientific theory. He had noted that milkmaids who caught cowpox rarely suffered from smallpox—at that time a serious scourge. It was not until the late nineteenth century that vaccination was put on a scientific footing by the Frenchman Louis Pasteur.

Pasteur discovered that by treating the causative

Dr. Jonas Salk, photographed in the Salk Institute for Biological Studies at San Diego, California, in 1973.

Opposite Salk injecting a child during the mass field trial of his vaccine in 1954.

23

Mobile clinic for mass vaccination. Both Salk's killed virus vaccine and Sabin's even more effective live virus vaccine made it possible to reduce polio dramatically by mass medication.

agents of disease in various ways, it was possible to weaken or attenuate them so that they became less lethal but still conferred immunity against subsequent attacks. The human body contains elaborate defense mechanisms that come into play when disease strikes. In combating a disease, the body produces antibodies that specifically attack particles of that disease. Consequently, once one recovers from a specific disease, there is less chance of contracting it again because the antibodies are already present in the body to ward off attack. This does not work with all diseases, because some viruses are extremely labile—that is, they can so change their makeup that the antibodies no longer recognize them. This is why it is extremely difficult, for example, to produce a satisfactory flu vaccine. However, many disease-causing agents are more stable and the possibility of vaccine development is good.

In the case of polio, there were two false starts before World War II. In 1934, Maurice Brodie, of the New York City Health Department research laboratory, announced the development of a killed vaccine, while John Kolmer in Philadelphia claimed to have produced a live vaccine. In a killed vaccine, all the virus particles are dead (that is, nonvirulent); however, the body still reacts to them by producing the appropriate antibodies. The difficulty, as Salk later discovered, is in insuring that all the virus particles are truly nonvirulent, for a killed vaccine is made from virus particles that have not been

attenuated to an extent that would make them harmless. In a live vaccine, the attenuation process is supposed to have gone further—although here again there are problems, for an attenuated virus may be able to revert to a virulent form. In 1935, Brodie and Kolmer vaccines were tried out on more than 10,000 children. By the end of the year it had become clear that both vaccines were unsafe: instead of providing protection from polio, they could cause it.

As a result many virologists considered the polio problem too difficult to solve. At this time much less was known about viruses; the electron microscope, for example, which first made possible the study of the structure of viruses, was not developed until 1937. Additionally, it was difficult to get polio viruses to grow in materials suitable for carrying out experiments.

The problem seemed intractable until the late 1940s. In 1949, John Enders, a Harvard University virologist, found that the polio virus could be grown in tissue culture—an important technique if extensive research on a particular virus is needed. In the same year, David Bodian and his associates at John Hopkins University showed that there are three types of polio virus, each of which produces specific antibodies. Consequently, a truly effective polio vaccine must provide protection against all three.

It was after Enders' discovery that Jonas Salk became interested in polio. Salk, educated at the New York University College of Medicine, had

24

gone to the University of Michigan in 1941 to work on influenza vaccine with Thomas Francis, who had been professor of bacteriology at New York University. His work was supported by an organization called the National Foundation for Infantile Paralysis.

In 1921, following an electoral defeat, Franklin Roosevelt had gone to Campobello Island in New Brunswick, Canada, for a summer holiday. There he had contracted polio, which crippled him. In 1938, the National Foundation for Infantile Paralysis was inaugurated in his name. This body, which later changed its name to the National Foundation, relied on voluntary contributions. Although its main concern was with the prevention and cure of polio, in an era when few people were prepared to work directly on the polio virus, it supported other research into virology, since this could all have some bearing on the polio problem. Hence its support for Salk even before he turned his attention to polio.

In 1947, Salk moved to the University of Pittsburgh School of Medicine, where he ran the virus research program. Two years later, following Enders, he became interested in polio and worked on a massive National Foundation program on typing viruses. This research, which required 30,000 monkeys for its execution, confirmed that all known strains of the polio virus belonged to the three types discovered by Bodian and his colleagues. It was found that strains produced cross-immunity within each type, but varied greatly in virulence. Thus, an attack of polio caused by any Type I virus would produce immunity from attack by any other Type I virus, but not from Types II and III. The severity of the initial attack would depend on the virulence of the particular strain with which the victim was infected. At this point, it became clear that there was a strong possibility that a satisfactory vaccine

could be developed. The question was, should it be a live or a killed vaccine?

Salk believed that the greater chance of success would come from looking for a killed vaccine. However, other scientists disagreed with him: Albert Sabin, then at Cincinnati, and Hilary Koprowski and Harald Cox, of the Cyanamid Company, favored a live vaccine. There were points in favor of both arguments. As a killed vaccine was, in theory, totally nonvirulent, because it had been killed, it did not matter how virulent was the strain from which it was made. A live vaccine, on the other hand, needed to be made from a relatively innocuous strain, which would then be further attenuated. To find a suitable strain and attenuate it could, Salk felt, be much too long a job to be worthwhile.

To prepare a killed vaccine, Salk cultured polio virus strains in monkey kidney tissues, then mixed the tissue culture fluid with formaldehyde—a chemical that had been used for many years for preserving biological specimens. In working out the actual "killing" technique, it was necessary to reach a compromise: all the virus particles had to be killed, but the process ought not to go on too long, as this would decrease the effectiveness of the vaccine in stimulating immunity. In 1952, Salk tried out a vaccine made from a Type I virus on a group of Pennsylvania children who had already had polio. These children already had polio antibodies in their bloodstream; however, it was possible to tell from the increase in antibody levels whether the vaccine was stimulating the body's defensive system. (And, by using children who had already recovered from the disease, the chance of causing harm, if the vaccine was a failure, was minimized.)

A "triple vaccine"—that is, one containing a strain of each of the three immunologically distinct types of virus—was then tried on children who had

Below left Type II polio virus strain enlarged approx. 90,000 times under an electron microscope, which is 100 times stronger than an ordinary microscope, employing electrons rather than available light to form real images.

Cases of vaccine being counted before being dispatched all over the U.S.A.

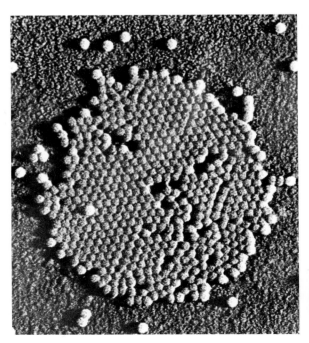

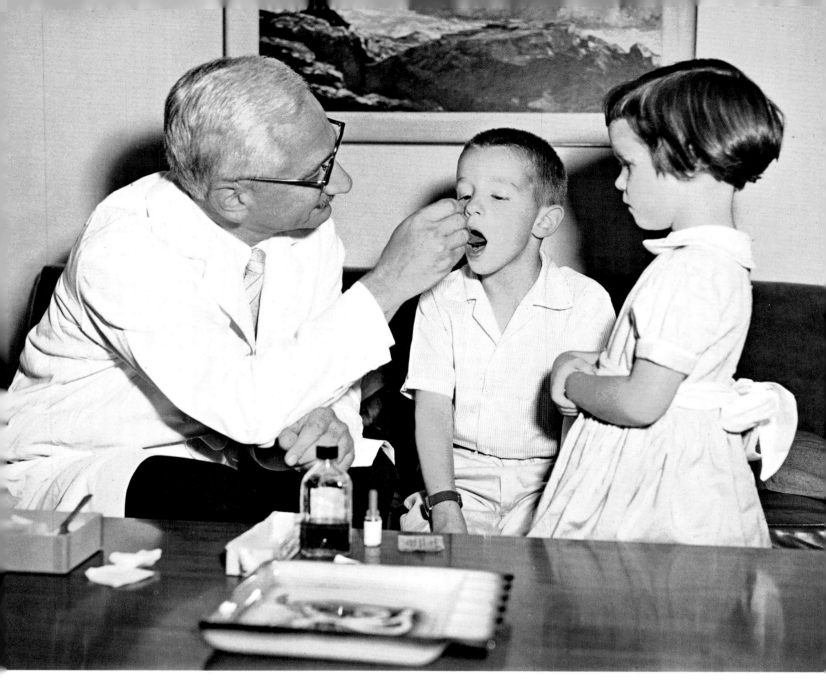

Dr. Albert Sabin administering his vaccine. A big advantage of the Sabine vaccine is that it can be taken orally—in syrup or on a lump of sugar —thereby conferring tissue immunity in the gut so that a "wild" polio virus subsequently taken in by mouth cannot multiply.

not had polio. Early in 1953, Salk published the results of this trial, which were encouraging, in the *Journal of the American Medical Association*.

It was then decided that a mass field trial of the vaccine was needed. Salk's mentor, Thomas Francis, agreed to conduct and evaluate the trial, which began on April 26, 1954. The National Foundation was the driving force behind the trial, although it did not meet with universal approval. A number of pharmaceutical companies had been called in to help prepare large quantities of Salk vaccine, and had found difficulties in producing the vaccine on a factory scale; Albert Sabin, the leading protagonist of live vaccine usage, opposed the use of the Salk vaccine. However, by the end of the trial, nearly two million children between the ages of six and nine had taken part in the experiment, all on a voluntary basis. Only a quarter of these actually received vaccine; an equal number received "placebo" injections, while the remainder received

no injections, but were observed to provide the statistical data against which the efficacy of the injections could be tested. "Placebo" injections— that is, injections similar in all respects to those of the material under test, except that the fluid injected is inert—are used in such experiments as a "double blind" to insure that the doctors administering the experiment are unable to bias the results, subjectively or otherwise.

On the tenth anniversary of Franklin Roosevelt's death, April 12, 1955, Thomas Francis made public his findings in a lecture at Michigan University that was telecast on closed circuit to invited audiences of doctors in theaters throughout the United States. His findings were favorable, although not unqualifiedly so: the Salk vaccine was effective in the majority of cases. However, the efficacy varied between virus types and was least effective against the commonest type, Type I. Different batches of vaccine also varied in efficacy, and some of those

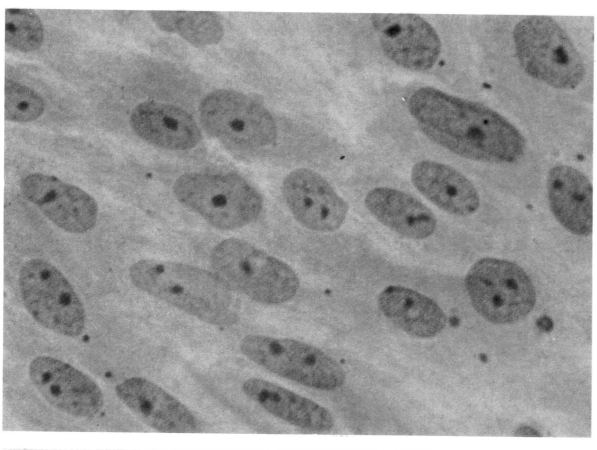

Healthy monkey's kidney
tissue.

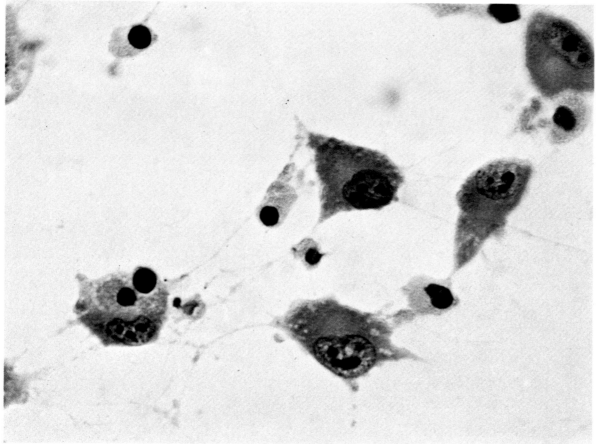

Monkey's kidney tissue after
receiving Sabin's attenuated
live vaccine.

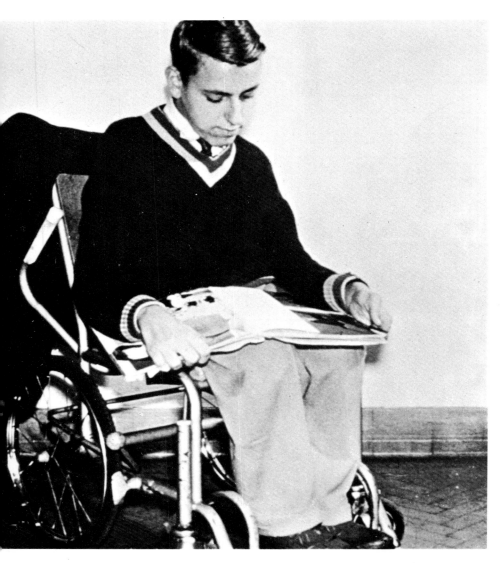

Although he has recovered from polio, this fourteen-year-old boy is condemned to life in a wheelchair because of the paralytic effects of the disease.

Chicago developed polio after receiving an injection of vaccine prepared by Cutter Laboratories. On April 26, exactly one year after the start of the mass trial, five California children injected with Cutter vaccine contracted polio: all of them suffered paralysis in the injected arm, an unusual place for symptoms to develop.

The United States Surgeon General withdrew all supplies of Cutter vaccine and set up a surveillance unit. However, it was too late to prevent further outbreaks. Twenty-two children in Idaho who had had Cutter vaccine developed the disease, and the infection was also reported in unvaccinated contacts. This meant, in effect, that the killed vaccine had still contained live virus particles. On May 6, at the Surgeon General's instigation, release of all further supplies of vaccine was banned. Further, it was discovered that all six pharmaceutical companies involved in vaccine preparation were having difficulty in manufacturing the material to Salk's specifications.

In June, a Congressional inquiry was held, at which Salk's method of inactivating the virus was attacked. However, once the public outcry had died down, new vaccine testing procedures were introduced and, by the end of 1955, seven million children had been vaccinated in the United States, with no further outbreaks of the disease among those vaccinated. In 1955, the incidence of polio in the United States was 29,000 cases; by 1957, this had dropped to 5,000. By 1961, the incidence of polio in the United States, as compared with the five-year period prior to the introduction of vaccine, had fallen by ninety-six percent. By this time, only fifty percent of the population had been vaccinated, and the greater reduction in polio incidence could be attributed to the "herd effect": by vaccinating part of a population, the amount of live virus in circulation was diminished, so that the disease incidence declined. For his work on the vaccine, Salk was awarded the Congressional Gold Medal.

However, this was not the end of the story—for there were still scientists, notably Albert Sabin, who believed in the greater usefulness of a live virus. Sabin, and others, had been working all the time on a live virus. However, once Salk's vaccine appeared to be a success, they found it difficult to focus public attention on their work, and even more difficult to arrange field trials. The Russian-born Sabin overcame this difficulty in a dramatic way. Despite the Cold War, in March, 1956, he sent samples of a Type I strain of polio, which he had attenuated in monkey kidney tissue, to Academician A. A. Smorodintsev, head of the U.S.S.R. Academy of Medical Sciences. In July, he sent samples of Type II and III strains which he had similarly attenuated. The Russians grew cultures of these live vaccines, tried them on monkeys, then in early 1957 began what must be the most massive medical experiment ever carried out. They started with small groups of children in 1957 and 1958, then, as they gained confidence in the vaccine, increased the numbers in the trials in 1959. On June 22, 1959, at

used in the trial had been ineffective. However, there was no evidence of danger from the vaccine. On the same day, Salk vaccine received a U.S. government license.

Running the trial and working out the results had taken nearly a year, and this had presented the National Foundation with a serious dilemma. If the results favored the vaccine, there would be a sudden demand for it; on the other hand, if it were unsafe, no one would want it. The pharmaceutical companies could not be expected to take the risk of manufacturing a product that nobody might want; and the U.S. government refused to take the risk. Consequently, before the results were announced, the National Foundation ordered 27 million doses of the vaccine (at a cost of $9 million) to keep the pharmaceutical production lines going. However, when the favorable results were made public, and the immediate demand for vaccine appeared, the 27 million shots were not ready. The companies involved were still having trouble making the vaccine. A public uproar broke out over the shortage of vaccine—to be turned on its head only days later by an even bigger uproar. A child in

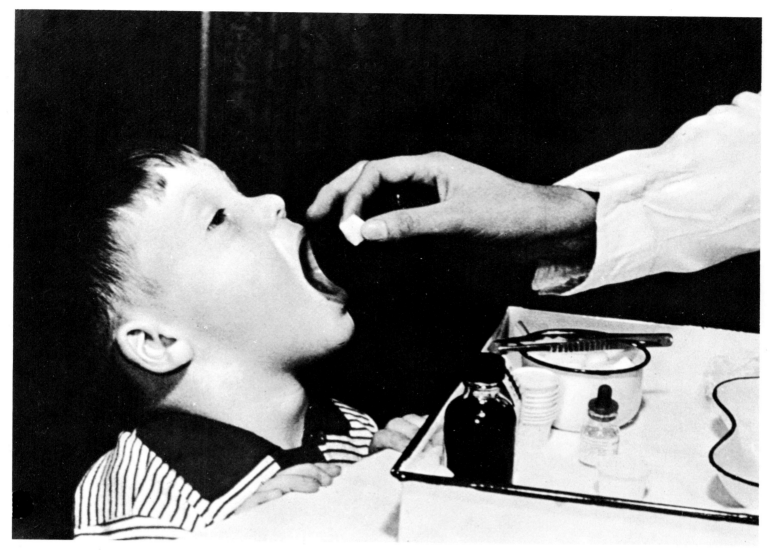

the International Congress on Live Virus Vaccines, Smorodintsev announced that four and a half million people in the U.S.S.R. had been dosed with live vaccine. He had been unable to find any reversion to virulence in the virus strains used, and the antibody response was good. In September of the same year, he announced that vaccinations had passed the six million mark, and, a month later in the United States, he announced that the Russians had now administered 10 million doses of Sabin vaccine.

At a conference in July, 1960, it was announced that during 1959 there had been twice as many cases of paralytic polio in the United States as in 1957. Part of the problem was the need for multiple shots of killed vaccine. The vaccine gave eighty percent of the population immunity after three shots, and ninety percent after four shots; but in many cases, people were not returning to clinics for the full number of shots. It also appeared that immunity gradually died away. By this time, the Russians had vaccinated more than 50 million people with Sabin's vaccine, and, on August 24, 1960, the vaccine received official U.S. government

backing. In July, 1961, the Pfizer pharmaceutical company produced the first commercially manufactured live vaccine. Early in 1962, Britain, which had been running a program of Salk vaccinations, officially changed to Sabin's vaccine.

About 500 million individuals throughout the world have now received doses of Sabin polio vaccine. Since 1961, Sabin has devoted much of his time to research on viruses that may cause cancer, although, from 1969 to early 1973, he was head of the Weizmann Institute in Israel. Jonas Salk, on the other hand, stayed in America: in 1963 he became Director and Fellow of the Salk Institute for Biological Studies at San Diego, California.

Poliomyelitis has not been completely eradicated. Partly this is due to the failure of government agencies in certain parts of the world to insure mass medication on a wide enough scale. However, the grand experiment in mass medication that began in 1954 has shown scientists and doctors that a concerted attack on a particular disease can, in a few years, reduce it dramatically.

MARTIN SHERWOOD

Child receiving Sabin's live virus vaccine on a sugar lump. Since its introduction live virus vaccine has been used increasingly throughout the world.

Death of a Tyrant

At his death, at the age of seventy-three, Joseph Stalin was about to embark on yet another series of purges—a means by which he had consolidated his power and kept his associates in a state of terror. His ruthlessness caused the elimination or relocation of millions of Russians—but it also resulted in creating modern Russia as an industrial nation, and in rebuilding her industry after the defeat of Hitler. "He fought barbarism with barbarism," said Nikita Khrushchev, "but he was a great man." Great or not, it seemed clear—and fortunate—that the circumstances that would produce another Stalin were unlikely to recur.

Floodlit memorial to Stalin prior to its unveiling in 1962.

Opposite Russians lining up to pay their last respects. Stalin's wartime leadership, personal charisma and state-fostered public image endeared him to the masses, despite the hardships caused by his coercive system.

When he collapsed of a brain hemorrhage on March 1, 1953, Joseph Stalin was seventy-three years old. Yet his resilience was such, and the strength of his heavy frame so great, that it was not until March 5 that the doctors finally pronounced him dead.

On the last day of February Stalin, together with four senior members of the Presidium of the Communist Party of the Soviet Union, had watched a movie at the Kremlin. Accompanied by these four, Lavrenti Beria, his chief of police, Georgi Malenkov, Nikolai Bulganin and Nikita Khrushchev, he then returned to his small country house outside Moscow for dinner. It lasted until the early hours of the morning, and when his guests left, one of them noted that he was jovial and a little drunk. They heard nothing more from the dictator until the next night, when he was found lying on the floor of his room, apparently asleep. It was not until the morning of March 2 that, at last, the doctors were called. There was little that they could do, though they administered oxygen, drugs and even folk medicine in the form of leeches. His close political associates together with his daughter, Svetlana, took turns watching beside the deathbed. In the last moments they looked on, powerless, as Stalin apparently choked to death. The official announcement was made early on March 6.

In many parts of Russia the news was greeted with something close to rejoicing. But celebration—if any—was muted and mixed with both fear and awe. Beria's security police were very much in evidence, and the newspapers reported in detail the lying-in-state and the burial of the embalmed body in the great mausoleum on Red Square, where it was laid to rest alongside the corpse of Lenin. The fact that it had been so placed, in the shrine dedicated to the memory of the supreme architect of the Bolshevik Revolution, seemed to indicate that there would be no drastic change in the nature of the Soviet regime.

But the pomp of the funeral was misleading. A press photograph of Stalin's lying-in-state itself provided indications of a new order. Behind the coffin of the dead leader were grouped twelve senior members of the Central Committee, in no very clear order. They included Kliment Voroshilov, an old and distinguished associate of Stalin from the days of the Revolution, Beria, Bulganin and Khrushchev; the picture projected was of what was described as a "collective" leadership. Stalin's policies would be continued, and his interpretation of Marxism would remain the essential theoretical basis for party decisions, but the style of leadership, the photograph implied, would change.

That style of leadership had been both personal and impersonal: personal in that the image of Stalin was everywhere, a figure both heroic and avuncular; impersonal in that what Stalin had built up was a monolithic and bureaucratic society, highly centralized and operating on rigid principles, which had been made to function properly by means of drastic and ruthless "purges." In practice this involved the death of millions of Russians and the imprisonment of many more. The justification for the price paid in human misery was the economic and industrial redevelopment of the country.

The process had begun with the economic plans formulated in 1928–29. The aim of these was to insure the maximum possible growth of heavy industry. So that this might be achieved many of the egalitarian ideals of the October Revolution were abandoned. The purpose of politics was to insure the triumph of this economic end, and the end itself was enshrined in the various economic plans. Individual initiative was discouraged, the last vestiges of a free market were systematically destroyed and, as a logical corollary, the peasants were forcibly collectivized. The purges served two purposes. They both provided a measure of flexibility where no such flexibility would otherwise exist and, because the "crimes" alleged against the victims

Destruction of the Stalin memorial in 1962, just after its completion. The de-Stalinization of Russia began in 1956, when Khrushchev publicly denounced the "personality cult" and crimes of Stalin's regime.

Stalin's body lying in state in the Hall of Columns in the House of the Unions near the Kremlin.

were held to be instigated by sinister forces working for foreign powers, they stiffened the morale of an embattled people.

Russia was soon to be embattled in reality. Anxious for the peace that his country needed if its economic development were to continue, Stalin had reached an agreement of kinds with Hitler. In June, 1941, Hitler showed how much he valued it by invading Russia. Before long German troops were within striking distance of Moscow and the Russian army, weakened by a recent purge of its most experienced officers, was in retreat. Stalin had done much to bring these disasters on his country, but he also proved to have the very qualities that the emergency demanded. His patriotic determination, expressed in speeches on the radio and on public occasions, gave Russians a sense of national cohesion and purpose. His ruthless expenditure of manpower held the Germans at bay and eventually turned the tide.

On June 24, 1945, at a victory parade in Red Square, Stalin expressed his thanks to his people for their sacrifices in the war. In the next few years it seemed his ambition to restore, as far as was possible, the state of things as it had been before the war. American possession of the atomic bomb gave a natural impetus to Russian fear of the capitalist countries; in foreign affairs this was the period of the Cold War. In domestic affairs it was equally a period of suspicion and rigidity. Stalin set about reducing the power of the army—which had naturally grown greatly in the war years, and was still of increased importance because it was needed to police the Russian sector of Eastern Europe. Successful generals were given remote and unimportant posts. A. A. Zhdanov, one of Stalin's most trusted colleagues, launched a campaign against freedom of expression in the arts, which extended to the proscription of works by well-known composers such as Sergei Prokofiev and Dmitri Shostakovich. Praise of Stalin in poetry and fiction was the only sure recipe for favor. And there were other, more brutal repressions. The war had given a chance for some of the national minorities in the Soviet empire to recover a sense of their separate identity, and Stalin resolved to stamp out such movements once and for all. Whole peoples, such as the Tatars from the Crimea and the Kalmucks from the North Caucasus and the Caspian Steppes, were forcibly relocated. There was a simultaneous, and deliberately fostered, growth of agitation against the Jews.

The war had cost Russia twenty million dead and many more wounded; the German invasion had devastated the areas that contained her heaviest concentration of industrial plant. Thus the return to the conditions of the 1930s was no mere whim of Stalin; the necessary work of reconstruction was vast. As Stalin saw it, the old methods would have to be used again. In 1946 he suggested that something like three more Five Year Plans were necessary in order to insure full recovery. Russia had to produce 50 million tons of pig iron, 60 million tons of steel, 500 million tons of coal and 60 million tons of oil if the economy was to recover fully and the country to be in a position to withstand the threat of yet another war. The Americans offered Marshall Plan aid, but this he rejected. It was not simply a matter of national pride; it was also essential to demonstrate the rightness of his system. In the countries of Western Europe the postwar period was austere; in Russia it was doubly so. The concentration on heavy industry meant that housing and consumer goods were in drastically short supply. The slave labor provided by the prison-camp system was an essential condition of economic recovery; the inmates who survived from the thirties or had been incarcerated during the war were joined by a new group, consisting of Russians who had been captured by the Germans. Former prisoners of war were seldom allowed to return to their families; because they had surrendered they were automatically suspect.

This return to the principles of tight planning and heavy industry recreated the necessary conditions for the purges. Bureaucracy developed on an even greater scale, and Stalin relinquished none of his enthusiasm for centralization. Management and workers were sharply differentiated, and the outlook and mentality of the Communist Party membership had changed accordingly. Lenin had seen the party membership as consisting primarily of intellectuals and workers, the intellectuals forming a cadre of ideologists who would demonstrate to the working classes their potential and their importance in the new order, and learn from the working classes the virtues of brotherhood and equality. Under Stalin the Communist Party became increasingly a party of managers, and the structure of management and

of the party came increasingly closer together. Workers still played their part, but membership was a matter of prestige rather than power. The extent to which the new order was hierarchical was reflected in the very considerable differentials of pay and status between managers and workers.

In 1949 there was a substantial purge of party members and senior officials; the most notable victims were Nikolai Kuznetsov, chairman of one of the constituent republics that make up the Soviet Union, and Nikolai Voznesensky, for some time head of economic planning. The early morning arrests and subsequent imprisonments and executions must have struck terror in the hearts of many of Stalin's colleagues. Yet, though his health had been impaired by the rigors of the war, and from 1946 onward he had taken to spending considerable periods away from Moscow in the South, Stalin's power seemed in no way diminished. From 1939 to 1952 there was no full-scale party congress. The supreme policy-making body, the Politburo, consisted of thirteen members, including Stalin. Stalin himself held three official posts: he was Chairman of the Council of Ministers, Minister of

Defense and First Secretary of the Party. He thus had control of the chief organ of government, of the armed forces and of the party machinery. Beria's security forces were an empire in themselves, but Beria was terrified of Stalin, who had dealt summarily with the two previous heads of the secret police, and served him loyally. Stalin's usual technique was to insure that his subordinates were split into opposing factions, to promote jealousy among them by giving and withdrawing favors, to maintain an atmosphere of uncertainty and to remain unpredictable himself. In his last years he had little contact with the people of Russia at large. Nevertheless there were times when some quite insignificant person in trouble might answer the telephone and find himself speaking to Stalin, who interested himself in many apparently trivial matters.

In the 1920s and 1930s Stalin had set much store by his abilities as a Marxist theoretician and seemed anxious to emulate Lenin in this respect. This preoccupation continued after the war, though his concern was more with other men's work than with the development of his own ideas. His public pro-

Stalin's funeral procession. In 1961 the dictator's corpse was removed from its place next to Lenin in the mausoleum in Red Square and cremated, and the ashes were interred by the Kremlin wall along with those of other leaders of the Revolution.

Lavrenti Beria, Stalin's chief of police. His execution at the order of the reorganized Presidium marked the beginning of collective leadership in Russia.

Berlin, June 17, 1953. East German demonstrators trample on border signposts. The change in Russia's leadership signaled a wave of unrest among her East European satellites.

nouncements embraced philology and biology, and he gave official sanction to the extraordinary and unscientific ideas of the geneticist Trofim Lysenko, who rejected the theory of heredity. Stalin's last major publication, *Economic Problems of Socialism in the U.S.S.R.*, appeared in 1952, in time for the first postwar party congress. In it he restated his central belief in the importance of heavy industry and planning. It could be seen as a statement of justified faith, for by the time of its publication Russia had just about recovered from the ravages of the war, and it was Stalin's ruthless application of these principles that had achieved this. At the same time it served as a stimulus for opposition; it epitomized all the restrictions and limitations of Stalin's outlook, and its consequences for Soviet society.

Awareness of this undercurrent of dissent seems to have prompted Stalin's final purge. This was heralded by an administrative rearrangement, by which the Politburo was abolished and replaced by a new "Presidium" of twice the size, and by complaints in the press about "lack of vigilance in the security forces." The next stage was the arrest of eight doctors, seven of them Jews who were active in a Jewish welfare organization, on the grounds that they had killed two members of the Politburo and plotted to poison a number of generals. Stalin was virulent in his demand that confessions should be extorted, and two of the doctors were tortured to death. The "confessions" were forthcoming, and it was alleged that the doctors were working for

British and American intelligence. A number of other arrests were made, chiefly of Jewish bureaucrats and academics. Diplomatic relations with Israel were broken off.

But the threatened purge, which had charged the air with the heaviness of a thunderstorm and lowered with all the menace of the worst times of the 1930s, did not break. The rumblings continued throughout January, 1953. Members of the Presidium were beginning to fear for their lives, yet only two senior officials were arrested and executed. Stalin's plans died with him, and if any trace of his intentions survived, his political heirs were quick to destroy them. A number of the inner caucus of the Presidium who lined up behind Stalin's coffin were surprised to have survived. But survival was not in itself an answer to the problem of how Russia should be ruled, and the supposedly "collective" leadership was a myth; technically there had never been a time when the leadership was not "collective." The question remained as to which men, and which policies, would emerge dominant, and as to the extent to which Stalin's methods and ideals would live on now that he was dead. There was nothing in the background or training of any of the men involved that made drastic change even a remote possibility.

Two of those present at Stalin's deathbed seemed, for a short while, to be in a position to take over something of his function. The first was Malenkov, who for a few days was both First Secretary of the

34

Party and Chairman of the Council of Ministers. But his post as Party Secretary was immediately taken from him by the Party's Central Committee, though he continued as Chairman of the Council—effectively Prime Minister. The second candidate was Beria, whose control of the security apparatus put him in an enormously powerful position. In June, 1953, the Kremlin was shaken by an outside event, a "revolt" by workers in East Berlin. Probably as a result of this there was a further reshuffling within the Presidium (now reorganized and reduced in size) and Beria was arrested and shot. The group had shown itself more powerful than the individual, and the death of Beria can be said to mark a turning point.

Malenkov lasted two years more, and insofar as it is possible to ascribe particular policies to him he appears to have placed an emphasis on the sectors of the economy neglected by Stalin. Consumer goods began to appear in greater numbers in the shops, the lines so characteristic of Russia after the war diminished in size and the official emphasis on work as the aim of life was relaxed. When, in 1955, Malenkov was forced to resign and replaced as Chairman of the Council of Ministers by Bulganin, the change was brought about publicly and without violence. Malenkov was relegated to the direction of a distant power station. His removal made possible a period of combined leadership by Bulganin and Khrushchev, who was now Party Secretary and ultimately the more influential of the pair.

Khrushchev, like Malenkov, was interested in those economic sectors that Stalin had ignored. His particular concern was with agriculture, and many of his policies, with an emphasis on controlled independence, ran counter to Stalin's ideals. His style of leadership was often distinctly personal, and he cultivated a public face as a frank, earthy man of the people. But it was never Stalinist, and his great achievement was to spell out what Stalin's death implied. At the Twentieth Party Congress, in 1956, 1,400 delegates heard Khrushchev denounce the "personality cult" that had grown up around Stalin, and the consequences of the accumulation of limitless power in the hands of one man. He recounted something of the inner history of the purges, and described the "Doctors' Plot" as "a fabrication from beginning to end." He defended Stalin's reputation as a revolutionary and a war leader, but made it quite clear that neither he nor his colleagues regarded such "disgraceful methods of leadership" as acceptable.

The speech could be seen as a development of the point that Khrushchev made to the American ambassador very soon after Stalin's death: "He fought barbarism with barbarism, but he was a great man." Nevertheless, there was a difference between such a comment and the public (at least within the party) condemnation of the whole philosophy on which Stalin had based his rule and his methods. A number of Khrushchev's colleagues considered that his denunciation was too extreme, and their case was given some support by the revolts

Marshal Joseph Stalin, by Alexander Gerasimov.

that troubled Poland and tore Hungary later in the year. It was not until 1961 that Stalin's remains were finally, after another round of denunciatory speeches, removed from the mausoleum in Red Square, and his name erased from the place that it had occupied beside Lenin's. The embalmed body was cremated and the ashes interred by the Kremlin wall, along with those of other distinguished leaders of the Revolution.

There is at present no clear-cut view of Stalin and his achievements in Russia. He is still officially honored, but the expression "heirs of Stalin" has become popular among intellectuals as a condemnation of what they see as the reactionary element in the government. His legacy of political prisoners has been reduced, but it still exists; outside their own country Soviet leaders have behaved in a way that suggests they have not wholly forgotten his example. It is equally clear that, with the death of Stalin, a phase in the history of the U.S.S.R. is over, and that the circumstances that made his rule possible ended with his death.

RICHARD LUCKETT

Opposite Prague, March, 1953. Stalin's death called for visible tribute from every Czech shopkeeper. Some, like this maker of false beards and wigs, did not succeed in conveying sincere sorrow.

South Africa

The rising chorus of nationalism in Africa and Asia in the postwar years led in many cases to a sharp reaction from the ruling white minorities, who feared that their domination was threatened. Nowhere was this better illustrated than in the Union of South Africa. The general election of 1948 had been lost by General Jan Smuts' conservative United Party. The National Party, which was devoted to "preserving and safeguarding the racial identity of the white population of the country; and of likewise preserving and safeguarding the identity of the indigenous peoples as separate racial groups," formed the new government. During the next few years under the leadership of D. F. Malan

Prime Minister Daniel Malan, father of South Africa's racial policies.

the Nationalists passed a stream of legislative measures designed to make possible the "separate development" (*apartheid*) of the different "nationalities." There was widespread opposition to the measures, particularly among the unenfranchised African population, who feared—rightly, as soor became apparent—that the government sought to restrict still further their political rights. In order to control the discontent, the government gave the police wide powers and drastically reduced civil liberties; the belief that those who opposed government policy must be Communists led to the passing

of the Suppression of Communism Act in 1950. In 1956 the government removed the last parliamentary representatives of Africans and those of mixed birth. Other provisions extended restrictive legislation for nonwhites and banned mixed marriages. During the next decade the white electorate showed increasing support for the government's harsh attitude. In 1948 there were seventy Nationalists in Parliament and eighty-three others; by 1958 there were one hundred and three Nationalists and only fifty-seven others. Among Africans, however, opposition—largely inarticulate—mounted.

The government was less successful in its desire to absorb the League of Nations Trust Territory of South-West Africa into South Africa. The refusal of the United Nations to allow incorporation was accepted by South Africa, but the government would not act on the General Assembly's resolution that the territory should be handed over to the United Nations. After 1949 South-West Africa was more closely linked to South Africa as a result of the South-West African Affairs (Amendment) Act, which gave the territory ten representatives in the Cape Town Parliament.

The Middle East

Southern Africa was not the only area in which the tide of decolonialization was resisted. The importance of oil to the Western

economy insured that the Middle East would be one of the world's problem areas in the postwar era. The Middle East, where Asia and Africa join and European involvement had always been large, had already become an important area of conflict as a result of the creation of Israel as an independent Jewish state in 1948. During the 1950s the importance of the Middle East both as a supplier of oil and as a stage on the trade route between Europe and the Far East grew.

An oil pipeline crossing mountainous terrain in Iran.

The increase in oil consumption both as a fuel and for chemicals grew rapidly, and only the Middle East could supply the growth in demand. At the end of World War II one-third of the world's proven oil reserves were in the Middle East; by 1955 this had risen to sixty percent. It was no longer possible for a handful of giant oil companies to dictate terms to the producer countries. In 1948, Venezuela, the only major producer in South America, had introduced a tax law guaranteeing the government fifty percent of the profits of Venezuelan oil, and during the next few years this formula was voluntarily extended by the major oil companies to most of the Middle East producer countries.

By 1951 all the Middle Eastern countries except Iran had adopted the fifty-fifty formula. In Iran the government had chosen to follow a complex policy in its dealings with the sole oil concessionaire, Anglo-Iranian (formerly Anglo-Persian and later British Petroleum). The opposition parties under Dr. Mohammed Mossadegh pressed the government to force Anglo-Iranian to accept a fifty-fifty split; unable to drive a better bargain or to withstand Mos-

sadegh's popular support, the government fell, and Mossadegh became Prime Minister. Believing that the British economy would quickly be strangled without Iranian oil, Mossadegh took an increasingly intransigent line, eventually ordering all the foreign personnel of Anglo-Iranian to leave the country. Over the next two years the British bought oil from elsewhere and refused to allow Iranian oil to be sold anywhere in the world; as a result Iranian oil exports—the main earner of foreign currency—dropped by more than ninety-five percent, and the Iranian economy lay in ruins. A military coup, perhaps with British and American backing, overthrew Mossadegh, and a new oil agreement was negotiated, giving all the major oil companies a share of Iranian oil. Anglo-Iranian was given ample compensation.

The Iranian dispute (which came to be known as the Abadan dispute, after the port through which Iranian oil flowed) caused a re-evaluation both among the producer governments and among the oil companies. The governments saw that they had to lessen their dependence on the major oil companies and began to give concessions to smaller independent companies. Meanwhile the major companies sought to expand their sources of supply by opening fields elsewhere. As a result, extensive exploration began to take place in states that were politically and economically more backward than the established producer countries. British protectorates on the Persian Gulf, such as Abu Dhabi and Dubai, soon became large-scale oil producers. The oil companies and the developed consumer states believed that this extension was enough to avoid the danger of further embargoes, and it was not until 1973 that a powerful producer group was able to threaten the developed world successfully with an embargo.

Egypt

Although the Middle East was outwardly calm in the wake of Mossadegh's fall there was a fundamental change in popular attitudes, particularly in Egypt, which had a higher standard of education and higher expectations than most other states in the region.

In 1951 the Egyptian government, under popular pressure, at-

feel threatened by the growing tide of nationalism

King Farouk of Egypt, deposed in 1953.

tempted to end the Anglo-Egyptian condominium of the Sudan by proclaiming the Egyptian King Farouk as King of the Sudan—a move that the British refused to accept. The Egyptian government's unwillingness to take strong anti-British action led to widespread rioting, and in 1952 the government was overthrown by a military coup d'état. Farouk, who was corrupt, licentious and incompetent, was forced by the army to abdicate. The real leader of the coup was Colonel Gamal Abdel Nasser, but its nominal head was General Mohammed Naguib; both soon showed their desire to modernize Egypt. The monarchy was swept away and other institutions were reformed or abolished.

Social reform and economic growth were, however, only secondary considerations to Egypt's new rulers; the first priority was to rid the country of the British troops who guarded the Suez Canal Zone and to settle the dispute over the Sudan. Naguib's success in his efforts to negotiate a satisfactory agreement with Britain did not prevent his fall from power, which took place in 1954 when he was replaced as President by Nasser. The new President pursued a neutral policy, which soon brought him into conflict with the British. Although British troops were now evacuating the Canal Zone, the British government sought to secure the support of Western interests by the Baghdad Pact, signed in 1955 between Turkey, Iraq, Iran, Pakistan and Britain. Nasser's desire to lead an independent policy brought him widespread support from the "Third World."

British support for Israel added to the difficulties between Egypt and Britain, and Nasser's government sought increasingly strong economic ties with Communist states. This led to an even more serious dispute. The United States refused to honor an agreement that it had made to finance the building of the Aswan Dam, which was no less important for Egypt's prestige than it was for her economy. Britain followed America's lead and Nasser took his revenge by nationalizing the Anglo-French Suez Canal Company.

Malta and Cyprus

In some parts of the world, such as South Africa, Britain had shed her colonial responsibilities, but she was involved in the government and defense of colonies elsewhere. The gradual transformation of the British Empire into a Commonwealth of Nations, united in practice only by a tenuous loyalty to the monarchy, helped to create enormous political tension in many of the remaining colonies. In the Mediterranean, for example, Britain's colonial power was coming under increasing pressure.

In Malta, where there was a major Royal Navy dockyard, there were proposals during the 1950s for complete integration with Britain, but despite the support of Dom Mintoff's Labor government these never gained majority support, and in the 1960s Mintoff's difficulties with the British and their allies in NATO drove him to take an increasingly independent line.

Malta's strategic importance for Britain lay in its position at the center of the Mediterranean. No less valuable was Gibraltar, which dominates the narrow strait that joins the Atlantic and the Mediterranean. Spanish claims to Gibraltar were unpopular with the local population, which enjoyed a far higher standard of living than the Spaniards over the border, but—as in Malta—the idea of political union with Britain never found widespread support, and "the Rock" remained a self-governing British colony.

The strategic importance of Gibraltar and Malta was to be diminished by the closing of the Suez Canal after the crisis of 1956. But the events of 1956 were to make the situation in the main trouble spot of the Mediterranean, Cyprus, even more critical. Since the end of World War II there had been agitation for the union (*enosis*) of Cyprus with Greece, but the large minority of Turkish Cypriots and the British authorities were firmly opposed to this. In 1955 the campaign for *enosis* took a new turn when George Grivas' EOKA (National Organization for the Cypriot Struggle for Union with Greece) began a campaign of terrorism against the British. Archbishop Makarios, political leader of Greek Cypriots, was exiled by the British. Cyprus was to remain a divided country with a U.N. force to keep the peace, and in 1960 the British finally recognized the impossibility

Archbishop Makarios, first President of Cyprus.

of continued rule and gave the island its independence. In 1974 the Greek Cypriot National Guard, influenced by the Athens junta, overthrew Makarios. This led to a Turkish invasion and to the political division of the island.

The troubles of the Mediterranean, however, were small compared with those of the Middle East. After the nationalization of the Suez Canal, Britain and France would have been unable to make the full extent of their anger felt if it had not been for Israel's attack on Egypt in October, 1956, which enabled them to intervene.

The dockyard at Valetta, Malta.

1956   Crisis at the Canal

In July, Gamal Abdel Nasser, riding the tide of Arab nationalism, nationalized the Suez Canal, to the outraged fury of the French and British, both major beneficiaries of the Canal and both staunchly anti-Nasser. Spurred by popular feeling at home, but hampered by their inability to persuade others—notably the United States—to go along with them, Britain's Anthony Eden and France's Guy Mollet sought a pretext that would allow them to make war on Egypt, regain the Canal, and topple Nasser. Israel was persuaded to attack Egypt, after which the French and British would intervene. Israel's forces quickly overran the Sinai, Anglo-French troops took Port Said, but world opinion and the U.N. called a halt to the affair. Israel had shown impressive military strength, Nasser emerged as the Arab world's most powerful leader, the French Republic crumbled and Britain acceded to the dismantling of her Empire.

Egypt's President Nasser and Britain's Prime Minister Anthony Eden in Cairo, 1955. Initially Eden had tried to enlist the support of the Arab nationalist movement for Britain's proposed Middle East Defense Organization.

Opposite British commandos raise the white ensign over Navy House, Port Said. Nasser's nationalization of the Suez Canal provoked Britain and France into occupying the Canal Zone in the guise of a peacekeeping force.

In Alexandria's Liberation Square on Thursday, July 26, 1956, President Gamal Abdel Nasser announced at a mass rally that the Egyptian government would take over the Suez Canal. "The Canal belongs to us," he trumpeted. "It will be run by Egyptians! Egyptians! Egyptians!" As his words echoed round the square the crowd erupted into wild applause. As soon as Nasser had finished speaking, Egyptian security police took possession of the Canal installations and the Suez Canal Company's central office at Port Said. News of the takeover, immediately transmitted around the world, would instigate one of the region's most fruitless wars.

Less than a week after the takeover a full meeting of the British cabinet agreed in principle to the use of armed force against Egypt. The reaction of the French government was equally militant. Guy Mollet, the French Premier, angrily denounced Nasser as an apprentice dictator, a new Hitler with whom compromise was impossible. Like Eden, Mollet instructed the French armed forces to draw up plans for an immediate armed assault on Egypt.

People naturally assumed that Nasser's seizure of the Suez Canal was the cause of the armed hostilities that were to follow. The British and the French had controlled the Suez Canal through their majority shareholding in the Suez Canal Company. In addition, they were heavy users of the Canal. "The Egyptian," Eden told his colleagues, "has his thumb on our windpipe."

Informed observers like John Foster Dulles, the American Secretary of State, however, concluded that the Suez Crisis was "fundamentally a business dispute about control over an international public utility in a monopolistic position." This contemporary consensus is echoed in most of the subsequent accounts of the Suez Crisis and has given rise to a new mythology. Britain and France's overreaction to Nasser's seizure of the Canal is explained away in terms of the domestic pressures

that beset British and French politicians at the time.

According to one fashionable view, public confidence in the Fourth Republic had been seriously undermined by the crushing French defeat in Indochina in 1954. The politicians saw in the Canal issue an opportunity to reunite France and build public support for the regime. Similarly the vulnerability of Eden's political position and the pressures to which he was subjected are said to be the basic causes of Britain's reversion to gunboat diplomacy during the crisis. Eden allegedly lived under the shadow of Churchill; his rise to power as Churchill's heir apparent created expectations, it was said, that he lacked the qualities to fulfill. The jibes of his colleagues ("Eden has to show he has a real moustache"), the demands of the press for "the smack of firm government" and rumors that even Churchill had turned against him are said—according to this interpretation—to have preyed upon Eden's sensitive nature. Moreover his judgment was said to have become seriously impaired by ill health. Thus, allegedly sensing that "the nation was in a mood for a spot of adventure," he plunged the country into war over the Suez issue in a desperate attempt to restore his political fortunes.

This caricature of history, which distorts the Suez Crisis into Eden's personal crisis, has become accepted academic canon. There can be no doubt that Eden concealed under his suave stiff-upper-lip exterior a mercurial temperament and that problems with his health contributed to the disastrous course of action pursued by the British government. But he did not deserve the role of scapegoat in which he was subsequently cast. If Eden labored under a neurosis, it was a collective neurosis, shared by most of his opponents as well as his supporters.

The true story of the Suez Crisis is more complex but no less dramatic. The Suez Crisis was not, in fact, primarily about the Suez Canal at all. It was the culmination of a power struggle in the Middle

Immediately after the capture of the airfield buildings at El Gamil, Port Said. The first British paratroops have just rushed the buildings while others are still dropping from the last aircraft.

East between the traditionalist pro-Western Arab regimes supported by the European colonial powers and the new Arab nationalist movement. Nasser's takeover of the Suez Canal was the issue that brought this confrontation to a head. But the real question was the future domination of the Middle East.

Successive British governments had been forced to reduce Britain's military presence in the Middle East during the first decade after World War II. But it was still Britain's policy to maintain her traditional influence in the Arab world by the creation of a network of client Arab states through loans and defense agreements. Eden's main concern had been to consolidate these defense agreements into a Middle East Defense Organization that would enable Britain to maintain her traditional influence in the Middle East cheaply. Initially, recognizing that Britain had to come to terms with political reality, he attempted to enlist the support of the Arab nationalist movement, and particularly Nasser's government in Egypt.

But Nasser was determined in his opposition to the Middle East Defense Organization, and turned to the Soviet bloc for economic aid and arms, thereby threatening to undermine the British system of patronage. He also encouraged domestic opposition to the pro-Western Arab regimes upon whom British hegemony ultimately depended. Eden came to the conclusion that Nasser was a major obstacle to British aspirations in the Middle East, who had to be removed. Ironically it was an incident for which Nasser was not directly responsible—the dismissal of Sir John Bagot Glubb, the English commander of the Jordanian army—that finally convinced Eden that headlong confrontation with Nasser was necessary. "I want Nasser destroyed," Eden bluntly told Anthony Nutting, his Minister of State at the Foreign Office, three months before Nasser's take-over of the Suez Canal.

The policy pursued by Eden was firmly rooted in the political consensus of the time. For the British government to have gracefully relinquished its traditional influence in the Middle East without a struggle would have required the adoption of a new national identity and relationship with the outside world. Eden was not alone in failing to perceive and

adjust to this new reality. British politicians across the political spectrum wanted to preserve Britain's traditional role in the Middle East. The renewed involvement of Russia in Arab affairs had if anything reinforced politicians' concern to protect the exposed lines of communication between Britain and her Empire, despite the independence of India and Pakistan. There was also a growing recognition of the economic importance of the Middle East as a source of oil, following a fourfold increase in Arab oil production since 1945. This served to reinforce Britain's concern to maintain her influence there.

Nor did British politicians understand the fundamental change in the power relationship that had occurred in the Middle East during the first decade after 1945. Eden himself was criticized by official spokesmen of all three parties, Conservative, Labour and Liberal, for failing to be sufficiently tough with Nasser. Yet Eden recognized better than many of his colleagues and adversaries the political importance of the new wave of nationalism that was sweeping through the Arab world. If he was basically out of sympathy with the new movement and inclined to regard Nasser as the cause rather than the consequence of Arab militancy, others were still more in error. Hugh Gaitskell, leader of the Labour opposition, declared Nasser's aspirations for Arab unity to be "exactly the same as that we have encountered from Mussolini and Hitler in those years before the war," and a former Labour Foreign Minister called Nasser a "pocket dictator." Politicians on both the left and right clearly believed that all that was needed to stem the tide of Arab nationalism was to avoid appeasement and take a firm stand.

Underlying this remarkable degree of unanimity was a belief in the nineteenth-century concepts of free trade and legality and an instinctive assumption of British superiority. Nasser had offended these creeds on various counts: he had nationalized the Suez Canal without prior consultation; he had contravened internationally recognized treaties and agreements signed by previous regimes in Egypt; he had blocked Israeli shipping, thereby forfeiting the right to manage an integral part of the free trading system; and it was almost universally agreed that, in the words of London's prestigious newspaper, The Times, "the Egyptians have neither the experience nor the money" to keep the Canal "going efficiently."

There was no disagreement among politicians or the national press (with the exception of the Communist Daily Worker) that Nasser's action called for reprisals. The only important difference of opinion was about the method. The Labour Party believed that the military intervention against Egypt should be based on United Nations rather than bilateral action. The fact that this difference later became a major point of controversy should not obscure the almost universal demands from nearly all articulate sections of opinion in Britain for a tough policy against "the new Hitler."

The French coalition government was under

even stronger pressure from public opinion to be "tough" with Nasser. Nasser's support of the Algerians, revolting against French colonial rule, made him a public enemy. Only the Communist Party offered token opposition to the French government's militant policy. Most French men and women were in favor of headlong confrontation with Nasser. The Suez Canal takeover provided the government with the opportunity it had been looking for—a respectable reason for going to war with Egypt.

By the summer of 1956 Nasser was also ready for a showdown with the European colonial powers. For a time he had wavered in his opposition to British foreign policy but when the American and British loans that had been promised for building the Aswan Dam were canceled on narrow—even punitive—political grounds, Nasser no longer had any cause to pull his punches.

Nationalization of the Suez Canal seemed to Nasser a desirable objective in itself. European shareholders of the Suez Company derived thirty-five times more profit from the Canal than did the hard-pressed Egyptian government. Nasser also wanted to step up the propaganda war in the Middle East. A showdown with the West was needed in order to strengthen his bid for leadership of the Arab world.

Nasser had previously shown himself to be an astute and nimble-footed politician. But this time he had made a serious miscalculation. He assumed that the Americans would restrain the British from going to war over Suez, as they had done when Mohammed Mossadegh had nationalized the Anglo-Iranian Oil Company. What Nasser did not appreciate was that the British and French governments would go to almost any lengths to overthrow his regime without awaiting American approval. Although it looked as though the nationalist government was doomed, it soon became apparent that the imperial reflex of the British and French governments was no longer appropriate to the changed circumstances of the modern world: military chiefs in both France and Britain told their leaders that an immediate military riposte against Egypt was impossible. Egypt had a powerful defense force, including an army of over 100,000 trained men and reservists and an air force of 100 MIGs and 30 Ilyushin

bombers. In addition, the Egyptian army possessed semiautomatic rifles that were superior to British breech-loading rifles.

The crisis revealed the strategic weakness of the British armed forces, which were equipped for an all-out nuclear war or limited counterinsurgency operations, rather than conventional warfare. Shipping and transport aircraft had to be collected from all over the world. Amphibious landing craft had not been used since the Normandy landings of 1944. Furthermore there was no suitable base from which to launch an attack on Egypt: Cyprus had no deep water harbor, and military bases in Arab countries could not be used. In the end Malta, two days sailing time from Egypt, proved to be the closest suitable starting point for an attack.

Delay created serious problems. It was one thing to attack Egypt quickly, which would provoke an ineffectual outburst of protest after the mission had been accomplished and Nasser had been ousted. But the launching of a twentieth-century armada requiring months of preparation raised serious diplomatic problems. World opinion needed to be mobilized against the intended victim to prevent other countries intervening on Nasser's side.

Eden's first move was to declare Nasser's seizure of the Canal illegal. But although Britain's stand on legality had impressed public opinion at home, it won few friends abroad. The Egyptian government claimed that as a sovereign power it had the legal right to nationalize the Egyptian-registered Suez Canal Company, and to compensate its shareholders.

Nor was international opinion convinced by the other arguments enlisted by the British government. Critics asked pointedly why it was that the British government was now demanding that the Canal should be administered by an international board when it had been opposed to such a board in the first place. They also pointed out that Britain had done nothing to enforce U.N. resolutions deploring the embargo on Israeli ships when it had British troops stationed in Suez, and that the Egyptians had demonstrated that they were perfectly capable of running the Canal without British or Western assistance.

Eden and Mollet then attempted to provoke Nasser into preventing British and French ships from using the Canal and thereby putting himself in the wrong. Egyptian reserves and assets were blocked in Britain and France and all British and French shipowners were instructed to refuse payment to the Egyptian government when they used the Canal. Nasser did not rise to the bait. British and French ships continued to be allowed to use the Canal without interference from the Egyptians.

Eden's next move was to convene an international conference of maritime nations. Issuing selective invitations Eden secured the support of the conference for the establishment of a Western-dominated international board to administer the Suez Canal. His intention was to go to the United Nations armed with his mandate and to provoke a veto on

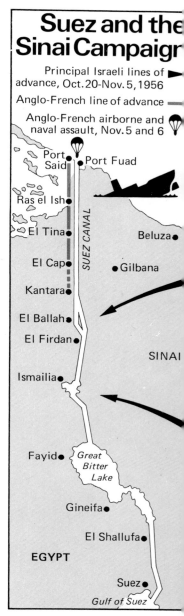

Troops examining captured Egyptian arms. Egypt's Soviet-supplied equipment was in many ways superior to that of the Anglo-French invasion force.

Ships scuttled by the Egyptians block the harbor mouth of the Suez Canal. The blocking of the Canal, and the speed of the Israeli advance, deprived Britain and France of their pretexts for intervention.

Ruined buildings in Port Said, key to the Canal Zone. Nasser would not allow the commander of the city to discuss surrender terms, and civilians were issued with arms.

the proposal from Russia. The deadlock at the United Nations would then provide the legitimate excuse he wanted for Britain and France to attack Egypt.

Much to his disgust, the American government refused to back up her allies to the hilt. Eisenhower was running for reelection as President on a platform of peace. Dulles had formed the Suez Canal Users Association, ostensibly with the purpose of forcing Nasser to "disgorge the Canal," but in practice with the objective of gaining more time. Eisenhower now bluntly told Eden that he would not stand by and see the United Nations used "as a cover for war."

The British and French governments were forced to enter into negotiations with Egypt in Washington; to the embarrassment of Britain and France, Nasser's representatives offered a compromise, suggesting that there should be joint management of the Canal by Canal users and the Egyptian government. It was difficult for Britain and France to refuse this offer. A further meeting to take place at Geneva was arranged. It seemed that Nasser had recaptured the initiative.

The French government was becoming increasingly exasperated by what Eden's Foreign Secretary, Selwyn Lloyd, called "the need for everything to be respectable." Even before the Washington talks the French had entered into secret negotiations with the Israeli government. The British now joined the conspiracy.

Israel was surrounded by hostile Arab neighbors who were committed to destroying the new Jewish state. The Israeli government was more and more alarmed by the apparently irreversible shift of the balance of power in the Middle East. The unification of Syrian and Egyptian armed forces under a single command hierarchy presaged a pan-Arab military alliance that could ultimately destroy Israel. The supply of Soviet-made arms to Egypt seemed a threatening gesture. The Israeli government was consequently predisposed to the launching of a preemptive attack designed to destroy the impending Arab alliance.

Egypt was the natural target. The Egyptian government had blocked Israeli shipping from the Gulf of Aqaba. It had also furnished active support for Palestinian guerrillas, who mounted raids into Israel. In addition, the Egyptian government had taken the lead in whipping up anti-Israeli sentiment. The Israeli government was already considering a limited assault on the Egyptian naval base at Sharm-el Sheik at the southernmost tip of the Sinai Peninsula and on guerrilla bases in the peninsula. The French government prevailed upon the Israelis to launch a more ambitious campaign, entailing the invasion of the Sinai, by offering to back the Israeli troops with air and naval cover.

The French needed British support, since the French air force could not alone provide the air cover that was needed. Secret negotiations were held in London and in Paris between the prime ministers and senior ministers of the two countries. It was decided that Britain and France would occupy the Suez Canal Zone in the guise of a peacekeeping mission after Israel had mounted an attack on the Sinai. The military expedition would be presented as a limited intervention to "separate the combatants" and "guarantee the security of the Canal." Its real objective would be to recapture the Canal by force and to overthrow Nasser.

Israeli troops were ostentatiously moved to the Jordan border, giving rise to speculation that Israel was about to mount a punitive raid against Jordan. The feint succeeded and a sudden four-pronged attack on the Sinai took the Egyptian armed forces entirely by surprise. Despite spirited resistance, one column of Israeli troops was able to break through as far as the strategic Mitla Pass.

On October 30, Britain and France issued an ultimatum calling upon both sides to withdraw to ten miles on either side of the Canal. An Anglo-

French force would occupy the buffer zone and use "whatever force was necessary to secure compliance" with the cease-fire terms.

The Egyptian government, not very surprisingly, ignored the ultimatum. Some Egyptian troops were engaged 175 miles to the east of the Canal, yet the Egyptian army was expected to withdraw west of the Canal, allowing the Israelis to advance unopposed. By ignoring this one-sided ultimatum, the Egyptian government gave the British and the French their excuse. The combined Anglo-French expeditionary force set sail from Malta after a series of preemptive air strikes against Egypt's air bases. Nasser, who had previously believed that the British and French were only bluffing, now attempted to regroup his forces around Cairo to fend off the impending Anglo-French invasion. Troop withdrawals from the Sinai and the inability of the Egyptians to attack the Israelis from the air led to a rapid collapse of the Egyptian army in the Sinai. With losses of less than 200 men, the Israelis occupied the entire Sinai Peninsula. The Egyptian army of 50,000 men had been routed.

At dawn on November 5 an Anglo-French commando force was dropped outside Port Said. It was followed by a wave of British and French troops backed up by full naval and air support. The Egyptian division stationed to defend Port Said quickly cracked under the pressure. Surrounded and cut off from water supplies, the Egyptian commander agreed to discuss terms of surrender, but Nasser would not allow it. Thousands of new Czech rifles and machine guns lying unpacked on the dockside were distributed to the civilian population. Loudspeaker vans were sent round the town to give the heartening news that World War III had begun, and announced Russian missile attacks on Paris and London. Civilian guerrillas, including young boys, proved more effective than the Egyptian army had been, but by November 6, Port Said and Port Fuad were occupied. The allied expedition had secured a strong bridgehead from which it could occupy the whole Canal Zone.

Events elsewhere had moved rapidly since the Anglo-French ultimatum had been issued. The Israeli attack had proved too successful. By the time the allied expedition had arrived to separate the combatants, fighting had virtually ended. The Israeli army had occupied the Sinai Peninsula and the Israeli government had no intention of advancing farther. The Suez Canal had been blocked by ships, which had been deliberately scuttled by the Egyptians. The Anglo-French pretexts for intervention no longer held good.

The whole pressure of world opinion was against the British and the French. Britain could not afford to ignore the almost unanimous vote of censure passed by the United Nations General Assembly in which the United States had joined hands with Russia—an extraordinary spectacle in the years of the Cold War—in condemning Britain and France. Britain's Middle Eastern oil supplies had been cut off; the pound sterling had come under severe

Men of the Royal Artillery 33rd Paratroop Regiment dig in a 25-pound field piece at El Cap. Britain's last imperialist venture brought her the opprobrium of the international community.

pressure, and Eisenhower was threatening economic sanctions. The British cabinet decided to accept the U.N. order for a cease-fire. The allied occupation of Port Said lasted until December, when British and French troops were evacuated to the hoots and jeers of the civilian population.

The allied expeditionary force achieved nothing. Nasser retained control of the Suez Canal and subsequent attempts by Britain and France to boycott the Canal proved ineffective. Britain's influence in the Middle East steadily declined, while the French Fourth Republic was subsequently destroyed by its vain battle to retain Algeria.

Bitterness in France, created by what was widely thought to be American sabotage and British betrayal during the crisis, left a lasting imprint. It was one of the contributory factors that led General de Gaulle to seek in the emerging European Economic Community a new power base that could act independently of the United States.

The impact of the expeditionary force's failure was even more decisive in Britain. The humiliation set in motion a fundamental reappraisal of Britain's role in the world, paving the way for the rapid dismantling of Britain's overseas possessions and the shedding of her role as international policeman east of Suez.

Two countries, Egypt and Israel, emerged from the conflict as victors. Israel had achieved a crushing victory over Egypt, even more decisive and humiliating than in 1948. Nasser emerged with his reputation enhanced as the courageous and unflinching leader of the Arab nationalist cause, who had "defeated" the Western imperialists. Yet the cause of neither country was decisively advanced by their victory. New guerrilla bases were established to harass Israel. Nor did defeat prevent Arab countries from again attempting to destroy Israel, although with equal lack of success. As for Nasser, his aspirations for Arab unity were never realized. While the Arab nationalist cause that he espoused was strengthened after Suez, it would probably have gathered support in any event from its own momentum.

JAMES CURRAN

The Hungarians' Revolt   1956

*In the 1950s, following the death of Stalin, life became somewhat easier for citizens of the Soviet
Union, but remained unchanged under the Stalinist leaders of Eastern Europe. In Poland,
Wladyslaw Gomulka took over the leadership of the nation, despite Soviet reservations.
In Hungary, the winds of change were blowing more strongly—and against stronger opposition.
Liberalism finally won the day with the accession to leadership of Janos Kadar and Imre Nagy.
But liberalism had gone too far. Alarmed, the Russians sent an invasion force, Nagy was
overthrown, and Janos Kadar became a new symbol of Hungarian repression.*

In the summer and early autumn of 1956, while the
attention of the West was focused on the Suez
Crisis, the Communist world was in a state of
turmoil. Events since 1950 had undermined the
position of satraps appointed by the late Russian
dictator to rule over the recently acquired empire
in Eastern Europe. These encouraged demands for
more freedom of expression. Nowhere was the
ferment greater than in Poland and Hungary. In
Poland it was to lead to the bloodless changes of
the "Spring in October"; in Hungary it erupted
into a bloody revolution.

The Communist leaders in the two countries
were in a difficult dilemma. They were expected to
follow Moscow's lead, relax the reins of terror and
give their peoples not only more consumer goods
but also a little more freedom of expression; but
they also had good reasons to be afraid of the consequences of this liberalization. They knew better
than their counterparts in Moscow how unpopular
their regimes were and how deep was the hatred of
the Soviet Union among their peoples. However,
in spite of appearances, the Communist leadership
was far from united, and this produced, especially
in Hungary, bewildering shifts from liberalization
to repression.

In 1953, Matyas Rakosi, the ruthless Stalinist
who had held both the posts of Premier and First
Secretary of the Hungarian Workers Communist
Party, suddenly handed over the leadership of the
government to Imre Nagy, while retaining the far
more important party office. Surprisingly, Nagy
was allowed to put Hungary on a genuinely new
and much more liberal course. But Rakosi was
only waiting for an opportunity to put the clock
back. In April, 1955, he had Nagy dismissed from
the premiership. In November Nagy was expelled
from the party for "right-wing deviation."

Rakosi tried to reverse the tide of reform, but
time was running out for the Stalinists, and the
party leadership was no longer able to use overtly

Stalinist methods. Instead Rakosi tried to steer
discussion onto "constructive" lines. During the
spring and early summer of 1956 the Petöfi Club,
a Communist-sponsored organization of young
intellectuals in Budapest, organized a series of "free
expression" meetings intended to provide a safety
valve for pent-up criticism, while offering a platform
for indoctrination in sound Communist thinking.
But the critics became more and more outspoken,
while the official party line found less and less
support. The series culminated in a nine-hour
meeting on June 27, at which writers and journalists
openly condemned the party leadership.

The party then tried to forbid further discussion
but could not stem the growing wave of criticism of
the regime. Finally, the Russians came to the conclusion that Rakosi had become a liability. On July
19, 1956, the Hungarians learned with joy and relief
that at long last Rakosi had been forced to retire.
In his letter of resignation, published in the press,
he admitted serious mistakes ". . . in the field of
the cult of personality and violations of socialist
legality."

The Hungarians expected a drastic change of
policy, but when they heard the name of the new
First Secretary of the Party, they knew that this
was not to be the case; Ernö Gerö was the most
faithful and the most hated of the Rakosi group.
On taking over the leadership he promised tighter
ideological control over the press, radio and
organizations like the Petöfi Club. Only ruthless
repression and terror could have stopped the great
public debate, but Gerö was unwilling, or more
likely unable, to resort to such methods. So the
debate continued through August, September and
October, with writers and intellectuals voicing ever
more outspoken criticisms of the regime, and
workers beginning to ask awkward questions at
public meetings. A feeling grew that Gerö was only
a temporary caretaker, and sooner or later Imre
Nagy—who was, however, still officially criticized—

In the streets of Budapest a
Hungarian insurgent reads a
leaflet calling for a general
strike.

Opposite Hungarian demonstrators dismantling the boots
of the gigantic statue of
Stalin.

Head of the Stalin statue decorated with a traffic sign and set at the main intersection of Budapest during the uprising. Souvenir hunters finally broke it apart.

November 12, 1956. Two patriot soldiers walk silently past the remains of members of the AVO (secret police) lying in the gutter outside their headquarters.

would be recalled to the helm. Meanwhile the Hungarians were watching developments in Poland with increasing attention.

There, in October, in spite of opposition from the Kremlin and a threat of Soviet armed intervention, the Polish Communist Party changed its leadership. Wladyslaw Gomulka who, like Nagy, had been expelled from the party, was now elected First Secretary and announced a program of reform, with more freedom and more independence from the Soviet Union.

Meetings of students and intellectuals in Budapest proclaimed their solidarity with the Poles. Many resolutions openly demanded Gerö's dismissal and the return of Nagy. For the first time voices were raised in public and reported in the press demanding the withdrawal of Soviet troops from Hungary and the release of the Primate, Cardinal Mindszenty, from house arrest. On Tuesday, October 23, Budapest was tense and expectant. University students had announced that they would be holding a public demonstration in support of the changes in Poland. The leadership of the Petöfi Club issued ten demands which included the expulsion of Rakosi from the Central Committee of the party, the return of Imre Nagy to the leadership and complete equality in relations with the U.S.S.R. The authorities adopted a vacillating line: in the morning the Minister of the Interior banned all public meetings and demonstrations until further notice; by the early afternoon the ban was lifted.

Thousands of students thronged the streets of the capital. As they marched, office and factory workers, soldiers and shoppers joined the demonstration, which, however, remained orderly. National flags and emblems appeared everywhere, makeshift banners proclaimed: "Away with Stalinism!," "Don't stop half way!," "Independence and Freedom!," "We trust Imre Nagy!" and "Hurrah for the Poles!."

There was little to suggest that the demonstrators were attacking the Communist system as such, but when Ernö Gerö went to the microphone at 8 P.M. he chose to give precisely that interpretation to the events of the day. "We must put it frankly. The question now is: do you allow the power of the working class and the worker-peasant alliance to be undermined, or will you stand up to defend the workers' power and the achievements of socialism?"

This was adding fuel to the flames. The demonstrators, now in an angry mood, converged on the Budapest studios of Hungarian Radio and sent in a delegation demanding that the resolutions adopted by them at the various meetings be broadcast to the nation. What happened next is not entirely clear, but most observers agree that when the delegation failed to return, the crowd attacked the building. A unit of AVO, the secret police, which was guarding the building, opened fire on the crowd, killing a number of people. A detachment of the Hungarian army was called to the scene, but it did not intervene; instead the soldiers started passing their arms to the demonstrators who stormed and occupied the lower stories of the radio headquarters. The Hungarian Revolution had begun.

News of the shooting outside the radio building spread quickly and led to an explosion of hatred against the AVO; angry crowds attacked various government buildings. The army and civil police either remained neutral or joined the demonstrators. A hurriedly summoned meeting of the Central Committee of the party sat intermittently through the night. Gerö resisted all pressure to resign. Without consulting the Committee he or the Premier, Andras Hegedus, asked the Soviet army for help. At 4:30 A.M. Russian tanks went into action in the streets of the capital, thus turning the

spontaneous anti-Stalinist demonstrations into a patriotic war against the Russians. Only the AVO remained loyal to Gerö.

Early in the morning of Wednesday, October 24, Gerö and his associates made a belated concession to popular demand and gave the premiership to Imre Nagy. The news of his appointment was broadcast just after 8 A.M.; forty-five minutes later came the announcement that "the Government" had asked for the help of the Soviet army, giving the false impression that it was Nagy's decision.

Changes in the Politburo of the party followed; Nagy became a member, but Gerö remained First Secretary. This was too little and too late to satisfy the insurgents fighting in the streets of Budapest. Workers from the industrial suburbs in their hundreds were joining the predominantly young demonstrators who had borne the brunt of the Soviet fire in the early hours.

At noon, with artillery and machine-gun fire reverberating in the city center, Imre Nagy went to the microphone. He appealed for an immediate end to the fighting, promising immunity to those who surrendered their arms. He went on: "I state that we shall realize the systematic democratization of our country. . . ." A Hungarian road to socialism and the fulfillment of the nation's aims were Imre Nagy's stated aims. He ended with this appeal: "Trust that we have learned from the mistakes of the past, and that we shall find the correct road."

His listeners, however, knew that as long as Gerö remained in the seat of power they could not trust Nagy to be able to fulfill his promises. The insurgents did not surrender their arms.

On Thursday, October 25, Budapest was in the grip of an undeclared, spontaneous general strike. Some two thousand demonstrators assembled in Parliament Square, carrying national flags and black banners to honor those who had died in the fighting. It was a peaceful demonstration and Soviet troops guarding parliament fraternized with the Hungarians. Suddenly shots were fired at the crowd from the rooftops. The Russians returned the fire and in the general fusillade scores of demonstrators were killed or wounded.

Unknown to the demonstrators, important political moves were taking place. Anastas Mikoyan, a first deputy premier of the Soviet Union, was in Budapest arranging for further changes in the leadership of the Hungarian party. At noon Budapest Radio announced the good news: Gerö was out. His successor was Janos Kadar, known as a tough Communist, but with the great advantage of having spent more than two years in Rakosi's prison.

Both Kadar and Nagy made speeches on the radio. What had started as peaceful demonstrations, they said, had been turned by counterrevolutionary elements into an armed attack on the system. This attack had to be crushed. Meanwhile Nagy announced "that the Hungarian government is initiating negotiations with the Soviet Union concerning, among other things, the withdrawal of Soviet forces. . . ."

Again it was a case of too little and too late. Only immediate Russian withdrawal and the dissolution of the AVO could have induced the insurgents to lay down their arms. The fighting went on and so did the Revolution. Workers' councils sprang up throughout the country, revolutionary committees were taking over administration in the provinces.

Friday, October 26, the fourth day of the Revolution: the Central Committee of the party proclaimed an amnesty for all those who laid down their arms by 10 P.M. that night, and announced that a new national government would be appointed to "make good without fail the mistakes and crimes of the past." It also repeated the promise to renegotiate relations between Hungary and the Soviet Union on the basis of equality in the same fashion as Polish–Soviet relations were being reshaped. But there was no mention of the AVO and no suggestion that Soviet troops should return to their bases at once. And so the Battle of Budapest continued.

On the morning of the fifth day of the Revolution, the composition of the new national government became known. It included for the first time in eight years representatives of non-Communist parties. Under Nagy there were three deputy premiers—one Communist, one representing the former Smallholders' Party and one the former National Peasant Party.

This constituted a great step toward democracy, but the skeptical Hungarians did not fail to notice that the key portfolios of the Interior, Defense and Justice remained in Communist hands.

On Sunday, October 28, Imre Nagy broadcast once more: a new security force would be formed from units of the police and armed platoons of the workers and youth (this meant the end of the AVO) and an agreement had been reached on the immediate beginning of the Soviet forces' withdrawal from Budapest. These were two vital concessions, but again they came too late. More demands—for

Premier Imre Nagy, whose neutralist government lasted a week after the Budapest rising; he was deported and executed in June, 1958.

Top Patriots arresting an AVO man. The Hungarian Revolution began when a unit of AVO opened fire on demonstrators at the radio buildings in Budapest.

47

the immediate withdrawal of Soviet forces from the whole country and for the establishment of a genuine parliamentary democracy—had already been made.

On Monday, October 29, some Soviet units did leave Budapest, but others still patrolled the streets firing at snipers and suspected centers of resistance. On the eighth day, Tuesday, October 30, the revolutionaries felt triumphant. At last the Russians were really withdrawing from Budapest. Imre Nagy announced the end of the one-party system and the formation of a new cabinet in which the Communists held only three out of seven posts. He also promised that the government would request a complete withdrawal of Soviet forces from Hungarian territory. Janos Kadar, on behalf of the party, endorsed Nagy's program. In addition Cardinal Mindszenty was released from house arrest.

In Moscow *Pravda* announced that orders had been issued for the withdrawal of Soviet troops from Budapest "as soon as this is considered necessary by the Hungarian Government," and declared Russia ready to discuss the question of the presence of its forces in Hungary. Mikoyan was again in Budapest, and was said to have agreed with what Nagy was doing. But new and massive Soviet formations were already entering Hungary.

The ninth day of the Revolution saw the last Soviet units pull out of Budapest. At last the Hungarians felt that they were masters in their own capital, though it was by no means clear who was in charge. Order in the streets was kept by the army, police and groups of revolutionary students and workers, but their loyalty to Imre Nagy's

government was in doubt, as Stalinists still held key ministries. In addition, the revolutionaries were an amorphous mass united only by their desire for freedom and their hatred of the Russians. The students and intellectuals who had been the first to raise the flag of revolt were still in the vanguard, but other groups and movements were beginning to crystallize, representing all shades of the political spectrum, except for orthodox Communism.

On that day, Wednesday, October 31, Imre Nagy disclaimed publicly any responsibility for having called in the Russians and disclosed that he had requested the Soviet government to start immediate negotiations for the withdrawal of Russian forces from Hungarian soil. Nagy also appointed a new Deputy Minister of Defense, Colonel Pal Maleter, who, having joined the revolutionaries, distinguished himself in leading a brave and successful fight against the Russians.

On Thursday, November 1, Janos Kadar, First Secretary of the Communist Party, in an attempt to rescue something from the wreck bequeathed to him by Rakosi and Gerö, announced the formation of a new party to be known as the Hungarian Socialist Workers Party. In a remarkably honest message Kadar said that the old party had "degenerated into a medium of despotism and national slavery." The new party, he continued, "will break away from the crimes of the past once and for all. It will defend the honor and independence of our country against anyone." Before the meeting convened to bring the new party into being was over, Kadar left the hall. His next public appearance was three days later in quite a different role. The movement of Soviet forces into Hungary that day reached such proportions that there could be no longer any doubt about their intentions. Imre Nagy personally took over the Ministry of Foreign Affairs and summoned the Soviet ambassador to protest vigorously against the Soviet invasion, demanding the immediate withdrawal of Russian troops. He also gave the ambassador notice of Hungary's withdrawal from the Warsaw Pact and proclaimed the country's neutrality.

This had the full support of the nation. For the first time since he became Premier, Imre Nagy was leading instead of following the revolutionary movement. But by then his fate was sealed.

On Friday, November 2, more Soviet troops entered Hungary. Imre Nagy protested again. In a message to the Secretary General of the United Nations he asked the Security Council to intervene. The Council met that evening in spite of Soviet objections, but the two-hour session was inconclusive. The Soviet delegate described reports about Russian troops moving into Hungary as "utterly unfounded."

On Saturday, November 3, Budapest was tense but quiet, awaiting further developments while still enjoying the intoxicating atmosphere of freedom. Imre Nagy announced more government changes; three prominent Social Democrats and Pal Maleter, the hero of the Budapest freedom fighters, joined the cabinet; at the same time twenty ministers, the

Streetfighting in Budapest: freedom fighters exchanging fire with Communist militia.

great majority of them Communists of the old school, lost their posts.

That morning in parliament, negotiations concerning the withdrawal of Russian forces began at last. Some progress was made and the meeting adjourned till the evening, when the talks were resumed at the Soviet military headquarters. From there at 11 P.M. Pal Maleter, leader of the Hungarian delegation, telephoned the commander of the Budapest military district to tell him that all was going well.

On Sunday, November 4, at 4 A.M. Soviet troops entered Budapest and started shelling the main strongpoints of the freedom fighters.

At 5:19 A.M. Imre Nagy went to the microphone for the last time to deliver his shortest and most moving broadcast:

Today at daybreak Soviet forces started an attack against our capital with the obvious intention of overthrowing the legal Hungarian democratic Government. Our troops are fighting. The Government stands firm. I notify the people of our country and the entire world of this fact.

At 6 A.M., probably using a Soviet transmitter, Janos Kadar announced that he had formed a "Revolutionary Worker-Peasant Government" in order to save the country from counterrevolutionary elements that had profited from the weakness of the Nagy government. "To help the nation smash the sinister forces of reaction" Kadar's government had asked for the help of the Soviet army.

The Hungarian army and armed detachments of workers and students fought bravely during their hopeless battle against the overwhelming fire power of Soviet armor. They struggled on for a few days, until their centers of resistance were reduced to rubble one after another.

Imre Nagy and a few of his political associates had to seek asylum in the Yugoslav embassy, while some two hundred thousand Hungarians fled the country, one in forty of the entire population. The United Nations were powerless. It was an internal Hungarian affair, claimed the Russians, exercising their veto. The West did not intervene either. It was thought at the time that only the Suez Crisis prevented it, but the case of Czechoslovakia in 1968 confirmed that all the West was prepared to do on such occasions was to protest and condemn.

The Russians and their Hungarian associates had displayed a high degree of duplicity during the Hungarian Revolution; they later improved on it still further. Maleter was arrested. Imre Nagy and his friends in the Yugoslav embassy were given a safe conduct and permission to live freely in Hungary; they were arrested by the Russians as they left the embassy and sent to Rumania. Two years later it was announced that both Nagy and Maleter had been executed following a secret trial. In Hungary itself Janos Kadar presided over a regime of grim repression. Devoid of any popular support, with the workers in a mood of sullen resistance, he resorted to methods that he himself had condemned in the past.

The international Communist movement, too, was a victim of the Hungarian Revolution and Soviet intervention. The Revolution demonstrated that the Moscow model of Communism had practically no support among the working population or among students who had received Communist education. The Soviet intervention proved that all the talk about respect for the sovereignty of other nations and concern for the wishes of the working class was utterly irrelevant when Soviet leaders decided that their interests were at stake.

Official history books in Hungary describe the Revolution of 1956 as a counterrevolution. Carefully doctoring the facts, they try to present the events of October and November, 1956, as a sordid attempt to overthrow the power of the workers. But the Hungarians remember what did happen. They have a long memory; after all they still remember their Revolution of 1848.

KONRAD SYROP

Aftermath of a street battle. With the breakdown of state control, order in the city's streets was kept by army, police and groups of revolutionary students and workers.

Left Budapest burns as Soviet tanks put down the Hungarian revolt. Despite their withdrawal by October 31, Russian troops reentered the capital on November 4, massively reinforced.

De-Stalinization

Russia's stranglehold on its European satellites tended to obscure an internal political development of great significance. It began in 1956 as a program of gradual "de-Stalinization" and it eventually caused a major rift between Russia and Red China. But its beginnings were so low-keyed that they passed almost unnoticed by the Western press. Khrushchev's program of de-Stalinization, introduced at the Twentieth Soviet Party Congress in Moscow

Marshal Zhukov and Nikita Khrushchev.

in 1956, called for an end to the "cult of personality" that had grown up around Russia's wartime leader. The Chinese Communist leadership, staunchly Stalinist, flatly denounced the change, which caused a serious breach between Moscow and Peking. This falling-out was accentuated by the Soviet reaction to China's sweeping program of communization in the mid-1950s. Khrushchev greeted the plan coolly, and when a subsequent economic crisis forced Mao Tse-tung's regime to abandon the program in 1959, Khrushchev's misgivings appeared confirmed. Domestically, too, there were changes, although the party retained its hold on society.

Europe united

Living under the shadow of the Soviet Union, West European states began to see that many of their problems were shared. What American Secretary of State Dean Acheson had said of Britain—"Britain has lost an Empire but has not yet found a role"—applied with little less force to the rest of Europe. The first half of the twentieth century had seen Europe

America's Dean Acheson with France's Foreign Minister Robert Shuman.

in political and economic decline. World War I had been above all a European war, although much of the world had become involved in it; but World War II had involved the whole world, although it had started in Europe. By 1945 the European states found themselves in a world that was dominated by the rivalry between Russia and the United States, a rivalry based on ideological principles rather than on the domestic and colonial squabbling that had characterized European disagreement up to 1918.

Both the great powers were federations of smaller states, and as early as 1948 a conference was called at The Hague to discuss

European unity, in the hope of establishing a third superpower. But early attempts at unity were heavily influenced by Winston Churchill's desire for a powerful European army; Russian hostility, treaty obligations and political disagreements soon led to the abandonment of these efforts.

Economic cooperation was to prove a more effective path to unity. The almost defunct European Defence Community and the flourishing European Coal and Steel Community formed the basis for a more effective organization, the European Economic Community (EEC). The Benelux countries (Belgium, the Netherlands and Luxembourg) had found a large measure of agreement with France, Italy and West Germany on procedure—although their ultimate aims were more varied, some wanting full-scale political union while others sought no more than a reduction in tariff.

Thus, the collapse of the European Defence Community and the equally ill-fated European Political Community in 1954 did not end the movement for European unity. On March 25, 1957, the "six" agreed, by the Treaty of Rome, to set up a European Economic Community that would ultimately remove all economic barriers between its members, would have common agricultural, industrial and social policies and would eventually

adopt common external tariffs.

A less ambitious organization had already been set up in 1956. This was the European Free Trade Association (EFTA), whose members—Austria, Britain, Denmark, Norway, Portugal, Sweden and Switzerland—intended to reduce tariff barriers gradually. It soon became apparent that EFTA was far less effective than the EEC, so there was little danger of serious rivalry that might lead to the increase of trading barriers between two organizations that had been set up with the purpose of abolishing them. Yet, it remained unsatisfactory that Europe should be at odds, and some countries, notably Britain, began negotiating to join the others. It was, however, to take thirteen years before the EEC was enlarged.

Scandinavia

Social change was characteristic of Scandinavia, too, in the postwar world. During the nineteenth century the Scandinavian states—and Denmark in particular—had led Europe in liberalizing their constitutions. During the early twentieth century the Scandinavian countries had extended the power of the state in industrial and commercial affairs, not so much by out-and-out nationalization as by taking large shareholdings in private companies. In Sweden, for example, Conservative governments during the first three decades of the century had nationalized about five percent of industry; the Social Democrat government that took office in 1932 and remained in power, either alone or in coalition with the Farmers' (or Center) Party, scarcely increased the state's direct ownership of industry. It did, however, have a major impact on both the economy and society. Large unemployment benefits were introduced during the Depression; an eight-hour working day was made mandatory and companies were not permitted to lower wages to compensate for the reduction in hours.

After World War II, all the Scandinavian states introduced far-reaching welfare schemes built on these prewar foundations. Although most other industrial nations had similar schemes by the 1970s, they were largely based on Scandinavian models. The main criticism by conservatives that the welfare state

"INNER 6"
EUROPEAN COMMON MARKET

"OUTER 7"
EUROPEAN FREE TRADE AREA

Maudling

"LOOK WHAT I MADE OUT OF THE SPARE WHEEL"

A cartoon attack on Britain's creation of the European Free Trade Association.

new role in a fast-changing world

Government-built apartment blocks in Copenhagen, Denmark. The Scandinavian states pioneered large-scale welfare services.

would become a "nanny state," producing citizens so pampered that they would be unable to help themselves, was disproved by events. The prosperity of the Scandinavian countries in the postwar years was in marked contrast to the rest of Europe, and standards of living remained higher than in most other parts of the Continent. Despite the continued existence of a predominantly private enterprise economic system, high and progressive personal expectations helped to raise the living standards of the majority by providing the most effective and extensive welfare and social services in the world.

Southern and Eastern Europe

In southern and eastern Europe the problems of unity were very different from those that dominated political discussions in the West. The Hungarian uprising and the contemporaneous disorders in Poland had shown that both in the eyes of the Soviet political and military establishment and in those of the population of Hungary the dominant question facing Eastern Europe was the relationship between the U.S.S.R. and its European satellite states. It was, therefore, not surprising that the effects of de-Stalinization were more widely felt in the U.S.S.R. itself than in its dependencies.

In Hungary, for example, the Communist old guard, reinstated by Russian arms, made substantial concessions to popular opinion,

particularly in rural areas: families were allowed to own up to forty acres of land; forced collectivization and forced deliveries of agricultural produce were abandoned. But the subordination of Hungarian to Russian interests remained, and in foreign policy the government followed the Moscow line without deviation. Any danger of deviation that might have existed was minimized by the continued presence of Russian troops in Hungary.

In Poland, the other Eastern European trouble spot of 1956, a more liberal attitude was taken. The Poles refused to join in the energetic denunciations of Yugoslavia that the Soviet Union encouraged. Indeed, the issue of

Yugoslavia became the measure of loyalty to the U.S.S.R. throughout the Warsaw Pact countries. The attitude that Chou En-lai had expressed during a visit to Poland in 1956 was one that the Russians could not approve of. He had said that "the relations between socialist countries . . . should be based on the principles of respect for their sovereignty, noninterference in their internal affairs, equality and mutual benefit." While other issues—such as the future of Berlin, attitudes to Israel and the question of international disarmament—continued to play an important part in the foreign policy of the Warsaw Pact states, it was the problem of Yugoslavia—itself a socialist state—that was most vexing.

Russia's need to reassert her leadership over the Eastern European states after the Hungarian Revolution made it particularly important that Yugoslavia should be forced to toe the Soviet line. In 1955, Russia had been willing to withdraw her troops from Austria, which then became a neutral but independent state. This would not have been possible after 1956. But President Tito, the Yugoslav leader, showed no intention of toeing any line that would put the uncommitted nations at a disadvantage.

During the late 1950s and the 1960s the Balkans were, indeed, to become a problem area for the U.S.S.R., equaled only by China. Yugoslavia continued to follow her independent line, which, by opening markets and financial op-

portunities to the West, made rapid economic progress possible. Rumania, formerly the most loyal of Russian satellites, began to take an increasingly liberal line during the 1950s under the party leader, Gheorghe Gheorghiu-Dej; after his death in 1965 the new party leader Nikolae Ceauşescu took a line that led Rumania still farther into disgrace with the Kremlin. The most extreme anti-Russian reaction of all came from Albania, a tiny and backward Adriatic state, which during the 1960s became more and more extreme in its espousal of the Chinese cause in the Sino-Soviet conflict. Although it would have been in Moscow's power to suppress the dissident Balkan regimes, this would have created difficulties at a time when the Soviet government was anxious to improve relations with the West, and the Russians confined themselves to energetic but harmless expressions of disapproval and to economic pressure of doubtful effectiveness.

The dispute within the Communist world made it increasingly important from Moscow's point of view to keep an effective and powerful army, even if only to avoid the danger of another Hungary. The loss of prestige that Russia had suffered as a result of the Hungarian rising was also a reason for joining in a new prestige race with the United States. Man had long dreamed of space travel, but it became a practical possibility in the 1950s for the first time, and the launching of Sputnik 1 was seen as a great national achievement for the Soviet Union.

A group of Albanian workers studying the works of Mao Tse-tung.

Earth's First Space Satellite 1957

At the end of World War II, the German rocket experts who had devised the V-1 and V-2 rockets were split up, some going to join their counterparts in the Soviet Union, others to the United States. Rocket technology was pursued avidly in both those—and other—nations. In the 1950s a number of countries were capable of space probes—rockets that were sent out into space to radio back information, but not to orbit the Earth. Then, in 1957, the Russians orbited Sputnik 1 and introduced the Space Age.

On October 4, 1957, an incredulous world learned that the Russians had put an artificial satellite into orbit around the Earth. On the radio, listeners everywhere could hear the bleeps from its transmitter as it passed a hundred miles and more over their heads once every ninety minutes. It seemed an astounding feat, yet, as it turned out, the launch of Sputnik 1 was only the beginning of mankind's conquest of space, and was itself a culminating point of many years of research.

In 1945, when the war in Europe had ended, the German rocket teams that had developed the v-1 and v-2 rockets at Peenemünde had been divided, some scientists going to the United States, others to the Soviet Union. On foreign soil they continued research into rocket propulsion, adding their own expertise to such indigenous rocket technology as they found. In the United States the organization of rocket research was fragmented; each of the military services had its own separate development program and exchanges of information between them were sporadic and infrequent. In the U.S.S.R. the work was coordinated on a much tighter basis, which was soon to prove more effective. Initially there were few spectacular results in either the Soviet Union or the United States; the research programs were primarily oriented toward military objectives, to extend the v-2 development to provide offensive and defensive rocket weapons. Most of this work was secret, but its ultimate aim was well enough known—to evolve rockets large and powerful enough to carry warheads between the Americas and Russia, to produce, in fact, an intercontinental ballistic missile (ICBM).

There was, however, a peaceful side to rocket development, and this soon showed itself in the use of sounding rockets (small rockets designed to carry scientific instruments high over the ground, above the lower and thicker depths of the atmosphere). Only in this way could the full gamut of radiation from outer space be studied; only with

rockets was it possible to reach regions where the air was too thin to support an aircraft, regions that needed examining to determine accurately the environmental conditions of our planet. Such small rockets, designed to reach heights of between 50 and 150 miles, were not expensive, and were not the sole prerogative of the Soviet Union and the United States. During the 1950s Australia, Britain, Canada, France, Western Germany, India, Italy, Japan, Poland and Switzerland frequently launched rockets that carried instruments. These were comparatively simple devices, working for the most part like a firework rocket with a solid fuel propellant; they became one of the accepted research tools during the special eighteen-month period from July, 1957, to December, 1958, known as the International Geophysical Year. This was an unprecedented example of international scientific cooperation to examine the Earth as a planetary body in space, and involved sixty-six nations making simultaneous observations and exchanging results.

It would have been of great scientific value if there could have been Earth-orbiting satellites, but although the Soviet Union and the United States had made feasibility studies as early as 1948, it had then seemed that the technical problems involved were too great. The primary difficulty was in launching a rocket with a velocity great enough to escape from the Earth's gravitational field, so that it would go into orbit and not fall back as a sounding rocket does. This in turn meant lifting the instruments (the payload) with a final velocity of not less than 17,450 miles an hour, which for a time seemed impossible to achieve.

Using chemical fuels, solid or liquid, together with an oxidizing agent so that the fuel would burn in the oxygen-starved upper atmosphere, the maximum speed attainable with a ground launching appeared to be 8,000 miles an hour if air resistance and gravity were taken into account. But it gradually became clear that if a second rocket could be mounted

Soviet astronaut Yuri Gagarin, the first man to orbit the Earth in Vostok I (April 12, 1961).

Opposite Sputnik II. Launched a month after Sputnik I, the first man-made satellite to orbit the Earth, Sputnik II carried a live dog, Laika (November 3, 1957).

V-2 rocket being elevated to a vertical position. Produced in Germany during World War II, the V-2 was an early stage in the development of effective rocketry.

Great Britain's Skylark rocket carrying scientific experiments into the upper atmosphere. Because of man's ability to study the universe from outside the Earth's atmosphere his understanding of solar activity has deepened considerably.

on top of the first, and be released from it once the first had reached its terminal velocity, a far greater speed could be obtained, even perhaps the crucial 17,450 miles an hour. On the other hand, if it was desired to launch a satellite into orbit not only must the rocket carrying it reach the required velocity, it must also be tilted so that the satellite could be ejected precisely into the correct orbit. To achieve such a tilt necessitates the use of thrusting jets firing at an angle and, therefore, more fuel. A two-stage rocket could probably do what was required as far as an Earth-orbit was concerned but a three-stage, at least, would be needed for any deeper space project.

It was also appreciated and even widely known that the velocity of an Earth-orbiting satellite would vary with the height of the orbit above the Earth's surface. Below about 100 miles, air drag would cause a satellite to lose velocity; it would drop below the crucial 17,450 miles an hour and return to Earth, burning up as it did so due to frictional heating in the atmosphere. Above 100 miles altitude the orbital velocity could be lower: at a height of 200 miles it could drop to 17,250 miles an hour, at 500 miles down to 16,660 miles an hour and at a height of 22,300 miles it could orbit with a velocity of only 6,872 miles an hour—a speed that carries the satellite around at exactly the same rate as the Earth's rotation so that, observed from the ground, the satellite appears to stand still in the sky. This property was made use of later in some communication satellites.

The successful launch of a satellite was a purely technological problem, but an expensive one to solve since it involved the construction of a large multi-stage rocket, the development of suitably powerful chemical fuels and elaborate automatic release mechanisms so that parts of the launching rocket no longer required could be jettisoned without delay. Moreover, to attain any desired orbit called for a high degree of precision workmanship, and this, as always, was costly. To solve the problem required expertise and money on a scale that demanded an effort of national proportions, but the prize was a tremendous boost to national prestige and might therefore be considered well worth the cost in manpower and finance. Clearly the Soviet Union felt that this was so, and set great store by being first in the field; when they launched Sputnik I in October, 1957, the International Geophysical Year was still in progress and they could be sure of maximum publicity in the scientific community as well as the world press.

Sputnik I weighed 184 pounds and the last stage of the launching rocket that followed the satellite in orbit weighed several tons, so it was immediately clear that the U.S.S.R. already had a large ICBM that could be directed with great accuracy. The American administrators were profoundly shocked, and the subsequent realization that all nations could extract useful scientific knowledge about the electrified regions of the upper atmosphere from the radio bleeps only added a greater sense of frustration. Then, one month later, on November 3, 1957, the Russians launched Sputnik II. This weighed half a ton, and carried a live dog, Laika; a careful analysis showed that the last stage of the rocket was at least sixty feet long.

Obviously the United States defense program, let alone the scientific one, needed reorganizing in the light of these results, and Congressional hearings were begun. The services' rocket programs were coordinated under one inter-service command, and early in 1958 the National Aeronautics and Space Administration (NASA) was established to run the entire United States civilian space program. But although the shock of the Russian success had been so electrifying, the American rocket engineers were not in fact so far behind. By January 31, 1958, they were able to launch a scientific satellite, Explorer I, using a hastily adapted four-stage rocket. Fortunately for national morale, Explorer I was highly successful. Carrying instruments designed by a team from Iowa University led by Professor James Van Allen, it distinguished itself by detecting the presence of two invisible halves of high-energy radiation around the Earth—now internationally called the Van Allen Belts. After this a whole series of American launchings occurred; other Explorer satellites were placed in orbit as well as a series of Vanguard meteorological and geophysical satellites. Even the launch of Sputnik III with a weight of more than one and a quarter tons in May, 1958, did not upset the American space effort, now fully under way.

It is clear that from early 1958, both the Soviet Union and the United States concentrated their military effort on effective large rockets to act as ICBMS and on smaller highly sophisticated Earth-orbiting satellites for spying on foreign territories. But since the military uses of space are, by their nature, cocooned in secrecy, no information is available. The civilian space program is another matter, and environmentalists, geophysicists, meteorologists and astronomers all owe an increasing debt to the satellite.

From 1960 onward, the American space program, at least, has contributed to better international communication. On August 12 that year Echo I was launched; this was a passive reflector acting as an orbiting mirror for radio waves so that very long-distance radio communication could be studied. Two years later it was followed by Telstar I, a satellite that acted as a television repeater, enabling the transatlantic reception of television programs. In ways such as these the instrumented satellite captured the public imagination and brought home in a simple way some of the advantages of the Space Age. In the United States, where Congress and the public apportioned expenditure, such support was a vital factor for NASA's continuance. But by far the most impressive achievements were those connected with a more speculative side of the American and Russian programs—the launching of satellite probes to the Moon and far into interplanetary space, and the attempts to put man himself into space.

If the problems of successfully launching Earth-orbiting satellites were hard to solve, those connected with probing further into space were even more of a challenge. This was due, primarily, not to the extra demands on rocket technology, although there were some, but to the immense increase in accuracy required. Instead of having an orbit a few hundred miles or so above the Earth, the probes were required to go accurately into an elliptical

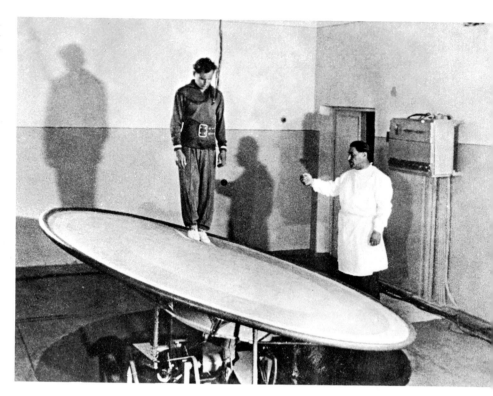

Major Gherman Titov in training. After orbiting the Earth seventeen times in Vostok II, Titov operated the retro-rockets that reduced his speed for safe reentry himself (August 6, 1961).

Instruments installed in Sputnik II for the study of cosmic rays.

orbit round both Earth and Moon (or round Earth and Sun for a planetary journey), and the immense distances involved meant that a small error in launch would be vastly magnified. For instance, an error of a couple of yards at the Earth end of an orbit for a probe on its way to Mars would result in an error of 50,000 miles at the other end. Added to this was the problem caused by the relative motions of Earth, Moon and planets during the probe's journey, all of which had to be allowed for in the prelaunch calculations.

The Moon is the closest celestial body to the Earth, lying at an average distance of almost 240,000 miles, a distance equivalent to that covered by ten orbits around Earth itself. Venus is much farther away; at its closest approach to the Earth, it lies about 100 times farther than the Moon. At its minimum distance, Mars never comes closer than 200 times the distance to the Moon. Yet it would seem that the difficulties and problems involved only succeeded in spurring the space technicians to greater efforts. As early as March, 1960, NASA gallantly attempted to dispatch a probe to Venus, and although it never arrived, it was able to

The first communications satellite, the American Telstar.

Opposite above Alan B. Shepard, the first American in space (May 5, 1961). The success of his suborbital flight enabled President Kennedy to announce with confidence that the U.S.A. would have a man on the Moon within the decade of the sixties.

Opposite Lunik I. Nearly two days after being put into orbit round the Sun (Jan 2, 1959), Lunik I passed within 4,660 miles of the Moon, thence to be lost in space.

radio back a considerable amount of scientific information about interplanetary space. For their part the Russians also attempted, eleven months later, to send a probe on the 26 million mile journey, and although it passed no closer to the planet than 62,000 miles and suffered a failure in its communications system as well, it showed quite clearly that "deep space" probes were a practical possibility.

In the first decade of the Space Age, the most spectacular results from purely instrumented probes came from attempts to reach and photograph the Moon. It was these that so appealed to the popular imagination. Unhappily for NASA the early American attempts made late in 1958 all failed: four Pioneer probes were launched but all suffered either from failure on the launching pad or inability to reach the target. The Soviet teams were more successful. On January 2, 1959, they launched their first lunar probe, Lunik I, which passed within 4,660 miles of the Moon nearly two days later, thence to be lost in interplanetary space. Two months later, the Americans followed suit, successfully sending a Pioneer craft to bypass the Moon. In September, 1959, the Russians crashed a probe, Lunik II, onto the Moon, but their most spectacular and scientifically important lunar success in these early years of the space race was achieved with Lunik III. Launched on October 4, 1959, this went into orbit round the Moon—a delicate maneuver that requires position

and orbital velocity to be judged to a nicety—and when behind the Moon, took photographs of the lunar surface. On emerging into visibility again, the photographic results were radioed back to Earth.

Since the Moon revolves only once on its axis every time it completes an orbit round the Earth, the same face is always turned toward us. The photographs taken by Lunik III gave the first view of the rear surface of the Moon in the whole history of mankind. That it was, predictably, very like the side we can see (the rear possesses fewer flat plains than the more familiar front) did not in the least detract from the achievement. Astronomers particularly were overjoyed at the innovation, and even more at the possibilities of further space observations. And the space technologists themselves were hopeful, for besides the instrumented probe, there had been a long series of experiments designed to launch animals and then man into space. If such accuracy as that displayed by Lunik III could be obtained by an unmanned probe, the possibilities for manned exploration appeared excellent.

As soon as Sputnik I had been put into orbit, the possibility of launching man into space, for so long the province of the science-fiction writer, had become more than a pipe dream. It seemed that at last techniques might soon be available to translate that hope into reality. The question, though, was not whether the rocket engineer could provide the hardware, but whether the human frame could stand up to the conditions of space. The Americans, as well as the Russians, believed that the difficulties would prove surmountable, and as early as 1958 NASA had decided it would work toward this goal. The international prestige of success in this field would be enormous, and in May, 1961, President John F. Kennedy felt confident enough in American progress to announce that the United States government had decided they must try to see a man landed on the Moon by the end of the decade. To some, it seemed a vain hope, but it proved to be no less than a sober statement of intent.

President Kennedy's announcement ushered in a heightened program of research and development in the American civilian space effort, both in rocket technology and in designing and building space vehicles suitable for carrying human beings. There were also astronauts to be selected and trained. So vast an enterprise was bound to take time, and in the early 1960s, the Russians quite clearly had the advantage over the Americans, at least as far as their rocketry was concerned, and were in a much better position to launch large man-carrying capsules into space.

The launch of living creatures and their safe return to Earth entails a host of problems not to be found when it is a question only of putting scientific equipment into orbit. Basically the additional difficulties arise because all animal forms require some life-support system—air to breathe, equipment to keep body heat within narrow limits, methods to take away waste products and an adequate supply of nourishment. In addition there is the phenomenon of zero gravity and the effect that this could have on all forms of life. Since it is impossible to generate zero-gravity conditions on Earth for any protracted period, the only way to investigate the effects was to launch animals into orbit around the Earth and examine them after their return. And this itself raised the difficult technical problem of slowing down the capsule on its return to Earth so that its velocity through the atmosphere would not generate more heat than could readily be dispersed. None of these questions arose over placing instruments in orbit since these required no life support, and did not have to survive reentry as they sent back their results from space by radio.

However, the Russians had long been busy preparing to put a man in space, and by May 15, 1960, were in a position to launch the first of a number of biological satellites. Known as the Korbal series, they carried plants, insects, frogs, rabbits, guinea pigs and dogs; four of them had recoverable capsules and of these three were successfully retrieved. These experiments were completed by March 25, 1961, but they were merely a preliminary. On April 12, 1961, Major Yuri Gagarin was launched into orbit around the Earth in a cylindrically shaped spacecraft, Vostok 1, which weighed almost five tons. After one circuit of the Earth, Gagarin—the first human being ever to leave the Earth and venture into space—returned safely. The Americans were not far behind: a little over three weeks later Commander Alan B. Shepard went into a sub-orbital flight successfully enough for President Kennedy to make his announcement about "Man on the Moon" with confidence.

As with the Russians, the American-manned launch was the culmination of a series of biological satellites, for the most part with monkeys as passengers. The two countries now seemed to be fairly close. In July, 1961, the Americans launched a second sub-orbital satellite, manned this time by Major Virgil Grissom, and with the information they then had on the use of flight controls and human reactions under operational conditions, felt ready to attempt a full-scale manned orbit. Meanwhile, the Russians did not rest on their laurels. A month after Grissom's flight, they launched Major Gherman Titov into space, and he remained aloft long enough to complete seventeen orbits before himself operating the retro-rockets that reduced his speed for safe reentry. The Americans still had to wait for NASA's response; at last, on February 20, 1962, ten months after Yuri Gagarin, Colonel in the Marines John Glenn was launched in a Mercury series capsule, and made three complete orbits of the Earth. Glenn's trip was not without its excitement, however, for just before reentry he discovered that the auto-control system was malfunctioning so that, like Titov, he had to fire the retro-rockets himself at precisely the right moment for a successful landing.

The Russian space program has always been covered by a veil of secrecy. The Americans, on the other hand, have carried out all their launchings, unsuccessful as well as successful, in a blaze of publicity, and this has led to widespread public confidence. Certainly both the Soviet and American projects have been extremely expensive, but nevertheless it would seem that later environmental, meteorological and purely scientific results alone have proved the viability of these new human ventures.

COLIN RONAN

"Perónitis" in South America

Despite the initial Russian lead in the space race, the U.S. soon made efforts to catch up, but American concentration on space achievement did not prevent continued diplomatic efforts in other directions. America's attention focused almost exclusively on Western Europe during the immediate postwar period, and relations with Latin America were largely neglected. For a time, at least, there seemed little cause for concern: the threat of Communist takeover, ubiquitous in Eastern Europe, had not yet spread to the Americas, and the United States' dealings with its Central and South American neighbors were amiable and progressive. In 1947, for example, every Latin American state joined the United States in signing the Inter-American Mutual Assistance Treaty, pledging reciprocal assistance in case of armed attack. A year later, the Pan-American Conference at Bogotá drew up plans for the Organization of American States, a pact that extended hemispheric cooperation into economic areas.

The amiability of the late 1940s was deceptive, however, for beneath the tranquil façade, two radically different forces were locked in bitter struggle. This clash between rebel forces—who were attempting to establish democracy in Latin America—and existing military dictatorships served to entrench the juntas that were to dominate Latin American politics for the next two decades.

The United States found itself intimately involved in the struggle. Enormous investment in most Latin American countries by United States companies made North American involvement in the South inevitable. In addition, United States politicians were influenced by the Monroe Doctrine and felt that it was their duty to interfere to preserve peace. Nor could the departments of State and Defense allow a situation to develop in which the United States might be threatened from the south.

The inability of Latin American governments to rule firmly without military support added to the economic problem of most of their states. In relatively stable Chile, for example, inflation was uncontrollable for nearly two decades,

and in other states the situation was still worse. In Uruguay the price index was to quadruple between 1958 and 1963. Continuous strikes, social unrest, the drain on the economy caused by the payment of interest and dividends to foreign investors and the need to retain the loyalty of the armed forces all contributed to the difficulties of Latin America and resulted in failure to exploit the continent's mineral wealth and industrial opportunities.

Many of the military dictatorships gained a well-deserved notoriety as a result of the brutality of the rulers and their paramilitary supporters. The enrichment of a few already wealthy families and the encouragement of future foreign investors were seen as more valuable goals than land reforms and the improvement of general standards of living. But there were differences between dictatorships. The most interesting among South American dictators was Colonel Juan D. Perón, the high-handed, high-living ruler of Argentina. Perón, whose *descamisados* (shirtless ones) had swept him into office in February, 1946, had subsequently embarked on a program of ruthless press censorship and rapid nationalization. His extremist politics did not initially lose him the support of the labor movement, but in June, 1955, resentment against the Argentinian President's tyrannical tactics reached its peak, and mutinous military officers engineered a coup that resulted in Perón's ouster. For almost two decades, Perón lived in Spain while Argentina's economic and political troubles made it a byword for corruption and disorder. The full significance of Perón's fall was first felt some eighteen months later in Cuba, where a series of events suggested that the days of all Latin American dictators were numbered.

The Cuban Revolution

In November, 1956, while Perón fumed and plotted in exile, revolutionary forces in Cuba launched the first of a series of attacks on the oppressive dictatorship of Fulgencio Batista. Led by a young lawyer named Fidel Castro, the rebel forces camped in the Sierra Maestra region of eastern Cuba. They survived repeated government efforts to eradicate them (including a campaign of terror

"Papa Doc," Haiti's President François Duvalier.

that resulted in some 20,000 executions over a two-year period), and in 1958—precisely two years after their initial uprising—Castro's forces initiated a final offensive.

Within a month the government was tottering, and when Castro's small force routed a government garrison ten times its size at Santa Clara, Batista fled. In the months that followed, Cuba rapidly entered the Soviet sphere, and in 1961 Castro's island was officially declared a socialist state.

In Cuba, the old order had proved incapable of coping with postwar demand for agrarian reform and truly representative government. However, the collapse of Batista's government did not lead to the end of the system of institutionalized disorder that had characterized South American politics. In Haiti, for instance, François Duvalier was elected President in 1957. He quashed all opposition, instituted a reign of terror that ended only with his death in 1971 and was as brutal as any despot in recent South American and Caribbean history.

Egypt and Arabia

While the Russians and the Americans pursued their space race, the countries of the Middle East were left to live with the effects of the Suez Crisis. The demonstration of the power of tiny Israel in the Arab world and the feeling, which was not to be confirmed for over ten years, that Britain and

President Perón of Argentina with his first wife Eva.

finds an echo in the Middle East

France had acted in collusion with Israel, was a cause of widespread change in Arab attitudes. It was not the only cause: the extension of education beyond a tiny elite; the spread of socialist ideas; improved communications; and a feeling that the Arabs were being deprived of most of the profits of their oil by the producer companies all added to widespread discontent that had existed even before the Suez Crisis had broken out. In addition, Nasser's status in the Arab world made it possible for him to act as a focus for the aspirations of those, throughout the Arab world, who wanted to

President Nasser with Ahmed Mahgoub, Sudan's Foreign Minister.

see political changes in the more conservative states.

Nasser made enormous efforts to use his position to create unity, at least among the more Westernized Arabs. He made recurrent efforts to create a united Arab republic, but these—like the later attempts by Libya's volatile chief of state Muammar al-Qaddafi—met with only limited and temporary success. In 1958 Egypt and Syria united, but when the army took over power in Syria in 1961, the union was dissolved. Nasser, undeterred, succeeded two years later in persuading a new Syrian government to try an even more ambitious scheme, but the new union, which was to include Iraq, was doomed from the start and never became effective.

In the more backward parts of the Arab world, where diplomacy was not likely to have much effect, Nasser used bribes and force to get his way. The coastline of Arabia was beginning to have some importance due to the vast increase in oil production in Saudi Arabia and the hopes of oil companies that further finds would be made there.

This coincided with a reduction in the military, economic and political commitments of the British, traditionally the dominant power in the area. Although the Yemen, on Arabia's southwestern tip, was not likely to produce oil, Nasser saw it as a valuable strategic base for extending his interests in the Arabian peninsula. Taking advantage of a rebellion that began in 1962, Nasser was able to dominate the republican side by supplying arms and troops. Despite the strong Egyptian presence—there were eventually around fifty thousand Egyptian soldiers in the Yemen—the loyalists continued to hold part of the country, and Nasser's ambitions remained unfulfilled.

Among the British protectorates along Arabia's southern and southeastern shores, Arab nationalist ideas were beginning to find an audience, and when the British announced their intention of withdrawing their troops from Aden this was the signal for the outbreak of fighting, which was to lead in the 1960s to the creation of an independent Republic of South Yemen. Farther east, however, the rulers of the states on the Persian and Oman Gulfs were able to use their new-found oil wealth to prevent or suppress rebellion. In Saudi Arabia, the pro-Western Prince Faisal deposed King Saud in 1964 and helped bring a measure of stability to the whole region.

Arab nationalism

The Egyptian example had a considerable effect in other parts of the Arab world. In 1958, for example, the Hashemite King of Iraq, who was striving for closer links in an Arab federation with his Jordanian cousin, was assassinated in a military coup d'état. The pro-Western premier, Nuri as-Said, and most of the royal family were also murdered, although there was little other violence. The President of the new republic, General Abdul Karem Kassem, quickly showed his determination to follow a socialist path. Even though a coup toppled Kassem in 1963, the Iraqi government showed little desire for change except to adopt an anti-Communist, pro-Nasser foreign policy. War with the Kurdish minority in the northwest added to the difficulties of the government.

Nuri as-Said, pro-Western Prime Minister of Iraq.

American fears that Lebanon would follow Iraq in overthrowing a pro-Western government were understandable as the country had been in a state of extreme political excitement for over a year. In 1958, in order to forestall the danger and to protect Western interests, U.S. marines were landed at Beirut to preserve the status quo.

Elsewhere in the Arab world, in Jordan and North Africa, the effects of the Suez Crisis and the growth of Arab nationalism were less immediately felt. The increasing inability of the French government to control Morocco had led to the granting of independence in 1956 by France and Spain. In Libya the discovery of substantial oil reserves gave great hopes for the future. In Algeria, too, which the French considered an integral part of France itself, there was a strong movement for independence, and during 1957 French politics were dominated by the question of its status—which led to the fall of five governments in that year. Although French public opinion was opposed to the granting of independence, many Moslems were appointed to civic office in Algeria during the year. At the beginning of 1958, as the government of Pierre Pflimlin seemed prepared to make further concessions, public disquiet grew. There were growing calls for a government of public safety. The government found that it could no longer rely on the loyalty of the army, and soon found itself faced with rebellion.

American marines guarding a country crossroad in Lebanon, 1958.

De Gaulle Returns to Power

By the spring of 1958, Charles de Gaulle had spent nearly twelve years in self-imposed retirement, following his resignation in 1946 as provisional President of France. Twenty-one unstable coalition governments had attempted to cope with the problems of postwar France. By 1958, the situation had grown grave indeed. On May 15, the commander in chief of the disaffected French troops in Algeria stepped onto the balcony of the Gouvernement Général in Algiers and declared: "Long live de Gaulle!" Deserted by the military, the troubled Fourth Republic was dying. Its final act was to call upon "the greatest of all Frenchmen" to form a new government.

Raoul Salan, commander in chief of the French forces in Algeria and one of the rebel leaders. He was sentenced to death *in absentia* in 1961.

Opposite General Charles de Gaulle.

At 6 P.M. on May 13, 1958, a European mob swept through the seat of Algeria's Gouvernement Général crying "Long live French Algeria!" For several years a bitter civil war had raged between Algerian Moslems, who were demanding self-rule, and Algeria's European settlers, who were implacably opposed to independence. Through demonstrations, strikes and incidents, the Europeans hoped to prevent the government in Paris from negotiating with the insurgents of the National Liberation Front (FLN), the leading nationalist group, for a political solution to the Algerian problem. By storming the Gouvernement Général, the Europeans, for the first time in the long history of Algerian colonization, were openly rejecting the authority of the French Republic.

The police showed few signs of serious resistance to the actions of the mob on May 13. By and large the police did not conceal their sympathies for the cause of French Algeria. At first the French army held back, but then, in the face of mounting tension, it showed its hand. One of the army's outstanding commanders was General Jacques Massu, who had made his reputation by cleaning out pockets of FLN resistance at the earlier Battle of Algiers. Massu made a dramatic public appearance before the crowds of demonstrators and proclaimed: "The Army is on your side!"

Shortly before 9 P.M. on May 13, Massu made a second appearance and read from the telegram that he had just addressed to the President of the Republic, René Coty:

I, General Massu, hereby inform you of the creation, under my presidency, of a civil and military Committee for Public Safety. This has been made necessary by the gravity of the situation and the vital need to maintain order and avoid bloodshed. We demand the setting up in Paris of a government capable of keeping Algeria as an integral part of Metropolitan France.

The army had crossed the Rubicon and the death throes of the Fourth Republic had begun. For several months, in fact, the Fourth Republic had survived only by a series of makeshift measures. Behind its façade, the structure was tottering. Ever since Charles de Gaulle had resigned as provisional President in 1946, the Republic had failed to achieve stability. Between December, 1946, and May, 1958, no less than twenty-one governments had come to power—having an average life of six months.

"The system," as de Gaulle nicknamed the Fourth Republic, had become the pawn of political parties. Since the liberation of France in 1944, the Communist Party had monopolized nearly a quarter of the votes at each election and had become the only substantial force in a rapidly declining democracy. By opposing all governments in power, the Communists had, in effect, joined forces with the Gaullist opposition.

France had emerged from war and occupation destroyed, pillaged and demoralized. The reconstruction had allowed all sorts of feudal systems to develop, and among these, political syndicates were not the least self-interested. The country was deeply divided. The German occupation had brought about a direct confrontation between the Resistance forces and the Vichyists. Since the war, international developments had brought the defenders of national independence and the partisans of European integration face to face. A permanent state of conflict existed between those who claimed they wanted to preserve the French Empire and those who, through idealism or self-interest, wanted a return to the limits of Metropolitan France.

Since November, 1956, war had been dragging on in Algeria. One million privileged citizens of European origin were living on an average yearly income of 450,000 francs and were paying only indirect taxes. On the other hand, there were 8.5 million Moslems living on an average yearly income of 16,000 francs. Although they represented 90 percent of the population, they provided very few of the elite and the intellectuals. Only one Moslem

Prime Minister Winston Churchill and General de Gaulle walk down Paris' Champs Élysées after honoring the war dead at the Arc de Triomphe in November, 1944. De Gaulle's wartime experiences as leader of the Free French led to a distrust of Britain and the United States that became apparent in French foreign policy after 1958.

child in seventy-five went to school. These desperate masses were increasingly turning their eyes toward the Third World, where colonization was giving way to independence everywhere.

In 1958 the whole of political life in France was carried on atop the Algerian volcano. In Paris, the word "government" had become a joke. On March 13 the Paris police, who were dissatisfied with their lot, had besieged the Chamber of Deputies and threatened the people's representatives. Then, on May 13, the army uprising in Algeria broke out. The regime, which had lost control of its own police force, now saw its own army turning upon it.

The news of the uprising threw political circles into complete chaos. The government of Félix Gaillard had been overthrown on April 15. Pierre Pflimlin was invested as the new Premier on the night of May

13, thanks to the support of the Communist Party. Indecisive, ill-informed and torn between the various political groups, Pflimlin struggled to maintain his position. One moment he would send a telegram expressing confidence to the army leaders, and the next he would cast about for the means of crushing their insubordination. Parliament became a humming beehive of rumors.

But throughout the whole country, an increasingly powerful trend was becoming apparent. The French people realized that "the system" was dead. From now on, people would listen to those who advocated changing the regime (either from the conviction that it was now essential to build a stable state, or from the desire to hang on to Algeria). Among all the solutions proposed, one stood out more and more clearly: appeal to General de Gaulle, the man who had symbolized resistance in 1940, the man who had liberated the country and restored its national sovereignty. He alone could stand up to the storm that had been let loose. On May 14, Hubert Beuve-Méry, the editor of *Le Monde*, made a resounding editorial appeal: "Speak to us, General!" *L'Aurore*, renowned for its stubborn anti-Gaullism, made the same plea. On the eve of the May 13 uprising, Alain de Serigny, editor of *Echo d'Alger* and a notorious opponent of Gaullism, caused some surprise. Despite his Pétainist convictions, he wrote: "I beseech you, General, speak, speak to us quickly— your words will be deeds."

The most decisive event of all took place on May 15, when General Raoul Salan, commander in chief of the French troops in Algeria, cried out from the balcony of the Gouvernement Général: "Long live de Gaulle!" After two days of confusion and uncertainty, the leaders of the Algerian secession— a secession that the official government in Paris was contesting—had made it known that they would

French parachutists landing at Dien Bien Phu in 1954. On May 7 the Communists captured this key stronghold, and shortly afterward they overran Hanoi, the capital of French Indochina. French power collapsed in Vietnam, Africa, Syria and Lebanon during the postwar period.

return to allegiance if de Gaulle came back to power.

The man to whom all these appeals were made was living in retirement in the village of Colombey-les-deux-Eglises in northeastern France. In 1946 he had voluntarily renounced power to avoid being involved in party intrigues. "We are near the end of the illusion," the General had written. "We must prepare the remedy."

In the face of the rapidly deteriorating situation, de Gaulle remained silent. His supporters were striving to influence all malcontents in his favor: Algerians, soldiers and citizens alike. Every Frenchman was waiting for a sign. It was only when the military leaders in Algeria made it clear that they desired continued allegiance to France that de Gaulle broke the silence. On May 15, at 6 P.M., the General's secretary in Paris broadcast de Gaulle's statement: "In view of the country's increasing tribulations, I declare to the people that I am ready to assume the powers of the Republic."

De Gaulle's message caused delirium among his supporters. In government circles there was complete panic. The hard-line ministers were pressing for a tough handling of the "sedition," and the government was vainly attempting to stifle the news by introducing censorship. Equally vain were the politicians' tortuous antifascist orders and the unions' attempts to call a general strike: at the Renault factories, scarcely three hundred workers out of 80,000 obeyed a union strike order.

In the French parliament there was panic and acute demoralization. Its corridors were the scene of maneuvers to rally or renounce support. Everyone was caught in the dilemma: on the one hand, there was the fear of de Gaulle (with his demonstrated hostility toward party intrigue), and on the other there was fear of an invasion by the French troops of Algiers. But little by little, the deputies came to accept the first of the two less-than-desirable options. Socialist leaders who had been corresponding with or making secret visits to de Gaulle were gradually tempted to finish the business by joining the appeal to the General, and the combined pressure of these new supporters forced Pflimlin to hold a secret meeting with the General.

The interview took place on the night of May 26 at St. Cloud. Even before Pierre Pflimlin could reach a decision about the issues raised in these discussions, a new communiqué burst like a bombshell: "I have taken the first step," said General de Gaulle, "in the regular procedure necessary to set up a republican government." It was generally thought that de Gaulle had accelerated developments to prevent an invasion by the mutineers; the process from this point was irreversible. The President of the Republic, René Coty, made an official appeal to General de Gaulle, "the greatest of all Frenchmen." On June 2, parliament elected him Premier by 329 votes to 224, adopted a constitutional law and entrusted the General with full powers of government for six months. The Fourth Republic was dead.

On March 25, 1957, France and five other nations had signed the Treaty of Rome, establishing the Common Market. But there had been no positive step taken toward executing these plans. Bogged down in the Algerian war and paralyzed by internal contradictions, the Fourth Republic could hardly devote itself to the reconstruction of Europe. Its economy was stagnant, its finances in ruins; France was definitely "the sick man of Europe." The return of de Gaulle—well known for his attacks on the Eurocrats, a resolute opponent of any submission to supernationality and a stubborn defender of national independence—seemed to other Europeans a formidable threat to the plans that they had momentarily cherished. All de Gaulle's skill was needed to dispel this prejudice. And, although he was to give life to the Common Market, he could not totally eclipse a certain mistrust.

On June 2, 1958, when Maurice Couve de Murville took up his duties as Foreign Minister—a position that he was to hold for ten years—France occupied an insignificant place in the concert of

General Jacques Massu, hero of the 1958 revolt.

Above left President René Coty and Prime Minister Félix Gaillard (left). Gaillard's government, the twentieth in twelve years, fell one month before the Algerian revolt erupted.

Voting cards used in the 1962 referendum that gave Algeria its independence.

63

nations. All its resources were incapable of bringing the war in Algeria to a satisfactory end, and the instability of its government had made France's pretention to the role of great power seem ridiculous. The return of de Gaulle was to dispel these uneasy specters. The world rediscovered the man who, almost alone, had embodied France during the war years. From the moment he returned to power de Gaulle occupied himself with the regeneration of his country. "France," he said, "must embrace her century." Within France itself, the foundations of a stable state were laid with the constitution of September 4, 1958. By the referendum of 1962, the President of the Republic was to be elected by universal suffrage, a move that indisputably gave increased power and prestige to the President.

Finances were put to rights, the foreign debt was paid back before it was due and the Bank of France accumulated reserves of dollars and of gold. France reestablished a strong currency, which it was able to maintain until the crisis of May, 1968.

Throughout the ten years of de Gaulle's rule, onlookers asked themselves two questions: how far-reaching were the changes that de Gaulle had imposed on France, and what would happen when he had gone? The terrible crisis that France experienced in May, 1968—and that led ultimately to the departure of de Gaulle in April, 1969—revealed how solid the Fifth Republic truly was. The crisis and its consequences also revealed the tenacity of those who clung to the past. Wealthy landowners, small industrialists, businessmen, farmers and local leaders

Below right An engraving of de Gaulle published in 1958, and (*bottom right*) a photograph taken ten years later. His Fifth Republic sought to restore France to greatness without the ties of a colonial empire.

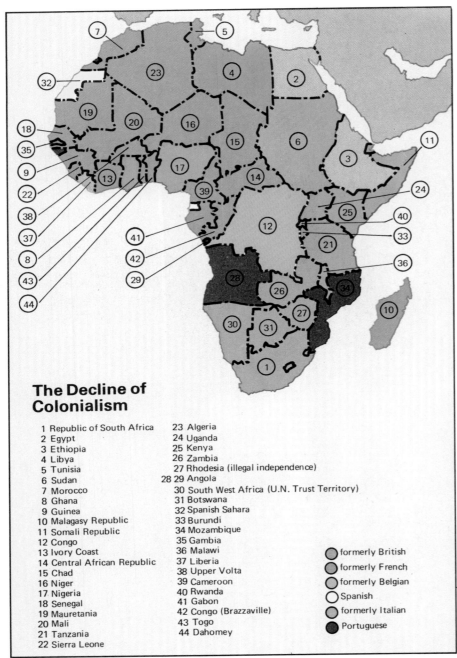

The Decline of Colonialism

1 Republic of South Africa	23 Algeria
2 Egypt	24 Uganda
3 Ethiopia	25 Kenya
4 Libya	26 Zambia
5 Tunisia	27 Rhodesia (illegal independence)
6 Sudan	28 29 Angola
7 Morocco	30 South West Africa (U.N. Trust Territory)
8 Ghana	31 Botswana
9 Guinea	32 Spanish Sahara
10 Malagasy Republic	33 Burundi
11 Somali Republic	34 Mozambique
12 Congo	35 Gambia
13 Ivory Coast	36 Malawi
14 Central African Republic	37 Liberia
15 Chad	38 Upper Volta
16 Niger	39 Cameroon
17 Nigeria	40 Rwanda
18 Senegal	41 Gabon
19 Mauretania	42 Congo (Brazzaville)
20 Mali	43 Togo
21 Tanzania	44 Dahomey
22 Sierra Leone	

○ formerly British
◐ formerly French
◑ formerly Belgian
○ Spanish
◐ formerly Italian
● Portuguese

all reacted violently against any reform that would erode their privileges or their way of life.

But the stability restored by the Fifth Republic also created new difficulties. Serving a strong state, the administration gave birth to a new race of young technocrats whose omnipotence could not be threatened by any ministerial crisis. At the same time, ministers who knew that their positions were safe only as long as the head of state approved them

were generally less preoccupied with making progress in their departments than with satisfying de Gaulle. It is undeniable, however, that French life underwent more transformations in ten years of Gaullism than it had in the preceding half-century.

As for the second question, "post-Gaullism" seemed to have found a temporary solution in the relative continuity that prevailed after the departure of the General. De Gaulle led France in an irreversible direction, but the principle of national independence, which had been severely shaken in the debacle of 1940, was no longer questioned.

The changes that de Gaulle brought about within his country and the consequences of his acts on universal developments make the General one of the few men who has shaped the history of the twentieth century. Powerless, he watched the fall of the Third Republic, which he had foretold in his prewar writings. The Free French, which he assembled, took part in the victory of liberal Europe against Hitler's Europe. He founded two republics. One, the Fourth—paralyzed by the impotence of the state and subject to political intrigue—lasted only twelve years. The other—the Fifth—also reached its twelfth year, but without its founder. Whatever its fate, it remains de Gaulle's Republic.

EDOUARD SABLIER

Rebel French troops in Algeria during the 1958 troubles. Their faces have been blacked out by Algerian censors.

De Gaulle on a visit to North Africa.

Crisis in the Congo

As the world's two richest nations allocated increasingly larger portions of their national budgets to the space race, the world's poorest nations moved toward independence. Sometimes the progress toward independence was smooth, with the colonial powers approving the aspirations to freedom. Often, however, as in Algeria, it was not.

Distressed by the persistent pattern of civil disorder in its only colony, the Belgian government called for round-table discussions regarding the Congo question in January, 1960. In April of that year, free elections were held in the Congo, and Patrice Lumumba's Nationalist Party won a clearcut majority. Lumumba became Prime Minister of the new Republic, while his closest political rival, Joseph Kasavubu, was President.

After less than a week of peaceful independence, the Congolese army mutinied and Kasavubu and Lumumba were obliged to call upon the United Nations to quell the insurrection. A U.N. emergency force responded promptly, but refused to place itself under Lumumba's command. The Congolese Prime Minister then requested—and received—Soviet aid, a move that prompted the rebellious leader of the rich Congo province of Katanga, Moise Tshombe, to declare his province independent of the central government. As matters worsened, President Kasavubu dismissed Lumumba—only to be turned out

Moise Tshombe, Prime Minister of breakaway Katanga.

of office himself by Colonel Joseph Mobutu, who promptly expelled the Russians. Lumumba was jailed, then freed, but ultimately turned over to the Katangans who claimed he died while trying to escape police custody in January or February, 1961.

Eleven months later, Tshombe and the central government settled their differences, and in June, 1964, the United Nations pulled its troops out of the Congo.

The Congo question was far from settled, however. Two months before the U.N. troops departed, secessionist forces in Kivu Province —followers of the slain Lumumba —staged a series of disruptive raids and skirmishes around Stanleyville

(now Kisangani) and it was not until 1966 that the central government was finally successful in establishing its authority everywhere.

The United Nations and Africa

A more encouraging development than the violence in the Congo was the growth in the influence of the United Nations. In March, 1957, one of Britain's former colonies, Ghana (previously known as the Gold Coast), became a member of the United Nations, and in the next six years twenty-three other African states followed suit. Fourteen of these newly independent countries joined the United Nations in 1960 alone, and by 1963 the map of Africa had been almost completely redrawn. By the mid-1960s the two great colonial empires of Africa, the British and the French, had become mere memories. The new

as the protector of the smaller states in a world that had become increasingly dominated by the rivalry between the United States and Russia. He wanted to make the United Nations Secretariat into an independent and powerful "dynamic instrument." The prompt action of the United Nations in the Congo was largely due to Hammarskjöld's efforts, which at first appeared to be successful. On September 18, 1961, however, while he was en route to a meeting with Tshombe, Hammarskjöld was killed in an airplane crash—which may well have been caused by sabotage. His death helped make the Secretariat more dependent on the whims of the great powers. No less serious was the covert support that was given to Tshombe's government by Britain and France, who were influenced by mining interests. As a result, the United Nations' efforts were ineffective

The funeral of U.N. Secretary General Dag Hammarskjöld in Uppsala, Sweden.

nations were often, however, more independent politically than they were in culture or economic affairs, and many former rebel leaders became firm supporters of the colonial powers they had struggled against with such energy. Membership of the United Nations General Assembly provided the new nations with a platform from which they could make their views felt. It also gave them a feeling of belonging to a wider community and encouraged a growth in the authority of the United Nations.

Under its brilliant Secretary General, Dag Hammarskjöld, the United Nations had shown itself increasingly effective in its attempts to deal with international crises. Hammarskjöld, elected Secretary General in 1953 and reelected four years later, saw the United Nations

and many of the developments that had taken place during Hammarskjöld's years in office were reversed.

Southern Africa

The quickening decolonization of Africa had affected the south more slowly than the rest of Africa. By 1963, as a result of the abandonment of empire by the British and French governments, Portugal with its colonies in Angola, Mozambique and Guinea had become the leading colonial power in the continent. Britain was reluctant to give independence to the Federation of Rhodesia and Nyasaland, and it was not until 1964 that Northern Rhodesia (Zambia) and Nyasaland (Malawi) were given their independence. Southern Rhodesia, with

Patrice Lumumba being carried shoulder-high by his supporters.

almost unchecked in Africa

African leaders meeting in London.

its greater wealth and larger white minority, remained under British rule; however, Southern Rhodesia's white settlers showed themselves unwilling to compromise at all with African nationalism, the root cause of the troubles that were later to afflict the country.

In South Africa the rule of the white minority became increasingly firm and ruthless during the late 1950s and the 1960s. The year 1958 saw the death of the National Party leader Johannes Strijdom, who had been responsible for introducing the first phase of apartheid legislation. His successor was Hendrik Verwoerd, a hardliner who saw that if South Africa were to remain a white-dominated state it would be necessary not only to intensify apartheid within the Union, but also to prevent the spread of African nationalist ideas from the north. He saw that the tide of decolonization could not be turned back in northern and central Africa, but said that "we must draw a line in Africa between the territories to be controlled by the white man and those to be controlled by the black man." As a result, while the South African government continued to support the white minority in the Portuguese colonies and to a lesser extent in Rhodesia, its links with the rest of Africa became increasingly tenuous.

Within South Africa itself, Verwoerd's hopes rested on an elaborate Act for the Promotion of Bantu Self-Government, passed by Parliament in 1959. He sought to remove black workers from "white" areas and to set up independent "Bantu homelands," mockingly referred to by the press as Bantustans. Although Verwoerd attempted to overcome the most pressing problem of giving the African population a measure of self-government by setting up university colleges to train black administrators, it was doubtful from the first whether the Bantustans could ever be viable economic units.

Verwoerd's legislation was opposed by members of the United Party, but without much energy, and a group of United Party M.P.s formed a more liberal Progressive Party, which attracted support from intellectuals and businessmen, but found little electoral backing. The reaction among black Africans to Verwoerd's hardening attitude and to the extension of increasingly restrictive "Pass Laws" was one of increasing frustration, which was fueled by resentment at the gap between the high-minded talk of separate development and the squalid realities of government action, massive unemployment and wage rates that were falling in real terms. Rioting became increasingly common in all parts of the Union during 1959, and led to the death of more than thirty blacks.

The visit of British Prime Minister Harold Macmillan to South Africa in February, 1960, brought the

British Prime Minister Harold Macmillan with tribesmen in Swaziland.

truth about South Africa home to many people in Europe for the first time. In a speech to the Parliament at Cape Town, Macmillan said that "the wind of change is blowing through the continent" of Africa, and that Britain could not support South Africa's large white minority against the national aspirations of the majority. This speech encouraged white liberals, and the African National Congress mounted a campaign against the Pass Laws, which began on March 21, 1960. The first day of the campaign ended in tragedy: at Sharpeville, south of Johannesburg, the police opened fire on a peaceful demonstration. As they did so the demonstration dispersed leaving sixty-seven dead and nearly two hundred wounded, most of them shot in the back as they tried to escape.

The government reacted sharply to its own violence. The main native organizations, the Pan African Congress and the African National Congress, were banned; Verwoerd, after recovering from an unsuccessful assassination attempt, asked Parliament for new and far-reaching detention and sabotage laws; South Africa became a republic and left the British Commonwealth in 1961. Internationally, South Africa found herself largely isolated for several years.

Russia and China

As the rift between the two great Communist powers, Russia and China, widened, diplomatic exchanges between them became increasingly strained, and in 1959 the Russians withdrew their promise to help the Chinese develop an atomic capacity. The Chinese retaliated in April, 1960, by publishing *Long Live Leninism*, an anti-Soviet broadside that so enraged Khrushchev that he summarily withdrew from China all Soviet technicians and all Soviet aid.

In the fall of that year, an extraordinary gathering of international Communist leaders was arranged, and representatives of eighty-one Communist parties met in Moscow in November to iron out the Sino-Soviet split. The delegates emerged from the meeting exuding amiability and spouting words of reconciliation, but in reality the dispute between the Communist monoliths was unresolved. In fact, the rift had grown worse, as the events of October, 1961, were to prove. In that month Russia publicly denounced the Albanian Communist Party for siding with the Chinese, and abruptly broke off diplomatic relations with the tiny Balkan nation.

Open antagonism turned into open warfare in 1962, when Turkic nomads in Sinkiang province in western China rose against their government, dealt the People's Army a severe blow, and fled across the border into Soviet Central Asia. Two subsequent incidents were to drive the wedge still deeper. The first was China's attack on India's northern border in October, 1962 —an act that the Russians regarded as a grave threat to the peace of the whole world. For the first time the rivalry between Russia and China involved a non-Communist state. The second incident, far more serious, occurred in Cuba, where Russia's tactical retreat outraged the Chinese.

Africans flee from police bullets during the Sharpeville riot, 1960.

The Cuban Missile Crisis 1962

President John F. Kennedy was still glancing over the morning papers when National Security Adviser McGeorge Bundy burst into his bedroom on the morning of October 16, 1962. Bundy confronted the President with "hard photographic evidence" that Russian technicians were constructing a series of offensive missile sites on the island of Cuba. During the next few days, Kennedy, Bundy and some fifteen other high officials and trusted advisers met regularly to ponder a response to the Soviet government's provocative move. In a dramatic televised speech to the nation on October 22, the President announced the Russians' action and called for a naval blockade to prevent further shipments from reaching Castro's island. The crisis was far from resolved, however; the missile sites remained, and it would take some highly unorthodox diplomacy to secure their removal.

In the nuclear age the greatest threats to international peace burst upon the world unannounced. The Cuban missile crisis of October, 1962, certainly happened that way. The first intimation that the whole of mankind was standing on the brink of a nuclear holocaust came on the evening of Monday, October 22, when President John F. Kennedy, in a broadcast to the American people, somberly warned them of the existence of "a deliberately provocative and unjustified change in the status quo which cannot be accepted by this country."

That "change in the status quo" was, of course, the construction in Cuba of a series of Russian-built missile sites—each with the power to point a nuclear dagger at the heart of any city in the southeastern United States. The construction of these missile sites had been a remarkably well-kept secret on the part of the Russians and the Cubans. Although work on them had almost certainly been going on throughout the previous two months, the President himself had heard of this clandestine development only six days earlier.

The U.S. government as a whole had been aware that from July on an unprecedented stream of Soviet ships had been moving toward Cuba. There were even reports from Cuban refugees of truck convoys on the island that were hauling long, tubular objects shrouded in tarpaulins. The U.S. intelligence community's view, however, was that all this activity betrayed only defensive precautions. It was, not surprisingly, a view that the Russians themselves did everything to encourage. On two separate occasions in September, messages were indirectly passed from the Kremlin to President Kennedy reassuring him that there was nothing alarming in this activity and that the Soviet Union had absolutely no desire to embarrass him in any way while the midterm elections were still unresolved.

The only American government official who appears to have been suspicious of these assurances—and to have convinced himself that all the goings-on in Cuba could bear a very sinister interpretation indeed—was John McCone, the Director of the Central Intelligence Agency. However, throughout this period McCone was not at his post in Washington: during September he was on his honeymoon in the south of France, and his warnings—sent in four separate telegrams from his holiday hideout at Cap Ferrat—seem to have been disregarded by his colleagues. Certainly they were not passed on to the President.

Four weeks later—on the morning of Tuesday, October 16—the President had to listen to a very different report. While he was still in his pajamas reading the morning papers, his National Security Adviser, McGeorge Bundy, burst into his bedroom to give him the grim news that "hard photographic evidence" now existed that disclosed that the Russians had imported offensive nuclear missiles into Cuba after all. The hard photographic evidence was the result of a stepped-up series of U-2 flights over Cuba that John McCone had personally ordered upon his return to Washington. The photographs left no room for doubt that the same telltale ground pattern of offensive missile sites previously seen only in the Soviet Union was now imprinted on the soil of Cuba, only ninety miles from the American coast.

President Kennedy had spent the previous day in a strenuous orgy of domestic political campaigning in New York State. But he lost no time in adjusting himself to the crisis. His first order was for the establishment of a task force to meet together in the greatest secrecy to consider the various options that the new situation left open to the United States. The first meeting of this informal group of presidential advisers (later to be called the Executive Committee of the National Security Council) took place in the White House that very morning. In attendance were some fifteen people. Only four of them (the Vice-President, Lyndon Johnson; the Secretary of State, Dean Rusk; the Secretary of Defense, Robert McNamara; the Chairman of the Joint Chiefs of

Ernesto "Che" Guevara, Castro's lieutenant and confidant whose life work was fomenting revolution in Latin America.

Opposite Soviet Premier Khrushchev and Cuban Premier Castro embrace at the United Nations in 1960.

69

Havana, no longer the cosmopolitan city it was before Castro's revolution.

Above right The General Assembly of the United Nations. The Cuban crisis was discussed at length by the United Nations.

Below right Fidel Castro haranguing a crowd.

A monument commemorating the Cuban Revolution; in the foreground is a statue of José Martí, a Cuban revolutionary leader of the nineteenth century.

Staff, General Maxwell Taylor) had been summoned chiefly because of the nature of the offices they held. The rest—the President's brother, Robert Kennedy; three of his most intimate White House aides; and private citizens like Dean Acheson—were made part of the group simply because they were types of people whom the President wanted at his elbow.

Most accounts of the Cuban missile crisis go out of their way to emphasize the smooth and well-ordered manner in which the American decision-making process worked. But the truth seems to have been rather different. At least in its early stages, the special ad hoc group charged with the responsibility of advising the President had difficulty in reaching any united conclusion at all. Certainly it was not in any position to put a collective proposal forward until the afternoon of Saturday, October 20, when, at the second of its meetings attended by the President, the decision in favor of a naval blockade of Cuba was made.

Even the decision to blockade was regarded by most of those present at that meeting as, at best, an interim measure. The general consensus was that if it was not enough by itself to convince the Kremlin that the missiles would have to be removed, then the United States would still have to be prepared to resort to an air strike, to be followed if necessary by a land invasion of Cuba. There were those, of course, in the Executive Committee of the National Security Council who wanted invasion to be the first move—and it was only at the Saturday afternoon meeting that they were finally overruled by the President.

On October 21—after the decision in favor of the naval blockade had been taken but before the President had announced it to the world—Dean Acheson (who, a decade earlier, had been President Truman's Secretary of State) slipped out of Washington with the delicate mission of warning the

governments in London, Paris and Bonn about what was to come; a similar arrangement was simultaneously made for the Canadian Premier, John Diefenbaker, to be forewarned.

Among the ships steaming toward Cuba—ships that the United States was now publicly pledged to intercept and, if necessary, forcibly board in a search for arms—were no less than twenty-five Soviet vessels. With his Monday evening broadcast announcing the naval blockade President Kennedy had, in effect, launched the first game of "chicken" of the nuclear era. If the approaching ships stayed

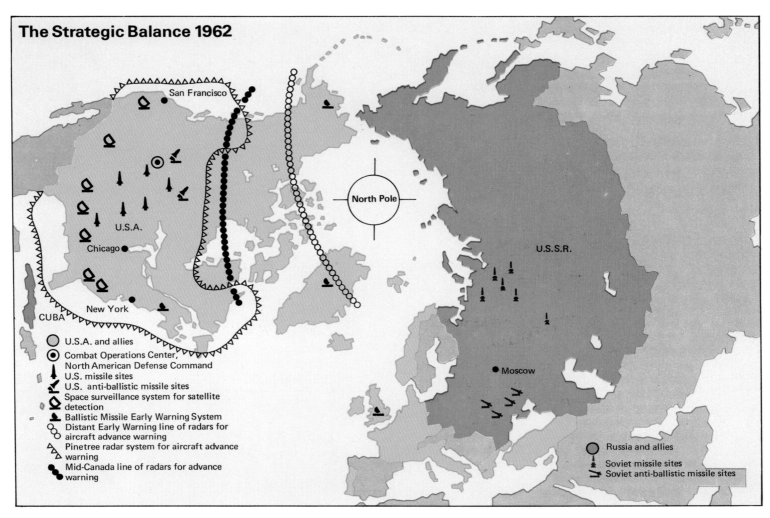

The Strategic Balance 1962

Legend:

○ U.S.A. and allies
◉ Combat Operations Center, North American Defense Command
⚓ U.S. missile sites
◀ U.S. anti-ballistic missile sites
◀ Space surveillance system for satellite detection
⚓ Ballistic Missile Early Warning System
○ Distant Early Warning line of radars for aircraft advance warning
△ Pinetree radar system for aircraft advance warning
● Mid-Canada line of radars for advance warning

○ Russia and allies
⚓ Soviet missile sites
◀ Soviet anti-ballistic missile sites

North Pole

San Francisco
U.S.A.
Chicago
New York
CUBA

U.S.S.R.
Moscow

on course, and if the U.S. Navy stood firm at the five-hundred-mile interception barrier it had thrown around Cuba, then sooner or later the two greatest powers in the world would necessarily be gazing at each other not across a conference table but at opposite ends of a gun barrel.

At the highest level of government in Washington the greatest anxieties were naturally enough fixed on what would happen on the high seas. After the signing of a presidential proclamation, the Cuban blockade was formally imposed at 10 A.M. on Wednesday, October 24. At that time two Soviet ships—the *Gagarin* and the *Komiles*—were within a few miles of the quarantine barrier; between them a Russian submarine had been detected moving into position. For the President's group of advisers, who were meeting in the White House at that moment, it was perhaps the tensest period of the whole crisis. What if the ships failed to stop or, worse, what if the Soviet submarine started to fire torpedoes at the shadowing American ships? So seriously was the danger taken that orders had already been given for depth charges to be dropped on the submarine if at a given sonic order it failed to surface. Dramatically, just before the moment of actual confrontation came, an unconfirmed report was received that the approaching Russian ships had stopped dead in the water. Within

the hour the U.S. Office of Naval Intelligence confirmed that all twenty Russian vessels nearest to the barrier had either stopped or turned around.

For President Kennedy, this was merely a temporary reprieve, not a solution to the crisis. The principal objection to the naval blockade tactic all along had been that it amounted in practice to no more than locking the stable door after the horse had been stolen. Intelligence reports reaching Washington confirmed that work was still going on furiously within Cuba on the rocket sites. The naval blockade might prevent the importation of further armaments into Cuba; it could not stop the Russians and the Cubans from making the most effective use possible of the nuclear arsenal they already had on the island.

President Kennedy had been only too conscious of this difficulty from the beginning; indeed it had provided the main argument for those (including all the Joint Chiefs of Staff) who advocated a "surgical" air strike as the only answer to the Russian challenge. The President, however, preferred to try the path of persuasion first. With that aim in view he had been in private correspondence with Premier Khrushchev from the time of the delivery of his broadcast. Initially, Khrushchev's reactions were not encouraging: his first letter simply accused the United States of "outright banditry" and his second gloat-

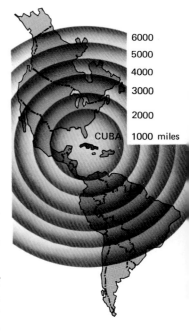

6000
5000
4000
3000
2000
1000 miles

CUBA

71

LAUNCH PAD WITH ERECTOR

CHERRY PICKER

LAUNCH PAD WITH ERECTOR

MISSILE READY BLDGS

OXIDIZER VEHICLES

FUELING VEHICLES

An aerial view of a Russian missile base in Cuba. It was on such evidence that President Kennedy ordered the blockade.

ingly pointed out that, as all the arms shipments needed were already in Cuba, there was no point in the maintenance of the United States' blockade.

But this second letter—which has never been published in its entirety—also gave the first signs that the Russian leader might be prepared for a negotiated settlement after all. In the course of what one who read it later described as "a confused, almost maudlin message," Mr. Khrushchev apparently suggested that he would be prepared to send no further weapons to Cuba and to withdraw or dismantle those already there if the United States, for its part, would call off its naval blockade and give a solemn pledge never to invade Cuba.

The relief in Washington was short-lived, however, for the very next day—Saturday, October 27—the Executive Committee of the National Security Council found itself confronted with a much more formal letter from the Kremlin raising the "price" on any deal. This time the Soviet leaders were insisting that in return for their taking their missiles out of Cuba, the United States must remove its nuclear bases from Turkey. Nor was this the only bad news received in the White House that morning. On his way into the meeting, the Attorney General, Robert Kennedy, received word from the FBI that Soviet diplomats in New York were preparing to destroy all confidential documents—an invariable

A Russian ship carrying aircraft as deck cargo, photographed by an American reconnaissance aircraft.

President Kennedy and the Joint Chiefs of Staff meet in the oval office of the White House.

embassy precaution on the eve of war. As if that were not doom-laden enough, the news also came that morning that an American U-2 had been shot down by a Russian surface-to-air missile while on a flight mission above the Cuban mainland. The understanding from the beginning of the crisis had been that once this happened, the United States would have no choice but to order a retaliatory air strike against the Soviet missile bases. Against the advice of many of his advisers, the President decided to stay his hand: there would, he directed, be no immediate act of retaliation while one final effort was made to reach a settlement.

The shape that effort took was certainly unorthodox. On the advice of his brother, the Attorney General, President Kennedy simply decided to ignore the formal letter that had been received that morning, which stiffened the Soviet terms. Instead a reply was drafted and sent to Mr. Khrushchev solely on the basis of his earlier, much more personal letter. In this reply the President made it clear to Khrushchev that the proposals he had made contained within them the ingredients of a settlement—but he insisted that the Russians must make the first move.

That Saturday night in Washington very few of those who had lived with the crisis during the past twelve days had any confidence that this final gambit—desperate, almost despairing—could possibly work. Indeed, arrangements went ahead for an air attack on Cuba early the following week, with the President even issuing a proclamation for the activation of twenty-four squadrons of the Air Force Reserve. But miraculously, the next morning, October 28, there arrived a dramatic message from Khrushchev agreeing to the President's terms. The Soviet government, the communication announced, had given "a new order to dismantle the arms, which you described as offensive, and to crate and return them to the Soviet Union." The Cuban missile crisis was over.

The American government's suspicion at the time was that the Soviet Union was trying for a trade or a deal, and there is some evidence to support that theory in the penultimate Soviet letter demanding the withdrawal of American missiles from Turkey in return for an agreement by the Russians to dismantle the nuclear installations they had built in Cuba. The rapidity with which the Soviet Union retreated from this position hardly suggests that it can have been a central part of the Kremlin's plan.

But a more plausible explanation remains: that the Soviet government was simply conducting a probe to see what it could get away with. Its miscalculation—if there was one—arose from its assumption that the U.S. administration would respond to the crisis according to the normal formulas of time-honored diplomacy. When the Russians discovered that the new and youthful American President—perhaps still smarting from his humiliation over the abortive Bay of Pigs invasion of Cuba in the spring of 1961—was determined instead to convert the crisis into a full-scale public nuclear confrontation, they had no choice but to back down. Certainly there is nothing in the Soviet government's behavior or reactions during those thirteen days to suggest that it had ever contemplated, let alone accepted, that a piece of classic, if reckless, *realpolitik* adventurism could lead to nuclear war.

In the end, of course, the Cuban missile crisis changed nothing in terms of the international power balance. Paradoxically, what it did do was to improve, if only fleetingly, the whole climate of Soviet-American relations.

What other fruits it might have had no one will ever know. By one of those ironic twists of fate the two men who, perhaps more than any others, had been brought to understand just how tenuous the thread of human survival is lingered only briefly thereafter on the world stage. Within thirteen months of those thirteen days that remain his principal claim to fame, President Kennedy was assassinated. Less than a year after that, Chairman Khrushchev fell from power in the Soviet Union. In much more than the obvious and direct sense, the Cuban missile crisis remains one of the great might-have-beens of history.

ANTHONY HOWARD

Andrei Gromyko, Russian Foreign Minister. It was his task to justify the erection of the missile bases to the United Nations.

1962　Pope John's Vatican Council

The College of Cardinals that convened in 1958 following the death of Pius XII found itself unable to settle on a successor to the austere and authoritarian Pope. To resolve the deadlock, the College settled on a compromise candidate, Cardinal Angelo Roncalli. Two and a half months after his election as Pope John XXIII, the supposedly uncontroversial Roncalli announced to an astonished world that he intended to call an Ecumenical Council. The Council—the first since 1870—was convened at the Vatican on October 11, 1962, and was charged with the task of adapting the Church to meet the challenges of the modern world. Weeks before the opening of the second session of the Council, John XXIII died and his work passed into the hands of his more conservative successor, Paul VI. The reforms that followed were small, but the spirit of reform that survived was substantial.

John XXIII, elected by a compromise.

Opposite The opening of the Vatican Council on October 11, 1962, in St. Peter's.

An Ecumenical Council of the Catholic Church is a curiosity in the modern world. Nowadays, grand ritual occasions are few and far between. A Pontifical High Mass in the basilica of St. Peter's before some twenty-three hundred bishops in resplendent dress is an extraordinary, impressive and photogenic event, and the Pontifical Mass that was celebrated in St. Peter's on October 11, 1962, naturally enchanted its worldwide audience. On that day a rather fat and undistinguished-looking, but peaceful, cheerful and kindly old man was carried aloft into the basilica where his elderly congregation awaited him. Papa Roncalli—Pope John XXIII— had come to open his Council. Many of the watchers were unsure what the Council could achieve, and many of the bishops were unsure what they would be allowed to achieve. But all agreed that the Second Vatican Council must take its course and its hope from John. He had called it into being; it was a child that he must educate and set on its way.

Four years earlier, the cardinals had been strongly divided on the choice of a successor to the austere and authoritarian Pius XII. They could not agree, and so decided on a stopgap measure. Cardinal Roncalli seemed to meet their requirements excellently. At seventy-seven he could not be expected to last too long. He had risen in the diplomatic service of the Church and was well regarded from Istanbul to Paris. As Archbishop of Venice he had performed his pastoral work with humble devotion and charm. Most important for a compromise choice, he was neither a theoretician nor a theologian, and he had little experience in the central Roman administration of the Church. It was therefore felt that the Curia—the civil service of the Church—would have no trouble keeping him in hand. When Roncalli became John XXIII, however, he quickly gave evidence of the strong and simple virtues of his peasant ancestry. His natural sympathy for all peoples had been happily fostered by diplomatic experience. His long absence from Rome left him

uncontaminated by the narrow and exclusive Roman outlook. Even his simplicity and lack of intellectual brilliance was turned to good advantage: theory never got in the way of human relations. "Are you a theologian?" he once asked an Anglican priest. "No? So much the better—neither am I!" He would talk to anyone, from Khrushchev to members of the Orthodox Church. He tried to serve where he could help most. He did not have a great mind, but doctrinal matters are only part of a pope's preoccupation; as Bishop of Rome he had a duty to comfort the sick, the poor and the unfortunate. He visited hospitals, slums and prisons as no other pope has done in recent times. The people listened to him because he could draw up from his own experience the right words for their condition. (He even told prisoners that his uncle had gone to jail for poaching.)

Pope John had his ear closely tuned to the stirring ground swell of twentieth-century humanity. He was far more able than the busy, efficient men in the Roman Curia to detect the widening separation between the secular world and the Roman Catholic Church. In January, 1959, two and a half months after his election, John XXIII announced to a surprised world that he intended to call an Ecumenical Council to be held at the Vatican.

"An Ecumenical Council," an unconventional churchman once said, "is a football match in which all the players are bishops." According to Abbot Butler's more prosaic definition, an Ecumenical Council is a meeting of the bishops in communion with the Holy See. "Together with the Pope, these bishops constitute the *magisterium*, or teaching body, of the Church and are also its supreme executive and governing body." An Ecumenical Council can define doctrine and make practical laws. In the past, Councils had been summoned to respond to special occasions—to fight particular heresies, or to formulate important doctrine. The first, at Nicaea in A.D. 325, was called by the Emperor Constantine to denounce the Arian heresy. The last before the

Three progressive cardinals: (*Left*) Cardinal Bea, a Jesuit reformer in the Vatican. (*Center*) Cardinal Suenens, Archbishop of Malines. He pointed out the dangers in the Church's traditional approach to contraception. (*Right*) Cardinal Frings, another leading liberal at the Council.

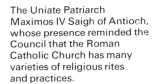

The Uniate Patriarch Maximos IV Saigh of Antioch, whose presence reminded the Council that the Roman Catholic Church has many varieties of religious rites and practices.

Second Vatican Council had been held in 1869–70. That nineteenth-century Council, also held at the Vatican, had promulgated the doctrine of papal infallibility.

What was the extraordinary occasion for the Second Vatican Council? The answer is: nothing in particular. What new dogma did John propose to define? The answer again is none. "I am not infallible," he once told some startled Greek visitors: "The Pope is only infallible when he speaks *ex cathedra*. But I will never speak *ex cathedra*." And he never did. The aim that John had in mind for his Council was both very simple and rather vague, quite unlike the obvious problems that had faced earlier Councils. The key to John's intentions was given by the word *aggiornamento*, by which he meant that the Catholic Church should be brought up to date and should adapt to the state of the world. On October 11, in his opening address to the Council, he suggested to the assembled fathers what their tasks would be: first to renew life within the Church—a revision of old thinking, old laws, old liturgy and old doctrine; then to attempt to promote Christian unity; and lastly to come together with the contemporary world and work toward a real understanding of modern conditions and problems.

Pope John put forward this revolutionary plan with his usual optimism. Others in the Church thought that his program would lead to either insoluble problems or appalling results. The Pope was proposing that the Church give up many of the habits that it had cultivated in the four hundred years since the Reformation. To many Catholics, particularly those in the Roman Curia, this was a very fearful idea. All commentators on the Second Vatican Council agree that the villain of the piece was the Curia, and it is understandable why this should be so.

For centuries the real power in the Curia had been held by a small group of elderly Italians who were convinced that Catholicism was an Italian, perhaps even a Roman, affair. Though in theory the Pope was above the Curia and the source of its power, in practice he was very often a prisoner to his curial

civil service. Ever since the Reformation, the centralizing and authoritarian traditions in the Church had encouraged the Curia to make the important decisions in Church government. The members now claimed this work as a right. They therefore viewed Pope John's Council plans with much apprehension. All three points in the Pope's program worried them. If John merely intended a renewal of the Church, then they claimed that a Council was not necessary: the Curia alone had the information and power to initiate reforms within the Church. But if the Pope really intended to push forward his other two points —Christian unity and adaptation to the secular world—then he was threatening the Roman Curia itself, which for hundreds of years had proclaimed Catholic exclusiveness and incompatibility with the temporal world.

On that Thursday in October when Pope John faced the bishops for the first time, the chances for the Council's success were finely balanced. In the last hundred years the Catholic Church had taken many steps toward reform and a revaluation of older attitudes. The encyclical *Rerum Novarum* (1891) of Leo XIII had shown that Rome was aware of modern economic and social problems. This promising direction was followed by Pius XI and by John himself in his encyclical *Mater et Magistra* (1961). Pius XII had been greatly interested in modern sciences, and his encyclical *Divino afflante Spiritu* had caused a great revival in Catholic biblical studies. For some time Rome had even edged demurely toward Christian unity. Here, too, John had made the decisive move: in June, 1960, he formed a Secretariat for Unity under Cardinal Bea, a Jesuit of liberal bent, and this body had a powerful effect on the Council. On the other hand, much about Rome was extremely backward-looking. The attitudes of curial cardinals such as Ottaviani and Ruffini were inflexible. Some hopeful progressive movements, such as the worker-priest movement in France and Belgium, had been frowned on and finally suppressed by Rome. And no one was certain whether or not a Council composed largely of bishops would be able to stand against the disapproval of the cardinals of the Curia.

Two reactionary cardinals: (*Left*) Cardinal Ottaviani, one of the leaders of the conservative opposition to the progressive bishops of Holland, Belgium and Germany. (*Right*) Cardinal Ruffini, Archbishop of Palermo. Most of the Italian bishops supported the Curia against outside interference.

The events of the Second Vatican Council have usually been presented as a struggle between the progressives and the conservatives—the progressives led by the cardinals of the northern European hierarchies, in particular France and Germany, and the conservatives ranging behind certain members of the Curia, supported by many Italian and Spanish bishops. Generally, this division was no doubt true enough. But the bishops were by no means consistent or united.

Pope John, in his innocent way, had hoped tha the entire Council would be over by Christmas, 1962 But the devious politics and the necessity to make speeches in rusty Latin insured a slow start. By the end of the first session, on December 8, only the liturgy had received a full discussion. But although the progress was slow, it was promising. Non-Catholic observers may have thought that the purpose of the Council was to conduct a flirtation with the outside world, but to Catholics the first aim of the Council was to encourage a renewal of life within the Church. The liturgy, dealing with the forms of Catholic worship, received the first attention. And from this, other benefits were reaped. The attempt to go back behind patristic sources and the accretions of tradition, back to the first biblical sources, was obviously pleasing to Protestants, and so a step toward Christian unity. Also, the translation of parts of the Mass into local languages helped to involve the laity in the service and fostered a kind of decentralization away from Rome. By the end of the first session, the reformers were reasonably pleased with the Council's efforts.

Then, in the months of preparation for the second session, a tragedy occurred. On June 3, 1963, John XXIII, the greatly loved and greatly admired Pope, died. The Council, into which he had breathed his own spirit of kindliness and tolerance, passed into the hands of his successor, Papa Montini—Pope Paul VI. Montini had been a member of the Curia for many years, yet on some matters he was known to have progressive opinions. However, no one was sure whether he could avoid the blandishments of his old companions in the Curia and continue the great reforming trend initiated by Pope John.

At the opening of the second session, on September 29, 1963, the signs were hopeful. In a fine and moving speech, Pope Paul outlined the work still to be done. He stressed the idea of service. He, the Pope, was "the servant of the servants of God"; and the Church was to serve the world, "not to despise it, but to appreciate it; not to condemn it, but to strengthen and save it." Within the Church, he looked on the bishops as a college that, together with the Pope, would play a large part in the doctrinal and practical government of the Church. The bishops, not the members of the Curia, were "the

Pope John XXIII giving his blessing at a Vatican ceremony.

Above Pope Paul VI, John's successor, closing the Vatican Council in St. Peter's Square, December, 1965.

Below Pope Paul meets Dr. Ramsey, Archbishop of Canterbury—Primate of the Church of England—in the Sistine Chapel.

heirs of the Apostles." He recognized the common religious patrimony that Catholics share with other Christian denominations, and he asked forgiveness for any damage that Catholics might have inflicted on the Christian community in the past.

The course of the second, third and fourth sessions did not run easily. Progressives and conservatives were as embattled as ever. The Curia still attempted to stifle promising movements. And Pope Paul, after his generous beginning, played a curiously ambiguous part—delaying, indecisive and often an apparent hostage to the Curia. In both the second session, in 1963, and the third session, in 1964, there were dangerous crises. None of the liberalizing measures had an easy passage. The question of the collegiate responsibility of the bishops was violently attacked by the Curia, which quite rightly saw here a threat to its own power. The Curia also went some way to persuade Paul that a synod of bishops would undermine his own primacy. The revival of the diaconate (an order of laymen with powers of assisting the priests), although begged for by the South American bishops, was strongly resisted by those reluctant to see laymen get a foot in the Church. The measure on religious liberty needed all the force and political ability of the North American cardinals and bishops to push it through. The Declaration on the Jews—although promoted with ardor by Cardinal Bea's Secretariat for Unity, and despite the German Cardinal's humble acknowledgment of the Nazi crimes against the Jews—still had to struggle for votes.

All these measures were to some extent theological matters. When the Council attempted to face the modern world, progress was even harder. In

78

November, 1964, the Council very cautiously approached the question of sexual morality. The Pope had already reserved to himself the decision on the contraceptive pill, but Cardinals Leger and Suenens and Patriarch Maximos IV Saigh discreetly tried to pour some light on the Church's traditionally dark view of sex, pointing out the human consequences of overpopulation. At least the Church was ready to discuss this fearful topic. The final document passed by the Council was the Pastoral Constitution on the Church in the Modern World. Tardily, but hopefully, the Church began to point the way forward.

The constitutions, decrees and declarations passed by the Second Vatican Council mark a definite shift in the attitudes of the Roman Catholic Church, the largest Christian community in the world. From the time of the Reformation until 1962, the Catholic Church was afflicted with Counter-Reformation mentality, a mentality mainly concerned with the preservation of the Church's rights, authority, privileges and exclusiveness. As a result, the Church naturally drifted apart from other religions, both Christian and non-Christian, and from the secular world. Whatever the value of its doctrinal truths, in human affairs the Church was becoming inflexible and out of touch with reality. Consequently, the Catholic religion had begun to lose its hold on contemporary man and no longer greatly influenced the course of modern life.

Taking its inspiration from Pope John, the most human of pontiffs, the Second Vatican Council gave the Church a chance to change its ways. If the suggestions of the Council are put into effect, the Church will become less centralized, closer to the people and to other religions, more able to answer the moral perplexities and practical dilemmas of modern life. Whether or not the leads will be taken up is the problem that is as yet unresolved. The habits of more than four hundred years are not easily set aside. The results of progressive action are not always what one would expect; sometimes they intensify the evils they hope to stamp out. Events in Rome since the close of the Council in 1965 have shown that the advance of reform is always slow and frequently painful.

MICHAEL FOSS

Pope Paul, surrounded by bishops, attending mass in St. Peter's.

Left Bishops leaving St. Peter's after attending a session of the Council.

Pope Paul entering Jordan on a visit to the Holy Land. Paul, a former Vatican diplomat and Archbishop of Milan, has traveled more widely than any previous pope.

79

A spirit of détente

For a time at least, the peaceful spirit of Vatican II seemed infectious. During the first years of the new decade, Cold War tensions abated, and the United States and Russia moved toward a genuine détente. Between 1959 and 1963, Soviet Premier Nikita Khrushchev purposefully pursued the policy of "peaceful coexistence" that he had first articulated in 1956 and reiterated in 1959 at the Twenty-First Party Congress in Moscow. According to Khrushchev, peaceful coexistence with the West was no longer a practical, temporary compromise—as in Stalin's day—but an enduring policy of Russia's new, consumer-oriented Communist state.

Détente seemed better suited to Soviet economic and military policy in the early 1960s than hostile confrontation, and Khrushchev actively and vocally sought improved East–West relations. In September, 1959, he paid a state visit to the United States and in June, 1961, the Soviet leader met with President Kennedy in Vienna. One of the topics they discussed was a nuclear treaty, discussions of which had become deadlocked. On July 15, 1963, these talks were revived, and on August 5 Great Britain, the United States and the Soviet Union signed a limited Nuclear Test Ban Treaty.

The new spirit of détente, which was embodied in the 1963 papal encyclical *Pacem in Terris*, was further evidenced by a meeting between German Chancellor Kon-

German Chancellor Adenauer and French President de Gaulle embracing.

rad Adenauer and French President Charles de Gaulle in Paris. As a result of this series of conferences, the strained relations between the two were eased and a program of mutual economic and military cooperation was agreed upon. In the same year, President Kennedy proposed a joint U.S.–U.S.S.R. space program, and Premier Khrushchev called for a NATO–Warsaw Treaty Organization nonaggression pact.

Southern Asia

Although the 1960s saw the beginning of a decline in the dominance of the superpowers, which went hand in hand with the gradual thawing of the obsessions that had characterized the Cold War era, significant events in little known

Nikita Khrushchev and John F. Kennedy at their first meeting in Vienna.

areas were still largely ignored by the media and the public in more advanced states. Important developments that took place in Malaya, Singapore and Indonesia, for example, aroused relatively little interest. Singapore and Malaya were given their independence separately by the British during the 1950s, but the rapid industrial development of Singapore—exceeded in Asia only by that of Japan—led Malaya to cast covetous eyes on its tiny but important southern neighbor. The British, fearful that the large Chinese population would bring Singapore under China's influence, advocated political union between Malaya, Singapore and the smaller territories of Sarawak and Sabah in Borneo. This was formed in 1963, but two years later Singapore left the Federation, although it retained close links with its neighbor.

Part of the reason for Singapore's departure from Malaysia was the hostile attitude of Indonesia, for-

Malaysia's Prime Minister Tunku Abdul Rahman on a ceremonial occasion.

merly the Dutch East Indies. Under President Sukarno, who had been largely responsible for gaining independence for his country from the Dutch, Indonesia followed an aggressive policy. There were no natural frontiers among the scattered islands that divide the Pacific from the Indian Ocean, and Sukarno sought to dominate the whole region, including the peninsula of Malaya. In Sarawak and Sabah and on the Asian mainland, Indonesia attempted to stir up opposition to the Federation, and until 1965 Sukarno followed a policy of *konfrontasi* (confrontation), which included military intervention. Sukarno had ambitions to the east, too, and sought to bring West Irian (Dutch New Guinea) under Indonesian rule.

Sukarno's policies, however, put the Indonesian economy under enormous strain. Politically he was forced to follow a careful balancing policy between the Communist Party, the dominant political party, and other groups—particularly the army. In September, 1965, the Communists, fearing a military coup, staged a rebellion. Within a few days it became clear that the army had managed to defeat them, and over the next few months thousands of Communists and suspected Communists were massacred. Sukarno's apparent sympathy with the rebels led to his gradual replacement as President by General Suharto, who moderated the ambitions of his predecessor.

Although fighting had been continuous in Vietnam since 1945, that conflict appeared to be no more than a sideshow in comparison with other events in Asia. India in particular found itself in conflict with its neighbors. Border disputes with China led to limited fighting in the Himalayas in 1962, in which the Chinese showed an overwhelming military superiority. Three years later, Indian soldiers were more successful in engagements against Pakistan in Kashmir and the Rann of Kutch, but the enormous disagreements between India and Pakistan were temporarily patched up by an agreement signed at Tashkent after Soviet mediation. As Pakistan found itself thrown into a closer alliance with China, Indian friendship with Russia increased, making it increasingly difficult for India to claim the leadership of the "Third World" nations. The breakdown of the Cold War alliance structure was shown by the ability of both Pakistan and India to retain close links with the U.S., despite their alliances with Communist states.

In most Asian countries, as was shown by the success of the Indonesian army against Communist insurgents, the army was usually a potent political factor that was able to ignore the democratically expressed views of the electorate. But military dictatorship was often coupled with extreme nationalism. In Burma for example, the ineffectiveness of the politicians forced the Prime Minister, U Nu, to ask the army to maintain order in 1958. Two years later, new elections were held and U Nu returned to power. In 1962, however, it became clear that political rule remained

America masks growing international problems

Indonesia's anti-Communist President Suharto.

as inefficient and dishonest as ever. The army chief of staff, General Ne Win, organized a coup d'état and seized power. His government took an increasingly isolationist line, seeking to find a Burmese road to socialism and gradually restoring the strength of the economy.

The ability of Asian countries to prosper despite fundamental social, political and economic difficulties was demonstrated most notably by Japan. Left by defeat in World War II with her economy and national morale shattered, Japan, which was in any case a poor country with little land suitable for agriculture, was yet able to emerge in the space of two decades as the great economic giant of Asia. During the early postwar years

A microphone factory in Japan, economic miracle of the postwar world.

enormous sacrifices were made to rebuild Japan's industrial strength. Between 1958 and 1964 world manufacturing activity rose by fifty-seven percent, while that of Japan rose by two hundred and sixty percent—far faster than any other country in the world. The Japanese rapidly established a key position in electrical engineering and automobile manufacturing, two of the main industrial growth

areas in the third quarter of the twentieth century. By 1965 Japan was second only to the United States as a manufacturer of television receivers and was poised to overtake Germany as the world's third largest manufacturer of motor vehicles.

Rebellion in Russia

Despite the easing of international tension neither the Soviet Union nor the United States was free from internal dissension during this period and as Premier Khrushchev's overtures to the West became more frequent and more cordial, opposition to his policy of peaceful coexistence grew. In mid-October of 1964, rebellious Politburo members ousted the seventy-year-old Premier and stripped him of his party rank. The fall of Khrushchev was not solely due to disapproval of his foreign policy. Industrial and agricultural difficulties had mounted steadily, and in 1963, for example, the U.S.S.R. was forced to import grain after the failure of a vast program to cultivate the Virgin Lands. Perhaps even more serious was Khrushchev's need to reverse his anti-Stalinist program. He had feared that liberal intellectuals were pushing him too fast, and in response to party pressure during the early months of 1964, he took an increasingly aggressive anti-intellectual stand. He showed less willingness to compromise on his rundown of military expenditure and this angered the party and military hierarchies. Party loyalists were suspicious, too, of his moves toward a more open style of government, particularly at the local level, and this was one of the major reasons for his removal. Khrushchev's successors, Aleksei N. Kosygin and Leonid I. Brezhnev, announced that they planned "no change in basic foreign policy," but in the ensuing months Western Kremlinologists grew increasingly pessimistic about the prospect of a continuing détente.

Kennedy

The new spirit of détente, which did to some extent continue after Khrushchev's fall, did not, however, end the problem of the Cold War: the nuclear arms race continued with unabated speed, despite all the talk of disarmament, and

China's explosion of an atom bomb in 1964 brought a new and politically undeveloped member to the nuclear club; the Cuban missile crisis had shown how narrow was the borderline between détente and nuclear war; and America was becoming increasingly involved in the as yet little publicized Vietnam war. Yet, the Kennedy years generated a new political interest both in the U.S. and across the world. Kennedy's ability to generate enthusiasm brought a new perspective to American policy. If the results were sometimes disappointing, the promise at least was golden. Kennedy hoped that the tiny majority by which he had been elected—only 112,811 out of sixty-nine million popular votes—would be increased during a second term. The "New Frontier" program which had been intended to improve social security, pensions and medicare, was largely rejected by Congress, and Kennedy, always a political realist, believed that it would be possible to push his program through only after the 1964 election. The obstructive attitude of Congress toward his program led to Kennedy's increasing reliance on a group of brilliant White House aides which ignored Congress—a change in the relationship between Congress and President that was to have far-reaching results in the 1970s.

Civil rights

The promise of the Kennedy years was, however, to evaporate on a bright November day in 1963 when the President was shot by a fanatic

in the streets of downtown Dallas, Texas. One of the last major problems that Kennedy had faced was the rise of a civil rights movement.

In the late summer of 1963, only days after the Test Ban Treaty was signed, more than 200,000 Americans—white as well as black—converged on the Lincoln Memorial in Washington, D.C., in what was described as "the greatest assembly for the redress of grievances" that the American capital had ever seen. A century after the signing of the Emancipation Proclamation, outraged blacks and sympathetic whites joined together in protest against what they saw as the nation's failure to insure that privileges granted to blacks in Lincoln's Emancipation Proclamation and guaranteed by the Constitution were truly available.

The demonstration in Washington was entirely peaceful, but it was both preceded and followed by "sit-ins" and "lie-ins" across the South and eventually across the whole country and these were often less peaceful as the demonstrators were a convenient target for outraged segregationists. Increasingly militant black organizations demanded an end to segregation in public transportation, public schools and housing; equal job opportunities; and the dropping of the so-called color bar in legislatures, the military high command and the civil service. The assassination of Kennedy left his successor, Lyndon Baines Johnson, a Southern Democrat, with the task of legislation; this was to bear fruit in 1964 with the passing of the Civil Rights Act.

The assassination of President John F. Kennedy.

"We Shall Overcome!" 1964

Ever since Lincoln's Emancipation Proclamation of 1862, black Americans had been striving vainly for equality and their constitutional rights. In the 1950s, the civil rights movement finally began in earnest, led by a soft-spoken, eloquent minister, the Reverend Martin Luther King Jr. As the movement gained force, John F. Kennedy tried vainly to write equality into law. It was only after Kennedy's assassination that Lyndon Johnson was able to persuade Congress to pass the most sweeping civil rights law ever passed in the United States.

During the second week of August, 1965, the black-populated neighborhood of Watts on the southern edge of Los Angeles broke out in 144 hours of rioting, burning and looting that left thirty-four people dead before the riot was quelled by the California National Guard. The "explosion" came at the end of a decade of unprecedented strides toward freedom and equality by the American Negro, a decade that promised something better; ten years of struggle had won the Civil Rights Act of 1964.

The movement toward racial equality had begun quietly enough in 1954 when the United States Supreme Court ruled in *Brown v. Board of Education* (of Topeka, Kansas) that "separate educational facilities are inherently unequal," thus abolishing the "separate but equal" doctrine that had dominated Negro-white relations in the United States since 1896, when the Court ruled in *Plessy v. Ferguson* that such accommodations were legal. Although the decision concerned only educational facilities, it indicated that the time was ripe for significant, society-wide change.

The civil rights movement began in earnest a year later when Mrs. Rosa Parks, a Montgomery, Alabama, seamstress, refused to give up her seat on a crowded city bus to a white man because, she later explained, "My feet hurt." Her arrest touched off a 381-day boycott of the Montgomery buses by blacks, who constituted seventy-five percent of the system's riders. After more than a year of walking, carpooling, and hitching to work, they finally won integrated seating, a promise of courteous treatment, and the hiring of Negro bus drivers. It was "the birth of the Negro revolt," according to journalist Louis Lomax, and from its first rally, the revolt had a leader: a new minister in town, twenty-six-year-old Martin Luther King Jr., whose charismatic advocacy of a nonviolent, "strength through love" approach was to dominate the movement until his assassination in April, 1968.

During the 1950s, President Dwight Eisenhower defended his lack of action on civil rights with the statement: "I don't believe you can change the hearts of men with laws or decisions." It was to the hearts and conscience of white America that the civil rights movement made its appeal. The extent of white resistance to change was vividly demonstrated in Little Rock, Arkansas, in September, 1957, when nine black students were escorted in army jeeps to attend previously all-white Central High School. The jeering, rock-throwing crowds that appeared on television screens that evening were to become a familiar news item long before full-scale school integration was achieved. The national mood was not to hurry integration if it would cause too much domestic dissension.

The civil rights movement continued to gain support, however. On February 1, 1960, four freshmen at North Carolina Agricultural and Technical College in Greensboro walked downtown to a whites-only lunch counter at Woolworth's, sat down and ordered coffee. No one would serve them; they remained forty-five minutes and decided to try again the next day. The "sit-in" had begun. Within four days, there were sit-ins at lunch counters in Charlotte, Durham and Winston-Salem, North Carolina. In thirteen months, the sit-in spread to sixty-eight cities and more than four thousand protesters went to jail. The Student Nonviolent Coordinating Committee (SNCC) was established in April to coordinate the movement and to school the participants in nonviolent, passive resistance. Despite repeated provocation, the protesters remained nonviolent and by the end of the summer, lunch counters in forty-three communities, including Greensboro, had been desegregated. The sit-ins, which had begun spontaneously, reflected a turning away from the established Negro leadership of the NAACP (National Association for the Advancement of Colored People) and Urban League toward active student demonstrations backed by careful organization, sophisticated tactics and the economic

Orval Faubus, Governor of Arkansas, on whose orders the National Guard prevented Negro students from entering Central High School, Little Rock, in 1957.

Opposite Funeral of Reverend Martin Luther King Jr. in Memphis, Tennessee, where he was assassinated on April 4, 1968. In 1964 he had been awarded the Nobel Peace Prize for his advocacy of nonviolence and racial brotherhood.

A black family. The condition of Negroes was such that their earning power and job prospects were half that of whites and their life expectancy seven years less.

Right National Guardsmen blocking the entry to Central High School, Little Rock, on Governor Faubus' order. A federal court injunction required Governor Faubus to remove the guards.

Opposite below Dr. and Mrs. Martin Luther King arrive in Selma, Alabama, leading the civil rights march from Montgomery, during which three people were killed (March 9–25, 1965). In response President Johnson secured the passing of the Voting Rights Act (August 6, 1965).

support of the adult community in the form of "selective buying."

Such tactics met a more severe test in 1961 when James Farmer of CORE (the Congress of Racial Equality) set out to test a Supreme Court ruling that passengers using interstate bus lines had the federal right to be free from racial discrimination in bus terminals. Farmer organized a "Freedom Ride," a bus ride through six southern states to challenge whites-only waiting rooms, terminal restaurants, washrooms and drinking fountains. The riders were attacked in Anniston, Alabama, by men with clubs and blackjacks who firebombed the bus and by mobs in Birmingham and Montgomery. Despite the hostility, the rides "did the job" with the help of more than one thousand people and at a cost of twenty thousand dollars in fares and more than three hundred thousand dollars in legal expenses.

The following year, 1962, was marked by the "Battle of Oxford" when James Meredith registered as the first Negro student at the University of Mississippi. He was accompanied by three hundred federal marshals through an angry white mob, which chanted "two-four-six-eight, we don't want to integrate." Rioting ensued, President John Kennedy addressed the nation on radio that evening, and after two men had been killed, federal troops arrived the morning of October 1 to clear the campus.

More than 1,600 demonstrators were held the following spring and summer in such places as Albany, Georgia, Nashville, Tennessee, and Raleigh, North Carolina, continuing the protest against segregated public facilities. The first major protest was in Birmingham in May. When Martin Luther King led an army of grade-school and high-school students in a march downtown, more than seven hundred of them, including King, were arrested and jailed. T. Eugene "Bull" Connor, the city police commissioner, promised to "fill the jail full" if Negroes kept marching. The next day, May 3, marchers were met by firemen using powerful fire hoses and by policemen with electrified cattle prods and police dogs. Before the marches ended, four black girls were killed when the Sixteenth Street

Baptist Church was bombed during Sunday School.

Such repeated violence in response to peaceful demonstrations, the cautious pace at which the federal government was reacting and the unwillingness of local authorities to bring white assailants to justice—while blacks were arrested by the thousands—led to a demand for one big "March on Washington for Jobs and Freedom." The idea originated with A. Philip Randolph, the only Negro Vice-President of the AFL-CIO, and was backed by CORE, SCLC (the Southern Christian Leadership Congress), SNCC, and eventually the NAACP. On August 28, more than two hundred thousand people converged on the Lincoln Memorial singing such songs as *Woke up this morning with my mind set on freedom.* Near the end of the day King addressed the crowd, which stretched more than a mile from the Washington Monument, with his famous "I have a dream" speech.

Now is the time to make real the promises of democracy. I have a dream that one day this nation will rise up and live out the true meaning of its creed: "We hold these truths to be self-evident, that all men are created equal." I have a dream that one day on the red hills of Georgia the sons of former slaves and the sons of former slave-owners will be able to sit down together at the table of brotherhood. . . .

Almost ten years had lapsed since the 1954 decision, but blacks were far away from real equality. In 1964 only one black child out of fifty was actually going to school with whites in the South, and the median black family income was only fifty-eight percent of that for white families. In a message to Congress in February, 1963, President Kennedy had listed some devastating comparisons: a black, compared with a white, citizen had half as much chance of completing high school, a third as much chance of becoming a professional, twice as much chance of becoming unemployed, the prospect of earning only half as much in his lifetime, and a life expectancy seven years less than whites.

The response of the federal government up until 1963 had been halting. The 1957 Civil Rights Act,

the first civil rights bill in eighty years, was aimed primarily at devices that impeded Negro voter registration, such as "constitutional understanding" tests and rules penalizing "mistakes in spilling," as one white registrar described them. It had also established the Civil Rights Commission. The Commission was strengthened by the 1960 Civil Rights Act, which plugged the loopholes of the 1957 act.

By 1960, both political parties had begun wooing the black voter. John Kennedy made a point of calling on Coretta Scott King while her husband was in jail during the presidential campaign. During the first two years of his administration, Kennedy considered the ballot the key to Negro advancement, but he soon realized that it was not enough. The televised reports of dogs assaulting Negro demonstrators in Birmingham were said to have been instrumental in prompting him to propose broad civil rights legislation on June 11, 1963.

Kennedy proposed the legislation at a time when nationwide support for civil rights was strong. A 1964 national opinion survey revealed that the majority of Americans no longer thought it inconceivable that they would vote for a Negro as President. Racist views were out of fashion, churches supported reform, and white middle-class suburbia seemed to recognize the justice of black grievances. Translating that moral consensus into legislation, however, would be an arduous process.

Kennedy sent a draft of his bill to Congress on June 19 and recommended that it be enacted before the end of the year. The bill prohibited discrimination in education, employment, labor unions and voting. The most controversial provision was a ban on racial discrimination in hotels, restaurants and other places of public accommodation, a section that Senate Minority Leader Everett Dirksen and Senator Barry Goldwater—both influential conservative Republicans—said they would oppose. Despite the March on Washington and strong backing by the executive branch, a bill with bipartisan support was not approved by the House Judiciary Committee until October 29. At the end of 1963, the bill was pigeonholed in the House Rules Committee whose chairman, Howard Smith of Virginia, was staunchly opposed to it.

The assassination of President Kennedy in November, 1963, seemed to spur the nation into more wholehearted support of a matter at the core of his administration's program. Lyndon Johnson said that nothing could honor Kennedy's memory more than the early passage of the bill, and he immediately began some very effective armtwisting. After a breakfast meeting with the new President in December, the Republican leader in the House of Representatives, Charles Halleck, announced his support of the bill; Johnson also wrested a promise from Smith that his committee would begin hearings on the bill in January.

As the hearings began, House Republicans were attuned to the pressures of a presidential election year. They did not look forward to making speeches

on Lincoln's birthday with civil rights still buried in committee. The added threat of a discharge petition prompted the committee to bring the bill to the floor of the House, and debate began January 31. It was passed eleven days later by a vote of 290 to 130. Only one major amendment had been added: the "May Craig" Amendment, named after a Maine television reporter, prohibiting job discrimination based on sex as well as on race. The House-passed version was called a compromise, but it retained almost all of the original Kennedy proposals, including the public accommodations section.

When the bill moved to the Senate, there were enough votes to pass it immediately, but a block of some twenty Southern Senators, led by Richard Russell of Georgia, had the power to delay the vote by filibustering and, with the aid of the more conservative Republicans, to force compromises. A vote on cloture—to cut off the filibuster—would require a two-thirds majority, for which Northern Democrats needed about twenty-five Republican votes. Dirksen's opposition to the public accommodations section would be pivotal.

The expected filibuster began March 9. Senator Russell called up the specter of racial "mongrelization" and Senator Allen Ellender of Louisiana said

Above "March on Washington for Jobs and Freedom," (August 28, 1963) the largest civil rights demonstration in American history.

National Guardsmen stand amid the rubble in Detroit where race riots in July, 1967, lost forty people their lives.

that white people in counties in his state "are afraid they would be outvoted." Mike Mansfield, the Majority Leader, began holding Saturday sessions to wear down the opposition, at the same time delaying a vote on cloture until he was sure of sixty-seven votes. Hubert Humphrey, floor leader of the sixty or so Senators in favor of the bill, opposed amendments to strengthen or weaken it, feeling it was the best bill that civil rights advocates could get through the eighty-eighth Congress.

While Southerners talked and supporters bided their time, the Negro revolt continued in the streets, particularly in Northern cities where it focused on school integration. In the South, SNCC demonstrations in Nashville led to one hundred arrests; in Jacksonville, Florida, rioting was triggered by the lack of progress toward desegregation; and tear gas was used on black demonstrators in Cambridge, Maryland. Schisms were beginning to develop in the civil rights movement, however, and even as legislation moved slowly through the Senate, there were indications that it was too little, too late, especially for Negroes in the North.

Electioneering continued simultaneously with street demonstrations. George Wallace, campaigning in Maryland, said the fair-hiring clause would force an employer to fire "Japanese Lutherans" and hire "Chinese Baptists." His strong showing in the Democratic primaries in Wisconsin, Indiana and Maryland revealed a discontent on the part of some whites with the pace of black gains. According to a Harris poll, three out of four whites thought the civil rights leadership had

been moving too fast. Goldwater, whose opposition to the bill was well known, won the California Republican presidential primary.

President Johnson continued to be a public advocate of the bill and public support for it increased from sixty-three percent in November to seventy percent in April. By the end of that month, there were indications that Senator Dirksen was willing to consider dropping his opposition. He introduced ten amendments to modify the Fair Employment Practices section. "Just what would *you* say about civil rights," he asked, "if you came to a convention in July and this thing was still hanging fire? . . ." The amendments primarily limited the Attorney General's right to initiate court action in cases where a pattern of discrimination existed and also required that complaints about public accommodations and employment be referred initially to state agencies. With the acceptance of these revisions, Senate leaders decided to seek a cloture vote, and on June 10, almost a year after Kennedy had requested the bill, the Senate voted seventy-one to twenty-nine to end the seventy-five-day filibuster—the first time cloture had ever been invoked for a civil rights measure. The NAACP's Roy Wilkins called it "a great day for Americans."

Cloture allowed only one hour's further debate for each Senator. After consideration of 115 amendments, which included 106 roll-call votes, and the adoption of agreed-upon revisions, the bill was passed on June 19, seventy-three to twenty-seven. Twenty-one Southern Democrats and six Republicans voted against it, including Barry Goldwater who said that its employment and public accommodations sections were unconstitutional. "There is an inexorable moral force that moves us forward," Dirksen replied. "This is an idea whose time has come." On July 2, the House approved the revised version and in a televised ceremony the same day, President Johnson signed into law the "most comprehensive piece of civil rights legislation ever proposed."

Among the act's eleven titles, in addition to the public accommodations section, were: a voting rights provision that set completion of the sixth grade as sufficient proof of literacy; provisions for the desegregation of public education through guidelines to be issued by the Department of Health, Education and Welfare; fair employment practices to be instituted over a three-year period; the creation of the Equal Employment Opportunity Commission to prevent discrimination in hiring, firing, promotions and union membership; and the establishment of the Community Relations Service to aid race relations on the community level.

The constitutionality of the act was unanimously upheld by the Supreme Court only five months after it was passed in *Heart of Atlanta Motel v. United States*, a suit brought by a motel that refused rooms to black interstate travelers. Ironically, the motel argued that being required to rent rooms to Negroes against its will was "involuntary servitude" and claimed relief under the Thirteenth Amendment.

The momentum gained by passage of the 1964 act continued into the summer and the following year as the civil rights movement reached its peak. "Freedom Summer," 1964, launched an intensive voter registration drive in the South, especially in Mississippi where slightly more than four percent of Negroes of voting age were registered. The project brought a large influx of Northern white students and was partially conceived to make the national government protect the civil rights of blacks in Mississippi. That such protection was needed became evident when three young workers, two white students from New York and a black Mississippi youth, disappeared after being arrested on a traffic charge and were later found brutally murdered. Among those finally convicted of the crime was the Neshoba County Deputy Sheriff. The voter registration drive was widely successful, however, and in October Martin Luther King was awarded the Nobel Peace Prize as "the first person in the Western world to have shown . . . that a struggle can be waged without violence."

Voter registration drives continued into the winter. Intimidation by local officials in Selma, Alabama, led to a march on that state's capital, Montgomery, in March. The protest group was met by state troopers using tear gas and eighty-seven people were injured. Although a federal judge ordered Governor George Wallace to provide protection when the march continued, three people were subsequently killed. In response to "Bloody

Mrs. Coretta King, widow of Martin Luther King Jr., the first woman to preach at a service in St. Paul's Cathedral, London.

Sunday" in Selma, President Johnson threw the force of the executive behind an effective voting rights law that was passed early in August, 1965. In 1967, more than fifty percent of eligible Negroes were registered to vote in every Southern state, and the gains began to be reflected in the election of black officials.

While progress was made in the South, President Johnson followed up with War on Poverty measures designed, in part, to bolster the educational and economic opportunities of blacks in Northern urban ghettos. "It's one thing for a Negro to get a cup of coffee, and another thing to have a dime to pay for it," summed up Whitney Young of the Urban League.

The effectiveness of the civil rights movement and the national commitment to racial progress were beginning to be depleted, however. Five months after Johnson pledged at Howard University in June, 1965, that his administration would help Negroes attain full equality, escalation of the war in Vietnam fatally distracted American attention from domestic concerns. The spontaneous riots in cities such as Washington, Chicago, Philadelphia and Newark during the "long hot summers" of 1965, 1966 and 1967 reflected a deep sense of frustration, spawned by rising expectations. White support and involvement in civil rights fell away as black leadership turned from those who had asked for "Freedom Now" to those who espoused "Black Power." Black militants rejected the tactics of nonviolence and the goal of integration for political, cultural and economic self-sufficiency.

Many said that the civil rights movement died at about the time the 1964 Civil Rights Act was passed. When Martin Luther King was assassinated by James Earl Ray in April, 1968, a particularly optimistic, idealistic era of struggle died with him.

JUDITH BENTLEY

Seven of the first nine blacks to serve in Georgia's legislature standing in the aisle of the House.

Johnson's America

The passage of the Civil Rights Act and the other changes that faced the United States during the Johnson administration made up his Great Society program, the most far-reaching program of social improvement in the whole of American history. Johnson's huge majority in the 1964 election, when he had received sixty-one percent of the popular vote against Senator Barry Goldwater, made it possible for him to promise widespread changes in his State of the Union address on January 4, 1965. Increases in spending for housing, education and the arts and an elaborate medicare program that earlier administrations had been too cautious to introduce were only the main measures to pass Congress during 1965. Some of Johnson's projects—notably a broadening of the minimum-wage law and improved unemployment benefits—were not accepted by Congress; more seriously, in the following year Congress refused to pass a bill making discrimination in housing illegal. Johnson had shown himself determined to press forward with social legislation of a kind that was already taken for granted in most European countries. Yet within two years of his landslide victory his whole program was in trouble. The difficulty of handling Congress was only one part of Johnson's problem. Finance was another; the War on Poverty program, for example, received only 200 million dollars instead of its expected 680 million dollars.

Johnson's domestic hopes were shipwrecked by his foreign policy. The Caribbean—an area that was always a measuring rod of U.S. foreign policy—came into prominence in 1965. After the assassination of the pro-American dictator Rafael Trujillo in 1961 the Dominican Republic became a trouble spot. Seeing the failure of both elected and unrepresentative military governments, and fearing that the republic would become another Cuba, the U.S. encouraged discontented army officers to start a rising. Johnson ordered the marines to land at Santo Domingo "to insure that U.S. lives should not be in danger." The marines eventually numbered nineteen thousand men. They quelled anti-government rioting in the Domi-

Anti-government soldiers in Santo Domingo with a jeep captured from the American marines.

nican Republic's capital, and were able to claim to have prevented an imminent leftist coup. By May 5, a truce had been negotiated and U.S. forces began to withdraw from the island.

Vietnam

The Dominican crisis showed that Johnson was willing to use U.S. troops in a twentieth-century equivalent of gunboat diplomacy. In Vietnam he showed that he was prepared to wage war to protect what he saw as U.S. interests. There is no evidence that this did more than delay what would have happened anyway in Vietnam, but at home it was to destroy Johnson's political reputation and to cause the United States one of the biggest crises of confidence in its history. Johnson did not begin the war in Vietnam. From the Geneva Conference of 1954, U.S. troops had been stationed in South Vietnam as advisers, but the Eisenhower administration had hoped that they could be removed soon after 1960.

In 1961, however, local Communist (Vietcong) activity became increasingly energetic. The U.S.-backed government of President Ngo Dinh Diem, which made little effort to disguise its nepotism and corruption, found its power being whittled rapidly away. Diem's re-

fusal to conciliate the large Buddhist population made his Roman Catholic government unpopular even among the least active political group. The number of American military personnel in Vietnam rose rapidly during Kennedy's presidency to more than twelve thousand men. Kennedy had stated: "We are not going to withdraw [from Vietnam] . . . for us to withdraw would mean the collapse not only of Vietnam but of Southeast Asia." These words, coupled with the overoptimism of the U.S. Army, which believed that 1965 would see a decisive military victory in

Vietnam, were to be Johnson's heritage from Kennedy. On November 1, 1963, a South Vietnamese military clique—with the knowledge, if not the support, of the Americans—deposed and executed Diem. The assassination of Kennedy later that month made Vietnam Johnson's problem. At first he was content to leave the conduct of the war to Secretary of Defense Robert McNamara. After less than a year, however, intransigent rebel troops with widespread popular support continued to resist combined U.S. and South Vietnamese efforts to expel or eliminate

President Diem, moments after an unsuccessful assassination attempt.

Caribbean and Vietnam increases

them. Repeated heavy bombing raids directed against supply depots and infiltration routes in North and South Vietnam and neighboring Laos hindered but failed to halt insurgent activity in the south, and the U.S. forces found themselves in a position little better than that of the French fifteen years before.

In March, 1968, President Johnson announced his intention severely to restrict American bombing in the north in an effort to break the stalemate. By this stage he had become increasingly disillusioned with the inability of his military advisers to fulfill their optimistic predictions. Besides, the unpopularity and high cost of the war were of enormous political significance at home, threatening his Great Society program and his hopes for reelection in 1968. Thus it was with high hopes that Johnson called for peace talks to settle the conflict. Hanoi responded promptly and affirmatively, and formal discussions began in Paris in May.

Cease-fire talks soon deadlocked over North Vietnamese demands for an unconditional bombing halt and U.S. demands for prompt withdrawal of North Vietnamese troops. As both the talks in Paris and the fighting in Southeast Asia dragged on, antiwar demonstrations and antiadministration broadsides grew more frequent and more vehement. With college students and the radical press—and later, college faculties and the established press—reiterating their demands for a solution to the Vietnam war, Johnson, as he had pledged the preceding March, did not seek reelection in November, 1968, but devoted himself instead to seeking "an honorable settlement" to the war during the remaining months of his term.

Great Britain

While the United States was divided by the problem of Vietnam, Britain had problems of other kinds. During the thirteen years of Conservative rule that had begun in 1951, Britain's economic troubles had increased dramatically, and by 1964 it was apparent that the government was no longer capable of running the economy effectively, or of reducing its massive balance of payments deficit. Leadership crises and the powerful stench of scandal—both financial and sexual—led to a Conservative defeat in

British Prime Minister Harold Wilson with Rhodesian leader Ian Smith during talks in London after Rhodesia's illegal declaration of independence.

the general election in that year. The new Labour administration under Harold Wilson saw the search for economic stability as its primary responsibility. During the next six years Britain's economy and balance of payments position strengthened, but the improvement was only possible at the expense of other social policies.

Other problems, too, demanded urgent attention, the most important of these being Ulster and Rhodesia. The compromise agreement of 1922 by which Ireland had been partitioned had long since begun to show signs of strain. The main problem was the attitude of the Protestant majority in Ulster (Northern Ireland) toward the Roman Catholic minority. The Irish Republican Army (I.R.A.)—although banned both in Ulster and the Republic—had long been the main forum for northern Roman Catholics who favored union with

Eire, and in 1967 the I.R.A. began to take a more militant line. A split in the I.R.A., with the foundation of a "provisional" wing in opposition to the "official" wing, led to outbreaks of sectarian violence. The government of Northern Ireland under Captain Terence O'Neill had already sought to avoid the more blatant forms of discrimination, but O'Neill's inability to act quickly led to his political isolation and fall from power. From 1970 the situation in Ulster was to deteriorate rapidly, and violence, both by the provisional I.R.A. and by Protestant loyalist extremists, mounted.

Rhodesia

The problem of Rhodesia was more distant, but no more tractable. With Britain abandoning her African empire, the white settlers

in Southern Rhodesia feared that it was only a question of time before they had to submit to a black-dominated government. To avoid this, in 1961 they had imposed a constitution that effectively disenfranchised the blacks. In 1964 when Northern Rhodesia (Zambia) and Nyasaland (Malawi)—which had formerly with Rhodesia made up the Central African Federation— became independent states, Southern Rhodesia found itself increasingly opposed to British policy. In 1965, angered by British pressure to improve native rights, the Prime Minister of Southern Rhodesia, Ian Smith, declared his country to be an independent state. This Unilateral Declaration of Independence angered public opinion in many countries. While refusing to use armed force to settle the dispute, the British government took the lead in imposing sanctions against Rhodesian trade, believing that this would lead to the speedy collapse of the Rhodesian "rebellion." But, despite the support of the U.N., the sanctions were never more than partially successful, as many governments—notably those of South Africa, Portugal (until 1974) and (from 1968) the Nixon administration—continued to trade with Rhodesia.

Rhodesia's position helped to polarize the opposition that already existed between white-dominated southern Africa and the states to the north of the Zambesi River. It also intensified the opposition to governments within the southern African states. In the Portuguese colony of Mozambique the nationalist movement gained momentum rapidly, and in 1966 Prime Minister Hendrik Verwoerd of South Africa was assassinated in Parliament by a white extremist.

Many of the black African states were disturbed by troubles of a different kind during this period. In 1964 the Arab ruler of Zanzibar was overthrown by Sheik Abeid Amani Karume whose government soon became notorious for its brutality. In April, Zanzibar and Tanganyika merged to form a new nation, Tanzania. In 1966 the flamboyant leftist rule of Dr. Kwame Nkrumah in Ghana was brought to an end by a coup d'état that led to a more pro-Western attitude. In Nigeria, too, discontent was brewing.

Meanwhile, in the Far East, China was plunged into civil strife as Mao Tse-tung fought his party.

A street barricade shuts off a Roman Catholic area in Belfast.

China's Cultural Revolution

The roots of the Cultural Revolution are to be found in the fundamental ideological and temperamental differences that had bedeviled the Chinese Communist Party from its earliest days—major contradictions that were to crystallize in Mao Tse-tung's declaration of war against the Party he had been largely responsible for bringing to power. Nonetheless Mao's victory in the Cultural Revolution was achieved at the cost of some of his most cherished ideals. The economic and social damage done to China was enormous and in the end economic principles rather than politics appeared to prevail. But China had begun to look outward—the necessary prelude to its acceptance into the community of nations.

Defense Minister Lin Piao, holding a copy of *Quotations from Chairman Mao*. The first edition was published for military use in 1965.

Opposite Part of Mao's wall poster campaign. Liu Shao-ch'i, portrayed as China's number one "revisionist," is wearing a yellow imperial robe. His protuberant nose is an additional touch of spite, as big noses are considered abhorrent in China. Despite his dismissal in the Cultural Revolution, Liu's policies could not be swept away.

In the huge Workers' Gymnasium in Peking on the evening of January 4, 1967, a vast crowd sang a rousing song that threatened vengeance on all who opposed Mao Tse-tung. As the song ended a group of Red Guards led General Lo Jui-ch'ing, former Chief of the General Staff, P'eng Chen, the recently ousted Mayor of Peking, Lu Ting-yi, who had been head of the Communist Party propaganda department and other "reactionaries" onto the platform. During the hours that followed speaker after speaker rose to condemn these men who until shortly before had been among the most powerful in China. As the crowd roared its approval of the treatment of the "despicable swine," the Red Guards knocked their victims to the floor and put their feet on them to show how the proletariat would triumph over all who threatened their rule.

The Peking rally was merely one of the largest of hundreds that occurred in almost all parts of China as the Cultural Revolution claimed victim after victim.

The roots of the Cultural Revolution stretched far back in the history of the Chinese Communist Party; they lay in the personalities of the small group of ageing men who formed the nucleus of the Party during the harsh years of the Long March and the Japanese invasion. The secrecy and the Byzantine intricacies of political maneuvering within the Communist Party and the complexities of political propaganda helped for a time to obscure the truth about the events that led up to the Cultural Revolution, but the truth gradually emerged during the late 1960s and early 1970s.

During the early years of Communist rule fundamental ideological and temperamental differences within the Party leadership were disguised by the need for economic growth to overcome the disruption caused by World War II and the Civil War. But Communist rule in China was already characterized by internal disagreement and contradiction.

The contradictions extended into almost every area of policy. There were major disputes as to whether revolutionary China should foment revolution in other countries. Defense Minister Lin Piao justified the withdrawal of substantial aid to North Vietnam by saying that "revolution or People's War in any country is the business of the masses in that country and should be carried out primarily by their own efforts.... If one does not operate by one's own methods . . . but leans wholly on foreign aid . . . no revolution can be won...." Although atomic weapons were officially viewed as "paper tigers" whose effect was far smaller than "the spiritual atom bomb" of the revolutionary warriors, China began work on nuclear weapons in the mid-1950s. The need to eliminate "warlordism" had been a major Communist aim from the 1920s, but in some provinces the governors were also military commanders, who could behave almost as though they were twentieth-century warlords. The mass culture that had supposedly taken the place of the traditional arts did not extend to the cinema where "Soviet realism" remained the major influence, even after Soviet Revisionism had come under fierce political attack. There were also fundamental disputes about the success of the Communist Revolution.

But the major contradiction was to be found in the role of Mao Tse-tung, who was Chairman of the Party Central Committee, Politburo and the Central Secretariat as well as head of state. His dominant position led inevitably to the formation of a personality cult and to fears about China's future after his death—understandable in view of the problems that had afflicted Russia after Stalin's death in 1953. Mao admired Stalin for the strong personal leadership he exerted, and one of the reasons for China's break with Russia was Khrushchev's attack on the Stalin personality cult. Although Mao's colleagues on the Party Central Committee emphasized that "he, too, obeys the Party," the strength of Mao's personality, charisma, self-confidence and his dominant role in Party development put him in an

Prince Norodom Sihanouk of Cambodia driving through the streets of Peking on a state visit. On the right is Chairman of the People's Republic, Liu Shao-ch'i, and on the left is Premier Chou En-lai.

unassailable position. Although he was not regarded as infallible, since the Party was the sole repository of infallibility, Mao's Thought was enshrined officially in the Party Constitution until 1957.

This almost divine role was emphasized between 1956 and 1959, when Mao began to divest himself of his title and "first-line" duties in order to deal more fully "with questions of the direction, policy and line of the Party and the state." His successor as Chairman of the People's Republic was Liu Shao-ch'i, whose hard work had done much to build up the Party organization in the 1940s. Mao found himself treated as a wise elder statesman, whose views were always respected but often in practice ignored.

Whether Mao's decision to reduce his administrative duties was entirely voluntary is uncertain. But if it was, Mao soon regretted his decision. He found himself increasingly at odds with the Party organization during the next few years. He was faced by many of the things that he most disliked in principle —the growth of bureaucracy and the spreading influence of intellectuals (university graduates) in particular—and was unable to do anything about it as the Party's power-base was in Liu's hands. At times he was able to overrule his colleagues but more often he was not, and this caused rapid swings in policy. In the "hundred flowers" campaign in 1956, for example, intellectuals were encouraged to "let a hundred flowers blossom, a hundred schools of thought contend." Instead of being rigidly bound by orthodoxy, Party officials and university graduates were encouraged to produce new ideas. A little over

a year later the importance of Marxist orthodoxy was being reestablished.

Such switches in policy were frequent in the years after 1956, and they suggest that there was tension in the Party's Central Committee. On the whole the Party machine tended to favor a bureaucratic system of government. It assumed that the Revolution of 1949 had brought with it the dictatorship of the proletariat, and involved a concentration on economic development. Mao, on the other hand, believed that the dictatorship of the proletariat was not necessarily secure, and that it was endangered by "representatives of the bourgeoisie who have sneaked into the Party, the government, the army and various cultural circles." He wanted to see the extension of the Revolution.

The "Great Leap Forward" of 1958 was, perhaps, an attempt to unite these divergent views by emphasizing the identity of socio-political and economic aims. Education emphasized that students should become "expert and red"—qualified but orthodox. The importance of economic growth was emphasized but the growth was to be built on human enthusiasm. As Mao said, "I have witnessed the energy of the masses. On this foundation it is possible to accomplish any task whatsoever."

The next three years proved him wrong. The three hard years from 1959 to 1961 were caused more by the wrong-minded overenthusiasm of the Great Leap Forward than by poor harvests. In 1958 the Minister of Defense, P'eng Teh-huai, was dismissed for expressing his view that "putting politics in command is no substitute for economic principles" too energetically; by 1961 most of the Central Committee shared his viewpoint, regarding the Great Leap Forward as a major disaster. Mao did not. Increasingly he identified those who disagreed with him on the Central Committee as bourgeois obstructionists—a criticism of attitude rather than birth—and Soviet revisionists. In his public statements criticism of the enemy within the Party became more and more frequent. Although the criticism appeared at the time to be largely rhetorical, like so much Chinese propaganda, it later became clear that by 1962 he had singled out Liu Shao-ch'i as the enemy; and since Liu controlled the Party machine, Mao was forced to take on the whole Party in order to triumph over him. This he justified by claiming the need for a state of continuing revolution. Thus the story of the Cultural Revolution is the tale of Mao's war against the Party that he himself had been largely responsible for bringing to power.

Mao's first step was to purge and reeducate the army. The new Defense Minister, Lin Piao, who had succeeded P'eng Teh-huai, dismissed a number of leading officers who favored an extension of China's commitment in North Vietnam. The most prominent of those who were dismissed was Lo Jui-ch'ing, Chief of General Staff. The first edition of *Quotations from Chairman Mao* was published for military use in 1964. In 1965, Mao was ready to move against his opponents, but his political isolation was so complete that he felt able to rely on only two supporters, his wife Chiang Ch'ing and his private secretary Ch'en Po-ta. The government, under Chou En-lai who had been Prime Minister since the Revolution, was suspect, with the sole exception of Lin Piao. Peking appeared to be firmly in the enemy camp, as the Mayor P'eng Chen was closely associated with Liu.

He was now ready to launch what came to be known as the Great Proletarian Cultural Revolution. This did not solely refer to culture in the sense of art and literature, but meant rather "a great revolution to establish proletarian civilization." The aim was political rather than artistic. But nonetheless the Cultural Revolution began on a cultural note.

The opening blow in Mao's campaign was against a distinguished historian and dramatist, Wu Han, who was a protégé of P'eng Chen and Deputy Mayor of Peking. Wu's play *Hai Jui's Dismissal*, published in 1961, had ostensibly been an historical drama, but was in reality an attack on the dismissal of P'eng Teh-huai. While Mao made a private and discreet criticism of the play in the Politburo's Standing Committee in September, 1965, he made arrangements for a more violent public denunciation. As the Peking newspapers, including the *People's Daily*, favored the Party apparatus, he sent Chiang Ch'ing and Ch'en Po-ta to publish an attack in a Shanghai newspaper.

P'eng Chen and his supporters leaped to the defense of the play in the Peking papers, and during the next few months controversy raged. It soon became clear, however, that Mao regarded Wu Han as no more than a pawn in a complex game of chess. By March, 1966, Mao felt strong enough to demand P'eng Chen's dismissal and arrest, and the Cultural Revolution claimed its first victim. Chiang Ch'ing and Lin Piao announced that the army, "the chief instrument of the dictatorship of the proletariat in China," would destroy the "dictatorship of the black line" that had defied Mao's wishes. They praised Mao's Thought as "the peak of contemporary Marxist–Leninism," a clear contrast to the importance of the Party as the lodestone of Communist orthodoxy. This was a reference to *Quotations*. The "little red book" that was soon to become a bestseller among students in many Western countries was now republished for general distribution. The importance of the *Quotations* was that, praising commonsense at the expense of formal authority, they by implication attacked the Party's bureaucratic structure.

Perhaps still not realizing the full implications of the Cultural Revolution that Mao was now publicizing, Liu Shao-ch'i had gone to Burma on a long state visit. On his return he must have realized his error; Mao was demanding that "counter-revolutionary revisionists ... of the Khrushchev brand" were still "nestling in our midst," and that they must be dismissed. A Cultural Revolution Group was set up under Ch'en Po-ta to coordinate radical activities. Students were encouraged to denounce their professors and the university authorities as bourgeois reactionaries. A campaign of wall posters—which carried the suggestion of grass-roots

On July 16, 1966, the seventy-three-year-old Mao Tse-tung (foreground) swam in the Yangtse River, in an attempt to quash rumors that he had died and that the Revolution was merely using his name.

support for the Cultural Revolution—denouncing Mao's enemies began in the universities, although the Mao-controlled newspapers were more moderate. But despite the revolutionary language and attitudes, few changes were made. The actors in Mao's revolution were still following the author's script. Indeed Mao was later to claim that even his enemies in the Party, such as Liu, had done as he had hoped when they set up "work teams" to cleanse the universities of Maoist supporters, whom they described as counterrevolutionaries; by doing so Mao claimed that they revealed themselves as his enemies.

Mao himself remained hidden from sight. Rumors that he was ill or dying added to the confusion. His remarkable swim in the Yangtse River—it was claimed that at the age of seventy-three he had broken the Olympic record by the splendor of his thought—did nothing to end the rumors. On August 18, 1966, the rumors were finally quashed as Mao appeared at a huge public meeting along with the first Red Guards, students who abandoned their studies in order to further the continuing revolution. In the next few months, however, Mao's control over his revolution effectively ended. During the rest of 1966, different groups of Red Guards, all claiming loyalty to Mao, fought each other in his name. Confusion in the universities became almost complete as no one knew which were the true Maoists. Vendettas that had nothing to do with politics were settled. Anarchy began to spread from the students to their elders in provincial and urban administration in some parts of the country. Mao's intention of using the Red Guards to sweep away Party organization in the universities had been all too successful. Yet outside the universities, despite their

belief that they were furthering the revolution, the Red Guards did little to overthrow those whom Mao had determined to destroy. Instead of attacking high Party officials they turned their attention to those whom they classified as "seven kinds of black," such as wealthy peasants; their activities merely expanded the chaos into which much of China seemed doomed to fall. Despite the appeals of the leadership for moderation many were killed. Even in Peking, which was now largely under Mao's control, mobs of Red Guards of differing hues attacked the Soviet and British embassies and denounced virtually all senior Party members—not excluding the most extreme of revolutionaries, Chiang Ch'ing.

Despite the follies and excesses of the Red Guards and the mutual recriminations of its members, the survival of the Party organization nationally was not threatened until January, 1967, when Mao ordered the Red Guards to "storm the positions" of the Party. In Shanghai and in three of the provinces anti-Liu groups were able to take power. In most other parts of China, however, the student radicals, instead of maintaining the offensive, found themselves attacked by industrial workers and peasants who supported the Party.

A moderate group in Peking, led by Chou En-lai, which had rallied to Mao's support had long criticized the economic damage caused by the Red Guards. Mao, now worried by lack of control over the Revolution, listened to their criticisms and in January, 1967, ordered the army, which had hitherto played a largely passive role, to come to the assistance of the radicals, but his real intention— that the army should take control—was clear.

The army showed little enthusiasm for its new task.

94

Senior officers feared that the defense of China might be impaired at a time when both the U.S.A. and the U.S.S.R. were making apparently threatening gestures and that soldiers would be influenced by the general lack of orderliness around them. Nor was it clear, despite Lin Piao's purges, that the army had any hostility toward the Party machine. Revolutionary Committees were set up in some parts of the country by the army, and senior Party officials were in most cases appointed through them. In many areas, however, not even the army was able to control events.

In Peking Mao's supporters were able to concentrate on the attack on Liu once again. By January he was being openly named as a bourgeois reactionary by the Cultural Revolution Group. His son and one of his daughters had been forced by the Red Guards to denounce him. On the pretext that another of his daughters had had an accident a group of Red Guards persuaded Liu's wife to go to

Mass rally in support of Mao Tse-tung.

Left Maoist poster. Here Liu is seen as the twin of Khrushchev, thus symbolizing the "supreme twosome of revisionism."

Far left Reciting the thoughts of Chairman Mao.

Propaganda break; agricultural workers in Canton Province taking time off from the harvest for a discussion of Chairman Mao's Thought. Such a study was supposed to be part of the workers' daily routine.

a hospital where she was kidnapped and forced to denounce her husband. Yet Liu still kept his formal position as head of state, and demanded that if he was to be tried it must be by the Party Central Committee. Mao knew that Liu still had widespread support on the Central Committee but was narrowly able to insure his condemnation by the Standing Committee. In addition, a huge publicity campaign against Liu was mounted. Attacks on other leading officials such as Chou En-lai and Ch'en Yi, the Foreign Minister, were little less virulent.

By the fall of 1967 the Cultural Revolution had run out of steam. Mao's increasing dislike of the Red Guards was apparent to all. Even Chiang Ch'ing, who throughout the Cultural Revolution had led the extreme radical campaign, was forced

to admit that the army, which she had been denouncing as recently as July, was "the cornerstone of the dictatorship of the proletariat."

But despite the efforts of Mao and his associates to end the Cultural Revolution, it was to take over a year for life in China to show much sign of recovery, and it was the army that was to be responsible for the eventual suppression of the Red Guards and other militant groups. This was eventually done by persuading or forcing hundreds of thousands of radical students to do agricultural work in the provinces.

The effect of the Cultural Revolution was mainly negative. For example, China's concentration on internal affairs made her unable to support North Vietnam at a crucial stage in the war with the

South. While Lin Piao could say "the victory of the present great Cultural Revolution is very great. The price we paid was the smallest, smallest and smallest, but the victory we gained is the greatest, greatest and greatest," the reality was different.

Mao had won a victory over his opponents; Liu died in disgrace after he was eventually forced to give up his office in 1968, and the Party bureaucracy appeared to be in ruins. But from 1968 onward many of those who had been dismissed during the Cultural Revolution returned to their former posts. At the Ninth Party Congress in 1969 only thirty percent of those elected to the Central Committee at the Eighth Congress in 1956 were reelected. But the reason for this was in most cases death rather than disgrace. Most of the new members of the Central Committee were soldiers, and almost none were noted radicals. Many of those—such as Ch'en Po-ta—who had risen to prominence during the Cultural Revolution were themselves purged after it had ended; those who had been most enthusiastic in their response to Mao's call for permanent revolution now found themselves under official attack as ultra-leftists. In economic terms the cost of Mao's attack on the Party had been enormous, and by emphasizing the existence of different classes—workers, bureaucrats, students, intellectuals, soldiers—within the dictatorship of the proletariat it was socially highly divisive.

Nor did the Cultural Revolution solve Mao's problems. The issue of his succession was less decided than ever. Lin Piao was Mao's heir apparent, but in 1971 it became clear that there had been a rift between the two men, and Lin was reported to have been killed in an air crash while trying to escape from China to Russia. The new heir presumptive was Chou En-lai. But Chou himself was seventy-three, only five years younger than Mao, and the Cultural Revolution had removed many of the rising younger officials. China's government remained almost totally dominated by old men who had risen to prominence in the Party during its early years.

Liu Shao-ch'i's policies were not swept away with his dismissal. Rather it was Mao Tse-tung who had to change his views after the Cultural Revolution was over. Although Mao could still say "no one must think that everything will be alright after one or two great cultural revolutions, or even three or four, for socialist society covers a very long historical period," the idea of permanent revolution seemed to have been abandoned. The Leninist idea of the Party as the "vanguard" of society replaced Mao's view that it was a "mass organization." Above all, for a time at least, China abandoned its inward-looking stance; instead of the search for ideological purity, China looked outward in foreign affairs and joined the United Nations. Economic principles rather than politics appeared to be in command in industry and agriculture. Mao's victory over the Party in the Cultural Revolution was more apparent than real and it was only achieved at the cost of some of his most cherished ideals.

ADRIAN BRINK

1967

Strife in Black Africa

The Federal Republic of Nigeria was a shaky coalition of four regions populated by various different, unrelated tribes, torn by tribal and political dissension and tormented by widespread corruption. When the nation was rocked by two violent army coups and a concomitant massacre of thousands of Ibo tribesmen, the surviving Ibos fled to their home Eastern Region and declared their independence as the Republic of Biafra. For thirty months the embattled Republic fought against the Nigerian federal army only to surrender at last at the cost of millions of dead, mostly noncombatants, mostly by starvation.

Lieutenant Colonel Odumegwa Ojukwu, Biafra's leader.

Opposite Starving Biafran children, rationed to two cups of milk a week. The majority of Biafra's casualties were noncombatants who died of starvation.

On May 30, 1967, the Eastern province of the politically troubled Federal Republic of Nigeria proclaimed its independence, taking the name Biafra. A political entity created by the British, Nigeria was composed of four regions: a vast and landlocked Northern Region and three smaller ones, fronting on the Gulf of Guinea and the Bight of Biafra, the Western, Mid-Western and Eastern Regions. It was into the last that federal troops went on July 6 in what was described by Major General Yakubu Gowon, Nigeria's Chief of State, as a "police action." It was in fact civil war.

Gaining its independence in 1960, Nigeria had almost from the outset been plagued by regional, political and tribal disputes. The instability of the nation was underscored in 1966 when two violent army coups culminated in General Gowon's seizing power. During the turmoil, tens of thousands of members of the Ibo tribe had been massacred and most of their fellow tribesmen had fled to the Eastern Region—their homeland. Their search for security ended in secession and war.

The war lasted thirty months, ending in January, 1970, with Biafra's total defeat and the flight of her leader, Lieutenant Colonel Odumegwa Ojukwu. By then the federal army had swollen to a force of more than 120,000 from a prewar strength of only 10,000. It was bound to remain an important political force. General Gowon's position as head of the federal military government was also secure. As for the future of a reunited Nigeria, Gowon's plan to replace the four regions with twelve states, a plan that had been one of the reasons for the Eastern Region's secession as Biafra, was now fully implemented.

If such radical redrawing of the boundaries, political as well as geographical, would not guarantee an end to domination of the federal government by the Northern Region, it was at least likely to promote a new relationship between the federal government at Lagos, now stronger and richer than

before, and the states at the periphery, some relatively small, weak and poor. The substance of dispute among Nigeria's various factions had always been the balance between power at the center and in the regions. That smouldering dispute finally erupted into action in 1966.

In mid-January of that year five majors assassinated some of Nigeria's leading politicians, among them the federal Prime Minister, Sir Abubakar Tafawa Balewa, and a number of the army's most senior officers. Although the coup was stifled at birth and its principals immediately arrested, the government of the country passed from civilian hands. The new head of state, Major General Johnson T. U. Aguiyi-Ironsi, suspended the constitution, set up a Supreme Military Council and appointed military governors for the four regions in place of the civilian premiers. One of these appointments, the Governor of the Eastern Region, was Lieutenant Colonel Ojukwu.

Ironsi did not survive long. In May, when he peremptorily announced his intention of abolishing the regions and unifying the regional civil services, his downfall was assured. Serious rioting broke out in the North, apparently instigated by civil servants afraid of losing their jobs, in consequence of the proposed unification, to men from other regions. On July 29, Ironsi and the military governor of the West were murdered at Ibadan, the capital of the West. Simultaneously, Northern troops mutinied. Three days later, with order partially restored, Lieutenant Colonel Gowon announced that he had taken power as Supreme Military Commander.

Like the federal civil service, the army was in principle a national institution. The danger was that its cohesion could be shattered if tribal and regional loyalties were invoked and came to be paramount, superseding allegiance to the nation. Once that happened, the command structure would break down, leaving mutually hostile remnants that would form the nuclei of tribal armies.

It was claimed by the makers of the January, 1966, coup, and subsequently by Ironsi as well, that the army had remained impartial throughout, acting only to cleanse the nation and to scourge corruption. The federal elections of the preceding autumn had been marked by outbreaks of organized violence and intimidation and were widely believed to have been rigged in favor of candidates of the ruling coalition. Army apologists cited this as an instance of the depths to which the politicians had stooped. But it was noted by skeptics that only the Northern and Western premiers had been victims of the coup, and that with one exception all the army men killed were Northerners; and as all five majors were Easterners, as was Ironsi himself, tribal factionalism seemed at least as compelling a reason for the coup as corruption.

The rioting in May and the army mutiny of July had an even clearer tribal slant and were regarded by Easterners as undeniable evidence of Northern determination to reassert that region's traditional grip on power and avenge the January murders. Although religious differences may not in reality have had much influence, Eastern Region propaganda at that time (and Biafran propaganda after secession) played insistently on Ibo fears of a *jihad*, or holy war, by the Moslem North and contrasted the more advanced Easterners with the more backward, feudal Northerners. The wholesale massacre of Ibos resident in the North in October, leading to the mass exodus back to the Ibo homeland and the beginning of the Biafran refugee problem, gave Lieutenant Colonel Ojukwu further grounds for arguing that the East should go its own way and make its own arrangements to secure the safety of its people.

There is good reason to believe that when General Gowon assumed power he did so with the intention

Federal troops crossing the Niger River Bridge on their way to Onitsha.

shortly thereafter of taking the Northern Region out of the federation. He was strongly advised against that course of action by, among others, the U.S. ambassador, and similar advice was tendered by senior civil servants. But the most influential counselors were those Northerners who spoke against secession: Colonel Hassan Katsina, the military governor, and the leaders of the Tiv minority tribe. So Gowon set himself the task of national reconciliation.

One of his first acts was the release of political prisoners, which was something more than just a gesture. Yoruba chiefs Awolowo and Enahoro, who had been jailed for conspiracy against the government in 1963, were freed in early August. They had previously been prominent in the Action Group, long the ruling party in the Western Region. Dr. Okpara, who came out of jail the day after the Yoruba leaders, had been the premier of the Eastern Region until the coup of January, 1966. The release of Tiv leaders, imprisoned following riots in the Middle Belt in 1964, was more prudent than generous. The Middle Belt was strategically placed between the Eastern and Northern Regions. Gowon wanted to be sure of that frontier and also knew that he could rely on the loyalty of the considerable numbers of Tivs serving in the army. Similar considerations no doubt prompted Ojukwu to exchange six hundred Northerners stationed at Enugu in the East for Ibo soldiers serving elsewhere in the federation.

At the end of August Gowon restored the status quo by revoking Ironsi's unification decree. The stage was now set for interregional consultations on new constitutional arrangements. Gowon made the opening address to the conference in Lagos on September 12. An interim report, setting out the differences between North and East, was ready at the end of the month. Then came the terrible massacre of Ibos over the weekend of October 1 and the conference was completely disrupted. It reconvened late in October, without a delegation from the East, and was adjourned indefinitely in mid-November. At the end of the month Gowon outlined his own plans for Nigeria's future, which included a strong federal government and the creation of new states. The East remained firmly committed to a form of association that left the regions with most of the executive functions of government and the center merely with a pool of common services to administer; each region should raise its own armed forces, legislate, and levy and collect its own taxes; there would be no effective central authority to exercise a veto.

In January, 1967, with the prospect of agreement more and more remote, Gowon met with the four military governors on neutral ground at Aburi in Ghana. Ojukwu was the star of this occasion, outshining his colleagues with ease. He pointed out that so far as the Eastern Region was concerned his authority alone was undisputed, and he refused outright to acknowledge Gowon as Supreme Military Commander. He argued that whatever his col-

Biafran junior officer being questioned by federal intelligence officer (*right*) at federal headquarters in captured Onitsha

leagues' hopes for the future, at present only the East's proposals were practical and realistic. The final communiqué showed that Ojukwu had carried the day. The press conference that he held on his return to the East was a triumphant exercise in self-congratulation.

In Lagos it was another story. The federal civil service, which had an interest of its own in the preservation of an effective central government machine, sent a strong memorandum to Gowon indicating some of the pitfalls in the draft document. These included the implicit threat to Gowon's own position as head of state. And when Decree No. 8 implementing the Aburi agreement was published in March, it was clear that it embodied a federal rather than a regional interpretation: federal law was to remain superior to regional law, existing federal law was safeguarded by veto power and the Supreme Military Commander had emergency powers that would enable him to intervene in regional affairs.

As March and the old fiscal year drew to their close, questions of finance came to the fore. The East had budgeted for an increase of expenditure in the new year (1967–68) of £9 million, but this was on the assumption that the region controlled its own assets and revenues, notably oil, which was not the case. On the contrary, over half the East's revenues were levied and collected by the federal government for remittance to Enugu. Ojukwu's solution to this problem was to sequester federal revenues collected in the East and to call in the oilmen and persuade them to pay their taxes directly to him. The federal government responded by placing an embargo on the East.

On May 27, Gowon repealed the two-month-old Decree No. 8 and announced that the four regions were to be abolished and replaced by twelve states, six in the North and three each in the West and East. Three days later Ojukwu proclaimed the Eastern Region's secession and the birth of Biafra.

Now it only remained to wait for the fighting to start. At the end of June Colonel Muhammad Shuwa, commanding the Northern troops, moved his headquarters south from Kaduna to Makurdi. In a few days the border was sealed. And on July 6 the attack was launched.

The federal battle plan was simple and direct: a two-pronged assault from the northeast and northwest, with the main commitment to the latter, along a line from Nsukka to Enugu, the East's capital, while the troops to the east secured the Cameroun frontier and then either turned west in a pincer movement on Enugu or continued south to the port of Calabar at the mouth of the Calabar River and the sea. It was expected that the fighting would last a couple of weeks. With the advantage of the initiative,

Biafran delegates arrive in Kampala for peace talks to be opened by President Obote of Uganda (May, 1968). The African states stood by the federal government as they opposed the disruption of the most important of the African states.

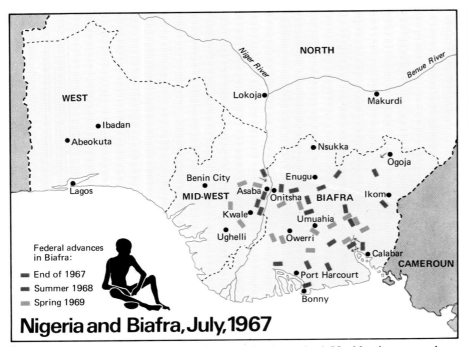

Nigeria and Biafra, July, 1967

Federal advances in Biafra:
- End of 1967
- Summer 1968
- Spring 1969

Above right Federal soldier. Both the federal government and Biafra underestimated each other's military strength and determination to pursue a long struggle.

Federal troops making for Benin after halting Biafra's westward push at Ore.

federal troops had reached Nsukka in seven days but then the advance bogged down. On July 25 a small amphibious force was landed at Bonny, an island in the mouth of the Calabar River, whose military significance was marginal but which owed its political and economic importance to the presence of the Eastern oil storage facilities of BP-Shell. Practically speaking, however, the presence of troops on the island made no difference so long as the federal navy could maintain its blockade of the Biafran coast.

August was the month in which Biafra came closest to winning the war. The key to victory lay in the attitude of the Mid-West and the West, the other two coastal southern regions. If Biafra could find a way to unlock the federal alliance and isolate the North then victory would be hers. Ever since

independence there had been close ties between the southern politicians of the opposition parties in the West and the governing parties in the East. Adebayo and Ejoor, the military governors of, respectively, the West and the Mid-West, had up until the very last opposed the use of force against Ojukwu. It is evidence of Gowon's awareness of the danger of such a split that four of the eleven civilian commissioners brought into the government in June were well-known as progressives, two Westerners (Awolowo and Enahoro) and two Northerners (Tarka and Aminu Kano). Chief Awolowo's statement, made earlier in the year, that if the East seceded the West should do so too, was also on the record to hearten Biafra and alarm the North.

On August 9 the door to the West opened. Federal troops mutinied in Benin, the Mid-Western capital. Their leaders were Ibo officers, among them Colonel Nwawo, Ejoor's second in command. Two Biafran columns immediately crossed the Niger River unopposed: one turned south, making for the oilfields at Ughelli, the other entered Benin. The Biafran commander, Lieutenant Colonel Banjo, was a Westerner, a Yoruba, who was alleged to have been assigned the task of killing Ironsi in the January coup of 1966 and who had been held in military detention in the East since then. His appointment may have been intended as a signal of Ojukwu's readiness to deal with the West, but Banjo soon showed that he had ambitions of his own. He announced that he was setting up an independent state of which he would be the head. Three days later he was relieved of his command and Major Okonkwo, a thirty-five-year-old doctor who had been in the army fifteen months, was appointed military administrator in his place. But the change of command had cost invaluable time. A relentless and uninterrupted drive on Lagos, three hundred and forty miles west of Benin, might well have captured the federal capital. Had that happened there is no way of knowing what effect it would have had either on the political calculations of Western leaders or on the loyalties of the air force and navy. As it was, Biafra's westward push was halted at Ore, a small town one hundred and thirty miles from Lagos. Here the opposing armies met, and here they stood and fought.

Meanwhile, the Yoruba leaders had made their decision. Chief Awolowo announced his support for Gowon and the federal government. No doubt the presence of federal troops in his region had some influence on the Western leader's decision to close the door on secession, as had his awareness of the demands from minority tribes within the region for separate recognition; it is likely that Gowon's appointing him to a government position also counted for something in his calculations.

Bitter fighting continued at Ore till the end of the month, with the Biafrans bringing in reinforcements from the east while federal troops moved in from north and south to support the main force. Elsewhere, fighting flared again on the northwestern front and Nsukka was retaken by the Biafrans.

But the tide of battle was ebbing for Biafra. By the year's end the federal army was engaged on four fronts. Enugu fell in early October and the push was continuing southward; federal troops had advanced east from Benin and were now in Asaba on the west bank of the Niger, unable as yet to effect a crossing to capture Onitsha; to the east, the capture of Ikom had cut Biafra's escape route to the Cameroun frontier; while in the south a sea-borne invasion force took Calabar in mid-October and turned west toward Biafra's only other outlet to the sea, Port Harcourt.

On paper at any rate Biafra's military situation was hopeless. Landlocked and encircled by federal armies with an overall numerical superiority of two to one, the Biafrans were already confined within the boundaries of the Ibo homeland. Yet the war was to drag on for another two years with few federal military achievements of consequence until Biafra's final collapse in January, 1970.

The outcome of four major federal offensives, the first announced in August, 1968, and the other three in January, June, and November, 1969, achieved, in 1968, the capture of Onitsha in March and of Port Harcourt in May, and, in 1969, the fall of Umuahia in April. Against these painfully limited federal successes must be set the Biafran breakout in April, 1969, which resulted in the recapture of Owerri and, in the following month, airstrikes against Port Harcourt and a bold raid on Kwale, during which some European oilmen were kidnapped. This proved something of an embarrassment because of the howl of international protest it provoked; and moreover the other Biafran "successes" represented propaganda victories rather than real gains. Nonetheless the question remains: why did the war last so long?

Partisan explanations go some way toward an-swering this question. One factor was de Gaulle's support of the Biafran cause, which he announced to the world at a news conference in September, 1968, and which was supposedly responsible for a flood of French weaponry to Biafra. Another was the degree to which the relief agencies were drawn into the partisan struggle and the cover that their operations gave to the arms lift. In addition General Gowon was reluctant to launch "all-out" war against densely populated civilian areas. But there were other factors as well, such as the heroic struggle of a united people for self-determination and the inspiring leadership of Colonel Ojukwu.

Some further considerations would be the following. Both sides were putting men into the field, most of whom had had little training and no battle experience. It unquestionably worked to the Biafran advantage that they were defending a relatively small area that was also their homeland. It was correspondingly to the federal side's disadvantage that their men were fighting in unfamiliar and inhospitable terrain, far from home, with poor lines of communication and coordination and desperately extended lines of supply. Indiscipline and indiscriminate violence against civilians were the inevitable results, and these in turn stiffened resistance and fostered belief in Biafran allegations of a federal policy of genocide.

Away from the battlefields, both sides consistently underestimated the determination and capacity of their opponent to pursue a prolonged struggle. Evidence of this is to be found in the dreary history of the wholly unavailing efforts of well-meaning intermediaries to bring the combatants to the conference table. Over and over each side reiterated its intransigent positions: Biafra never abandoned her demand for recognition and the federal government never wavered in its call for the rebels to surrender. At the bitter end the only resolution was to be found in military victory.

TOM RIVERS

Colonel Adekunle, the most dashing of the Nigerian military commanders.

Skeleton of a soldier. Both sides suffered high casualties as the majority of troops had had little training and no battle experience.

103

The Six Day War

Far less drawn out than the Nigerian Civil War and far less costly in human life was the outbreak of fighting in the Middle East six days after Biafra's declaration of independence. During the spring there had been border clashes between Israel and Syria; tension mounted, and in May, Egypt became directly involved. Nasser ordered the United Nations expeditionary force, the observer force that separated Israel from Egypt and the Gaza Strip, to leave. This warlike gesture might perhaps have been regarded by the Israelis as no more than an attempt by Nasser to retain the leadership of Arab opinion, but on May 22 Nasser also announced the closing of the Strait of Tiran, the entrance to the Gulf of Aqaba, to Israeli shipping, thus cutting off oil and other supplies to the port of Eilat. While Palestine Liberation Organization leader Ahmed Shukairy threatened to drive the Israelis into the Mediterranean and a Syrian minister promised that Israel would be destroyed in four days, the Israelis put the finishing touches to a plan of a preemptive military strike that would shatter the Arab air forces at a blow.

Arabs drop to the ground as the shadow of an Israeli jet passes.

Early in the morning of June 5, Israeli aircraft attacked airfields in Egypt, Syria, Jordan and Iraq. After flying far out into the Mediterranean the Israelis penetrated Egypt's defenses at 6.30 A.M., attacking more than fifteen air bases. Some 400 airplanes—many of them newly supplied by the Russians— were destroyed on the ground during the morning. The next few days were to show that Arab counterclaims to have shot down 180 Israeli jets were untrue, as the Israelis were able to demonstrate their complete control in the air.

On the ground, deprived of air support, the Arabs were able to do little. Egyptian tanks were destroyed in their hundreds in the Sinai Desert by Israeli aircraft, and Israeli armored columns were able to move quickly across the desert, passing the burned-out wrecks of Russian tanks in the strategic Mitla Pass, and to reach the Suez Canal on June 8. The Strait of Tiran was opened to Israeli shipping on the same day after Israeli troops occupied Sharm-el Sheikh—which commands it—without a fight. Now Israel was able to use the Gulf of Aqaba, while Egypt's revenues from the Suez Canal were lost as a result of Israeli guns and hastily sunk ships.

The Israelis were no less successful elsewhere. After an heroic defense of the Arab part of the city of Jerusalem, the Jordanians were forced back across the Jordan River, losing the relatively fertile West Bank and its tourist revenues. Syria, more cowardly or more prudent, did no more than bombard the Israeli settlements in Galilee from the Golan Heights. Even this mild support for the Arab cause from the most militantly anti-Israeli of the Arab states brought swift reprisals, and Israel occupied the Golan Heights, a region from which Syrian guns had been able to dominate much of low-lying Israel.

The loss of Arab territory was enormous, but the loss of prestige was far greater. Nasser, who had been widely regarded as one of the most far-seeing statesmen in the world, was now discredited—although in Egypt itself his attempted resignation caused riots by mobs who had not yet grasped just how seriously Egypt had been defeated. Nasser's ambitions were, however, much curtailed and he was forced to abandon the war in the Yemen and to purge his army. The loss of military matériel was, perhaps, the least important aspect of the Arab defeat, since within a few months the Russians had replaced—at what cost is unknown—aircraft and tanks.

Yet, despite the extent of the Israeli victory in the Six Day War, the importance of the war is easily overrated. It was in reality merely another battle in the longer struggle between Israel and the Arab states. A root cause of Arab objections to Israel—the plight of Palestinian refugees—was largely overlooked, although the size of that problem grew enormously as a result of the Israeli victory. The Israelis saw their frontiers as more secure than before, but the dangers of overconfidence were vastly increased; while the Arabs, shattered by defeat, looked for lessons from their defeat, as the 1973 Yom Kippur War was to show. The dependence of both Israel and the Arabs on the great powers remained, and Russian-American disagreement both helped to keep up the tension in the Middle East and at the same time obscured its cause.

Czechoslovakia

If 1967 had seemed a gloomy year internationally, 1968 was no less so. The Nigerian Civil War dragged on, peace in Vietnam seemed increasingly distant to all but a handful of American generals and politicians, and in the Middle East tension between Israel and the rearmed Arabs threatened several times to explode into war. To this international picture, which United Nations Secretary General U Thant was to describe as bleak, were added signs of domestic conflict and tension that threatened to disrupt society and economy in several of the more advanced states in both East and West.

Since the Hungarian rising of 1956 had been crushed, Russia's satellite states in Eastern Europe had been reluctant to court a similar fate by adopting liberal reforms that might antagonize the Soviet Union. But change in Eastern Europe could not be avoided for ever. The Communist old guard in Czechoslovakia under Antonín Novotný, a Stalinist who had been the country's virtual dictator since 1953, had been forced to resign by a rising chorus of criticism in 1967, both because of its failure to deal with inflation and other economic difficulties and because of public dissatisfaction with its strongly anti-Israeli line during the Six Day War. On January 5, 1968, the sixty-three-year-old Novotný gave way under popular pressure and finally resigned his post as the First Secretary of the Central Committee of the Communist Party, although he retained the presidency

Alexander Dubček, the Czech Communist Party leader ousted by the Russians.

of the Czechoslovak republic

The new Party Secretary, Alexander Dubček, soon showed his lack of sympathy with the hardline policies of his predecessor. He announced that the party would try to introduce "socialism with a human face." During the spring of 1968 a large number of reforms were announced and the government sought to weaken the hold of the bureaucracy, and many leading trade unionists and party officials—including the President —were forced to resign. An investigation into the mysterious death in 1948 of the non-Communist statesman Jan Masaryk was opened and many non-Communists were appointed to government posts.

The Soviet Union had initially appeared to favor the changes, but the Czechs soon noticed that the media in Russia and the East European states did not mention the changes that were taking place. The pressure on Czechoslovakia from the Soviet Union mounted steadily, particularly after the publication of *Two Thousand Words*, a document calling for the rapid liberalization of the whole government machine. Although the Soviet Union repeatedly denied that it had any intention of interfering in Czechoslovakia's internal affairs, plans for invasion were being prepared. The fears of the U.S.S.R. were probably due less to Dubček's reforms than to the possibility of the creation of a bloc of non-

Soviet-aligned Communist states— Rumania, Yugoslavia and Czechoslovakia.

On the night of August 20, with the assistance of the traffic controllers at Prague airport, the Russians began to ferry Warsaw Pact troops and tanks into the capital. All the main towns were quickly occupied. The Russians claimed that they had been asked by ministers and party officials to intervene, but this claim never achieved widespread belief either in Czechoslovakia or abroad. The Czech government realized that its troops could not overthrow an invasion force of half a million men, and confined the army to barracks. The people, too, were asked to show no violence toward the Russians, an appeal that was not universally heeded. Radio stations continued to broadcast anti-Soviet messages, and a newly (and secretly) elected Central Committee demanded the end of the occupation.

But the tanks and men of the Warsaw Pact could not be ignored and would not go away at the request of the Czech government. Dubček and other revisionist leaders were briefly imprisoned in Moscow, and in Czechoslovakia itself the process of "normalization" began. Gradually, over the next three months, progressives were forced out of office and replaced by conservatives. Nonetheless it was not until 1970 that the pro-Soviet element in the government felt sufficiently sure of itself to carry out a thorough-going purge of party membership.

Paris in the spring

In France, too, social conflict erupted in 1968. The government of the Gaullist prime ministers in the years after 1958 had shown itself increasingly unable to satisfy the aspirations of large sections of the community—most notably the trade unions and the students—and had chosen instead to build an electoral base among rural and small-town groups. The discontent that was caused came to a head in 1968 for economic reasons—inflation, unemployment and high taxation for wage earners hit the working population and city dwellers particularly hard. De Gaulle's complacent inability to believe that "the crises of former times" could upset his government was not, however, enough to unite the

A Kent State University student throwing a teargas bomb back at guardsmen.

tangled parties of the parliamentary opposition to overthrow him, but among working people the President was increasingly regarded as an outmoded fossil.

The government was unpopular among workers, but the students had no rivals in their hatred of it, and the "events" of May, 1968, were begun by student militants. At one of the campuses of the University of Paris, in the suburb of Nanterre, student discontent led to rioting that spread at once to most other universities. The motives were mixed—anger at overcrowded and uncomfortable conditions, discontent with outmoded rules and a desire to sweep away an "unjust" society—but the appeal seemed universal. Fighting broke out almost daily between students and police

A street battle between Paris students and police.

in the Latin Quarter (the student quarter of Paris). The students made little impact on the well-armed ranks of the police, but the violence of the police made an immediate impact on public opinion. Strikes spread rapidly throughout France's more industrialized areas. Demands for widespread industrial and social changes were made by the strikers, while the irresolution of the government was apparent to all. On May 30, however, de Gaulle broadcast a

firm message denying rumors that he was about to retire; he also announced that there would be a general election and attempted to split the opposition by agreeing to an increase in legal minimum wage levels. During June the troubles evaporated almost as quickly as they had arisen, and the Gaullists were returned with an increased majority in the elections. But the events of 1968 had illustrated the gap that existed between the underprivileged industrial majority and the pampered rural minority, and Gaullists began to show an increasing awareness of economic reality.

U.S. presidential election

Student discontent was not confined to France. Throughout the world students felt a new confidence, often regarding themselves as a "fifth estate" able to influence political decision-making for the first time. The United States election of 1968 was to show how far-reaching student hopes were. The threat that the Vietnam war posed for American society had all along been vigorously expressed by students, partly because of a desire to avoid conscription and partly for more unselfish reasons. The 1968 election appeared to give them an opportunity to help bring about the end of the war. At the first of the primaries—that of New Hampshire—Eugene McCarthy, standing on an antiwar platform, astonished everyone by matching the votes for Lyndon Johnson for the Democratic nomination. The entry of Robert F. Kennedy and Johnson's decision not to run for reelection changed the balance within the party and made it

possible for the Vice-President, Hubert Humphrey, to enter the race. By the end of the California primary it was clear that Kennedy had achieved an overwhelming lead, but the hopes of his large constituency were shattered by the bullet that killed Kennedy at the moment of his victory.

The Democratic convention in Chicago was the scene of an attempt by students and radical "hippies" and "yippies" to influence the voting of the delegates. But the students were violently subdued by the police: their tactics were to prove no more of a match for the police than their wishes were to prove for the party bureaucracy. As a result, Hubert Humphrey's selection as candidate left the Democrats deeply divided. By comparison, the selection of Richard Nixon as the Republican candidate seemed a peaceful affair and the lack of serious divisions in the Republican Party helped Nixon to victory at the presidential election.

The failure of student leaders to make their voices heard led to an outbreak of campus violence that brought increasingly harsh reaction from federal and many state authorities. This was to reach its climax in May, 1970, when four students at Kent State University, during a protest against the extension of the Vietnam war into Cambodia, were shot by the National Guard. Although the Justice Department under Attorney General John N. Mitchell refused to allow an inquiry, a federal grand jury in 1974 found that the National Guard had a case to answer. But, while the world was conscious of student violence and the reactions to it, the excitement of the space program seemed for a time more important.

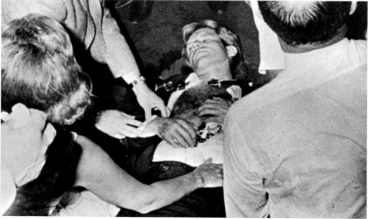
The assassination of Robert Kennedy.

Man on the Moon

Some 350 years after Galileo Galilei first trained his improved refracting telescope on the Moon and studied its craters, two American astronauts landed in one of those flat, dry, dusty basins. By that time, the Apollo Space Program inaugurated by President Kennedy was eight years old, and the Apollo 11 mission was four days old. Six additional hours were to elapse before Neil A. Armstrong, civilian commander of the Moon flight, was ready to announce to an impatient worldwide audience of more than 350 million people that he was about to descend the lunar module's ladder and step out onto the Moon's surface. At 10:45 p.m. on Sunday, July 20, 1969, Armstrong took his first tentative step—and the world exulted. Few could deny that on purely technological terms the U.S. Space Program's remarkable achievement was indeed a "giant leap for mankind."

A Saturn rocket blasting off from Cape Kennedy.

Opposite The Moon, photographed by the Apollo astronauts from their capsule.

A sharp command cut through the relaxed atmosphere in the Mission Control Center in Houston. It was the voice of Eugene Kranz, the Apollo 11 flight director. "Everyone at his desk, please," he called out curtly. "I want absolute silence." He then ordered the doors to be locked and guarded. There must be no risk of anyone's bursting in and distracting attention—even for a second—while his engineers were helping Neil A. Armstrong and Col. Edwin E. ("Buzz") Aldrin Jr. to land on the Moon.

A poll was taken to ascertain, in these last seconds, whether the landing attempt should proceed. "Communications?" Kranz called out. "Go," replied the communications engineer. "Medical?" The answer again was "Go." Some twelve times Kranz asked the question, and the verdict was unanimous. If there had been a single "No go," the landing mission might have been aborted. But all answered in the affirmative, some quietly and others with an emphatic shout.

Now Mission Control was resolved. The capsule communicator spoke swiftly to the two astronauts who were circling the Moon, 239,000 miles away. "Eagle, you're to go for PDI." The initials "PDI" meant "power descent initiation," prelude to the trickiest part of the mission. Few people at Mission Control had any fears that the astronauts would be marooned on the moon after a safe landing. The takeoff had been rehearsed dozens of times with mock-up lunar modules. But landing was very different. The lunar module was so delicate, and the Moon's gravity so much less than the Earth's, that the only place a lunar landing could be practiced was on the Moon itself.

After clearance for the landing had been given, Buzz Aldrin replied, "Roger, understand." Aldrin was the co-pilot of Eagle, code name for the lunar module. Neil Armstrong, the commander, pressed a button on his instrument panel to initiate Eagle's computer landing program, and Eagle's descent engine flamed immediately. The lunar module

paused in its 50,000-foot lunar orbit. Lower and lower it approached the Moon's surface, ever more slowly.

At an altitude of 39,000 feet there came a second of terror. Eagle's landing computer was flashing its alarm panel. For a split second nobody knew whether or not something had gone dangerously wrong, and back at Houston, General Samuel L. Phillips, head of the Apollo Space Program, bit clean through his cigar. (Christopher Kraft, the director of flight operations, later called this computer malfunction "a matter of grave concern.") The computer had become saturated with the demands placed upon it. If Eagle had been unmanned, there is no doubt that it would have crashed. The astronauts were compelled to take partial manual control. Armstrong directed the craft while Aldrin called out speed and altitude.

No sooner had this danger passed than a fresh one appeared. The gravitational pull of mysterious "mascons," great lumps of solid matter beneath the Moon's surface, were throwing Eagle off course. Armstrong stared through one of Eagle's triangular windows and saw to his horror that she was about to land in a jagged crater "big enough to house the Houston Astrodome." He took over full manual control. Finding a smoother place, he began his final descent. Mission Control's nervousness was intense; if the descent engines faltered now, the two men would perish. The engine held. The landing probes on Eagle's legs signaled "lunar contact," and Armstrong cut the engine. Eagle settled into the Sea of Tranquillity. "Houston," radioed Armstrong, "Tranquillity Base here. The Eagle has landed."

The Apollo 11 mission had begun four days earlier, on Wednesday, July 16, 1969, at the Cape Kennedy Space Center in Florida, and the occasion provoked the most passionate excitement. Five hours before liftoff, which was due to occur at Launch Pad 39A at exactly 9:32 A.M. local time, thousands of carloads of people converged on the Space Center,

The Flight of Apollo 11

1 Liftoff from Cape Kennedy.
2 The burned-up first stage of the *Saturn V* launching vehicle falls away.
3 *Saturn* second stage falls away and *Saturn* third stage puts the craft into Earth orbit.
4 *Saturn* third stage is fired to put the craft out of orbit and into Moon trajectory.
5 The command-service module (C-SM) detaches from *Saturn* third-stage.
6 C-SM turns to join up with the lunar module (LM).
7 LM and C-SM dock.
8 LM and C-SM jettison *Saturn* third stage.
9 The spacecraft nears the Moon.
10 The spacecraft fires rockets to put it into low orbit. As it orbits the Moon two astronauts enter LM.
11 LM separates from C-SM.
12 LM descends to Moon firing retro-rockets.
13 LM lifts off from Moon leaving its descent stage behind and goes into orbit.
14 LM and C-SM dock. Astronauts return to C-SM.
15 LM is jettisoned.
16 Rockets fire C-SM out of orbit and into Earth trajectory.
17 Before entering Earth's atmosphere, the command module with the astronauts inside detaches from the service module.
18 Command module enters Earth's atmosphere.
19 Parachutes break the module's descent to Earth to 25 mph.

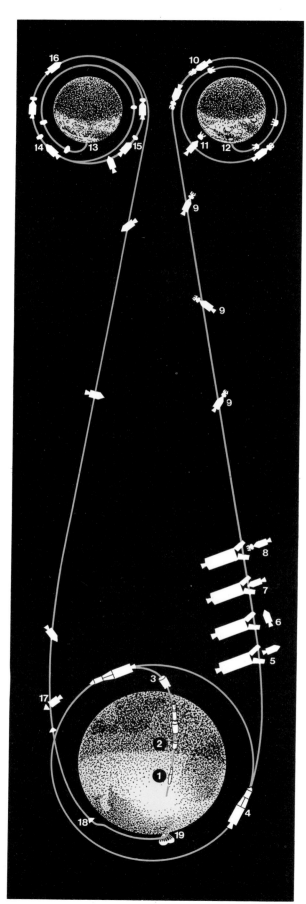

causing solid lines of traffic for nearly twenty miles. At 5 A.M., the entire eastern night sky blazed with one great light—the white glare from a floodlit Saturn v rocket. The Saturn, which was 364 feet in height and capable of putting a weight of 150 tons into orbit, was, at the time, the most powerful rocket ever made. The dazzling beacon was visible for thirty miles, and it sent a glare out over the horizon that seemed to call men's spirits to it like a modern Star of Bethlehem.

By 8 A.M., astronauts Armstrong, Aldrin and Col. Michael Collins, pilot of the command ship Columbia, were inside their spacecraft on top of the rocket. Everyone listened to the crisp voice of Jack King, the official launch commentator. "We are still go for Apollo 11." The minutes passed. "Astronauts report it feels good. T-minus 25 seconds. Twenty seconds and counting. T-minus 15 seconds; guidance is internal. Twelve, eleven, ten, nine—*ignition sequence starts*. Six, five, four, three two, one, zero—*all engines running, liftoff! We have liftoff on Apollo 11!*"

The blinding explosion of light was like a signal to the crowd. Hundreds of thousands of people rose from their seats yelling: "Go! Go! Go!" The rocket appeared to hear them and obey. With the equivalent combined horsepower of 543 jet fighters, the roar of five giant engines struck the spectators with a force that made every wooden and metal structure tremble. When three-quarters of its 7 million pounds of thrust had built up, the rocket began to rise, making the earth shake almost visibly. Great clouds of ice, which the supercooled propellant had deposited on the hull, were shaken loose by the monstrous vibration and they showered down on the launch site.

The journey from the Earth to the Moon, a voyage that had caused considerable wonder in the previous missions of Apollo 8 and Apollo 10, had by now become almost routine. After the first two stages of the rocket had burned out and been jettisoned, and after the spacecraft had made several orbits of the earth, Mission Control in Houston advised the astronauts that they were "Go for TLI" (the abbreviation stands for "translunar injection"). The third stage was then fired to accelerate the spacecraft to 25,000 mph, the velocity needed to break away from Earth orbit and fly to the Moon.

An ingenious maneuver then took place. The three astronauts in the command ship Columbia separated their craft from the third rocket stage, and moved on ahead until they were some one hundred feet away. They slowly turned the module around and retraced their path until their front "docking probe" faced the front end of the third stage. The third stage then unfolded its flowerlike "petals," revealing Eagle packed up inside. Columbia's docking probe locked on to Eagle, and the two craft were fixed together. A short burn of her side engines was sufficient to push Columbia away from the third stage. The journey to the Moon was now well under way, with the two craft tumbling continuously over each other so that the fierce heat of the sun would not burn too long on any part.

At 1:26 P.M. (Eastern Daylight Time) on Saturday, July 19, the three-day coast to the Moon was complete, and the trajectory of the two linked spaceships carried them behind the Moon. During the thirty-four minutes that the craft were out of touch with Houston, Columbia's powerful rocket engines slowed the ships' speed and thrust the two into a low lunar orbit.

On Sunday morning, Armstrong and Aldrin crawled through a hatch and into Eagle's tiny cabin. When they were certain that the lunar module's instrumentation was in working order, they initiated Eagle's separation from Columbia. Leaving Collins orbiting some seventy miles above the Moon's surface, Armstrong and Aldrin began their hazardous descent to the Moon. At 4:17 P.M. on Sunday, July 20, the lunar module touched down at Tranquillity Base. The Eagle had landed.

More than 350 million people sat before their television sets that night, impatiently awaiting the first steps on the Moon. At last, at 10:45 P.M., they heard Armstrong's voice: "The hatch is coming open." A few minutes later, he was on the porch at the top of Eagle's ladder.

Armstrong had begun to operate the television camera, and Houston interrupted: "Man, we're getting a picture on the TV. Okay, now we can see you coming down the ladder." As he reached the foot of the ladder and took his step on the lunar soil, Armstrong uttered the sentence that will surely be remembered a thousand years from now: "That's one small step for a man; one giant leap for mankind."

Aldrin soon followed him down the frail ladder, confidently jumping the last two rungs. They then set in motion three scientific experiments: a laser reflector to detect minute movements in the Earth's crust—and thereby warn of impending earthquakes; an experiment to measure the gases of the solar wind; and a seismic device to detect rumblings beneath the Moon's surface. In addition, they collected several bags of rocks that were carried home for analysis. Their "walk"—in gravity one-sixth that of the Earth's—consisted of swift hops and jumps. It was interrupted by a radio telephone call from President Nixon, who told them: "Because of what you have done, the heavens have become a part of man's world."

These events produced popular excitement on an extraordinary scale. In New York, crime dropped to a fraction of its normal rate, and one police chief wished it were possible to have a moonwalk every

Yuri Gagarin, the first man to orbit the Earth, seen in the cabin of his spaceship *Vostok* before his flight.

A photograph of the large crater of Goclenius, taken as the space capsule orbited the Moon.

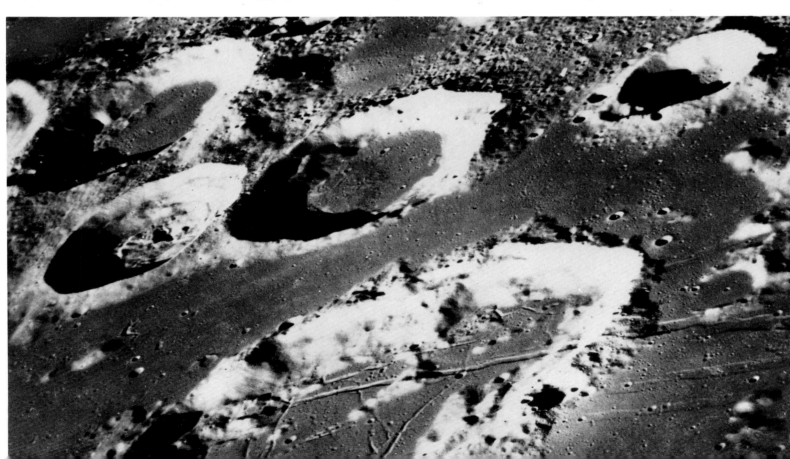

The Apollo astronauts leaving their quarters for the ride out to the launch pad at Cape Kennedy.

The Earth as seen from space. South America is visible on the left and the African coast on the right.

night. In London, hundreds of thousands of people stayed up all night to watch the moon landing on a giant television screen in Trafalgar Square. In Rome, Pope Paul VI solemnly performed a blessing as he watched his screen. In North Vietnam, the Communist leaders were so concerned over the Moon landing's effect on the morale of their fighting men that they told them that the Russians, not the Americans, had walked on the Moon. In Russia itself, parts of the moonwalk were shown on television with the grudging official comment that it was "a great scientific achievement." In America, Monday, July 21, 1969, was declared an official holiday.

As the weeks passed and calmer minds began to appraise the importance of Apollo 11, it became apparent even to the least imaginative men that a milestone in history had been reached. The changes it produced would be subtle and gradual, and its impact might not be felt on a substantial proportion of mankind for several generations. But in the future, when the colonization of the solar system should begin in earnest, with whole planets climatically altered to support large populations in a healthy atmosphere, and when the first manned expeditions to the stars should depart (perhaps to settle in some remote world and never to return), Apollo 11 would be recalled as the decisive act that opened the way. Significantly, only churchmen, not historians or sociologists, challenged President Nixon's remark that the week of the Apollo mission was "the greatest week in history since the Creation." Evolutionists might argue that the Creation lasted somewhat longer than a week, and clergymen lament that the President had omitted the life of Christ from his catalog—but it is difficult to see the decisive moment that liberated man from his own planet in any other context than one of gigantic consequence.

Just as modern astronomers have abandoned all concepts of the universe that gave a special or central position to Earth or the solar system, so an increasing number of scientists had abandoned the thesis that man may have evolved on our planet through a vast series of accidents. It is asserted that evolution might have taken one of millions of other possible routes, and those scientists agree that it could well have done so. But if that had happened, they say, the result would have been essentially the same as if it had not: one species would have acquired intelligence and grown to dominate the others. All that was needed was eyesight that distinguished perspective and color, a well-coordinated brain, the ability to stand several feet off the ground, and members resembling fingers. Armed with these tools, there would be nothing to prevent such creatures from establishing a machine technology and traveling through space.

Such thinking leads at once to two fantastic implications. Apollo 11, or something like it, may have happened millions of times before, and will probably happen millions of times again. Even if only ten million stars, from the hundred thousand million suns in our galaxy, bear technologically intelligent life, then countless alien civilizations must have passed the critical moment of a first landing on another celestial body. The second implication is that Apollo 11 was inevitable from the moment when life first appeared on Earth. The human species, which finally prevailed over all other life-forms, was impelled into technological progress by those inventive powers and exploratory urges that it had acquired during millions of years of struggle for survival. To believe that this tough creature could refrain from expensive and dangerous exploration is to ignore man's biological nature. Forty centuries of urban civilization is too short a time in which to cast off the aggressive habits of three million years.

Access to the far side of the Moon will enable an

An astronaut with his cumbersome life-support pack The Moon's thin atmosphere enabled the astronauts to move freely despite their bulky equipment.

Bottom One of the first tasks the astronauts performed was to plant the American flag on the Moon's surface.

A footprint left by the Apollo 11 astronauts in the dust on the Moon's surface.

experiment to be performed that may confirm the truth of all these suspicions. A search will be made for intelligent radio or optical messages from civilizations on planets in orbit around other suns. To await this shattering communication, an automatic radio-receiving device will be installed among the remote craters. It will switch itself on during the fourteen-day-long lunar nights, when there will be no radio interference from the Sun or from the busy people of Earth. The moment it detects an artificial pattern in signals from any of the neighboring stars, it will trigger an alarm, and a cautious reply will be sent into space.

Earth at that point will have become listed in what Arthur Clarke has called the "galactic telephone directory." Because of the vast distances, resulting interstellar conversations will take many years to complete. Even the nearest star, Proxima Centauri, is four and a third light years away (a light year is the distance light travels in a year, moving at 670 million miles per hour.) A radio message would take just under nine years to make the trip there and back. But to some scientists, the prospect of such a long drawn-out conversation is undaunting. "Imagine that a reply to one of your messages was scheduled to be received forty years from now," writes Professor Edward Purcell of Harvard University. "What a legacy for your grandchildren!"

ADRIAN BERRY

Scientific and medical advances

Scientific developments

Nothing could better illustrate the accelerating speed of historical change than the first manned Moon flight a mere sixty-six years after the Wright brothers' first hesitating powered flight. Technological and scientific developments came with ever-accelerating speed as the century progressed. Industrial reconstruction after World War II provided enormous opportunities for the introduction of modern techniques and of fully automated machinery—on which the postwar prosperity of Germany and Japan was built. The introduction of a new process utilizing oxygen in the 1950s increased steel production, especially in Europe and Japan, making possible a rapid expansion by heavy industry. The use of transistors and printed circuits revolutionized radio—and television—design and cost, so that radios particularly became available even to the relatively poor practically throughout the world.

The space program that had led to the Apollo 11 flight produced many valuable scientific and technological spinoffs, which helped to justify the enormous expense involved. For example, the use of satellites for the transmission of television broadcasting and telephone messages brought a major improvement in long-distance communication. Man's knowledge of the Earth was also enlarged by the use of satellite weather forecasting. But set against the vast advances in scientific knowledge that took place from 1950—of which the discovery of DNA (deoxyribonucleic acid, the molecular basis of heredity) was among the most significant—the space program produced very little of real value in relation to its enormous cost, one reason for its deemphasis in 1973.

By that time, however, as a result of man's ability to study the universe from outside the Earth's atmosphere, astronomical knowledge had advanced considerably. Not only was knowledge of the Moon's geological make-up available, but in addition it was possible to study the atmospheres of Venus and Mars, and to gain a new understanding of solar activity. But argument about the origin of the universe continued unabated, and the new knowledge threw little light on this. The increasing effectiveness of radio telescopes, however, made it likely that some of the more contentious issues would be resolved as the century entered its final quarter.

Other technological developments brought important increases in scientific knowledge. The rapid development in computer technology during the 1950s and 1960s, which had been made possible by the use of the binary system, led to the growth of a new science, cybernetics; but in many other fields, too, the relationship between science and advanced technology was closer than it had ever been before. The development of low-temperature physics, for example, promised to have important practical results for electronics. Research into the use of nuclear power led to significant developments for both peaceful and military uses: in 1950 electricity was produced from atomic energy and in the following year the first hydrogen bomb was tested. By 1970 there were already over 600 nuclear reactors in operation in Europe and the United States. During the early 1970s, argument over the safety and cost of nuclear power stations became more critical and there was considerable disagreement as to design, fuel element and coolants as the development program expanded.

Chemical knowledge continued to advance rapidly, as the extension of the periodic table of elements showed. As early as 1940 the tables extended beyond uranium (element 92), and by the 1960s the table had been extended to 103. Agricultural research and biochemistry came to play an increasingly important role; knowledge of proteins and vitamins began to overlap into medical research during the 1950s, and during the late 1960s assumed a new importance as a result of concern about the long-term deleterious effects of pesticides.

Science and society: medicine

Many of the scientific and technological discoveries and developments of the third quarter of the twentieth century had important social implications. The widespread use of computers, for example, made the misuse of confidential information given to government departments a real danger, and there were fears about nuclear power, as the debates about power-station safety and nuclear disarmament made clear. But in no field were the social implications of science so clearly marked as in medical and biological research.

Improvements in medical knowledge had a profound effect on social life as the age patterns of society changed rapidly; it appeared that, as a result of the eradication of previously widespread and serious diseases, most of the world's advanced states would be largely made up of inactive "senior citizens" by the year 2000. The development of the Salk vaccine was merely the most notable of many major advances. The great epidemic diseases—cholera, typhus, typhoid and bubonic plague—and many other serious infections—such as yellow fever and malaria—were already being brought under control, but the battle for their complete eradication continued. Disasters, whether manmade or natural—civil wars, earthquakes, floods—were often followed by outbreaks of disease, and many diseases fought back vigorously against the advances of medical knowledge by taking on new and sometimes more virulent forms.

Cures were being found for many less dangerous diseases. The use of synthesized substitutes for insulin helped control diabetes, and it was discovered that thrombosis could be cured by doses of warfarin, the active agent in common rat poison. In addition, a vaccine was developed against measles—a "childhood disease" that posed more dangers than were generally recognized.

The increasingly sedentary nature of society in the mid-twentieth century, however, brought with it new dangers to health. The incidence of heart disease grew steadily, and medical research was forced to pay increasing attention to it. The development of artificial "pacemakers" that regulated otherwise irregular heartbeat, marked a great step forward, but a complicated form of surgery—transplantation—caught the public imagination more effectively. Although few patients of the early heart transplant operations at Groote Schuur Hospital in Cape Town, South Africa, survived and there were objections on the grounds

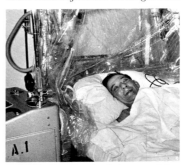

Louis Washkansky, the first successful heart transplant patient.

that surgical resources could be better used, it was soon clear that mechanically this operation would present no insuperable problem. However, considerable research remained to be done on how to circumvent the body's immunosuppressive system, which tended to attack—and to destroy—the "alien" transplanted organ, thereby causing death.

Medical research also concentrated increasingly on cancer, another illness that had spread rapidly in advanced industrial countries. Although no cure had been discovered by the mid-1970s, cancer researchers had discovered

Francis Crick and James Watson with a model of DNA.

give man a new understanding of himself

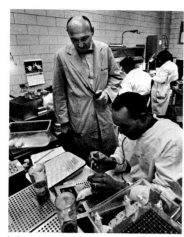

Laboratory work on cancer research in Chicago.

much that was of interest about the disease—not least the high incidence, strongly suggesting causality, of cancer among heavy cigarette smokers. Other avenues of research were not, however, ignored; researchers at Uganda's Makerere University, for example, discovered that some forms of leukemia appeared to be caused by a virus infection, a finding that won wide credence, although it was not universally accepted.

However, despite all of modern science's ministrations, age-old diseases maintained their grip. Throughout much of disaster-stricken Africa and Asia, malnutrition and its accompanying ills—such as kwashiorkor—remained endemic, as did such scourges as schistosomiasis and even the ancient curse of leprosy, a serious medical and social problem, especially in Korea. In the technologically advanced countries, the results of carelessly or inadequately researched products caused additional suf-

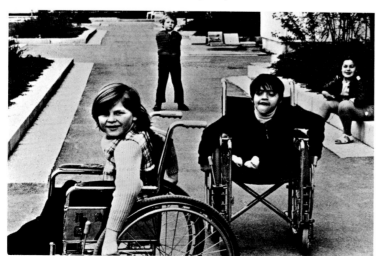

Children deformed by the drug Thalidomide.

fering. Thousands of children in the 1960s, for example, were born malformed as a result of their mothers' taking the tranquilizer Thalidomide during pregnancy.

No less of a problem were the ethical difficulties caused by the success of scientific research. It was not merely that science had found the causes of many illnesses, but also that, for the first time, it was expected that the fruits of scientific research would be available to all instead of only to a tiny privileged minority. Although the use of effective birth-control methods helped to reduce the very real danger of world overpopulation, it brought with it other problems, notably the very rapid spread of venereal disease. Although attacks by conservative churchmen on the use of contraceptives did little or nothing to prevent the spread of "the pill," the questions raised could not be ignored totally. Other related problems such as abortion, euthanasia (mercy killing), test-tube babies and the preselection of a baby's sex, continued to arouse popular discussion and showed clearly that the potential of scientific research had far exceeded man's vision of his own society.

Economic troubles

The speed of scientific and technological change had an immense impact on man's life, but the change was not always reflected by developments in social structures or political institutions. Primitive headhunting tribes in New Guinea, Brazil and the Philippines, that had changed little in thousands of years, continued to live almost

unaffected by the airplanes that flew overhead. Bureaucratic society adjusted sluggishly to change but the police powers of government generally made it possible to preserve the domestic status quo or to make sure changes came gradually. Internationally, however, the problems were far greater. Political disagreements could be solved by direct contact—whether diplomatic or military—so that the weakness of the United Nations did not prove disastrous. In economic, and particularly monetary, affairs, however, changes in relations between states had a worldwide effect. The setting up of the International Monetary Fund and the International Bank for Reconstruction and Development (World Bank) at the Bretton Woods Conference of 1944 had been an attempt to create a new international monetary order. But despite the activities of these new institutions and the optimism of their Keynesian founders, the postwar world was bedeviled by endemic financial difficulties.

Steel production at a Japanese works.

The weakness of the pound sterling and the French franc and the dollar shortage were the main problems during the immediately postwar years, and European currencies were substantially devalued in 1948–49, which damaged the assumption of the Bretton Woods Conference that the pound, like the dollar, would act as a "reserve currency." During the 1950s the situation eased somewhat as the deficit in the American balance of payments became normal, which helped to weaken the dollar. It was only in the second half of the 1960s that international finance reached a critical point. This was in large measure due to the rigidity of exchange rates that remained ulti-

mately based on gold (although most currencies had abandoned the Gold Standard and were valued in relation to each other, the price of gold remained fixed at $35 an ounce and other currencies were valued against the dollar), but other factors included the accelerating rate of inflation in most countries and the problems caused by large surpluses and deficits in trade balances.

As a result even the semblance of financial stability was abandoned. Starting with the long overdue devaluation of sterling in 1967 the world was thrown into a monetary crisis that was to grow graver during the 1970s. The sterling devaluation created a new speculative interest in the gold price, which was met by the introduction of a two-tier system, with central bank dealings fixed at the old price of $35 an ounce and a free market price for other dealings. By 1971 it was clear that as a means of increasing stability this had failed. Economic cooperation declined as the free price of gold rocketed, and the United States was forced to upvalue gold against the dollar. In 1972 the situation appeared to stabilize and the European Economic Community tried to impose a measure of order on its member states: the EEC currencies were to have only a limited freedom of movement, seen on a graph as a "snake," which was seen as a prelude to the introduction of a common European currency. As a prelude to joining the EEC Britain joined the "snake" but was forced within a few months to allow its currency to float freely (downward) outside the "snake," and by 1974 France too had left the "snake" and European monetary cooperation was in ruins. The inevitable result of the monetary uncertainties and the fact that the value of the dollar was still expressed in terms of gold was that the price of gold leaped upward, adding enormously to the monetary problems of the developed world.

The price of other commodities rose too. This was partly due to currency uncertainties and partly to world shortages. Rising prices had a disastrous effect on many poor countries. In 1970, for example, many Pakistanis starved as a result of high rice prices after a disastrous cyclone and flood. This was to be a major cause of the civil war that split Pakistan in 1971.

Birth of Bangladesh

Power in the unwieldy state of Pakistan was vested in the West. Thus in the election of 1970, the resentment at years of neglect in geographically remote East Pakistan resulted in a sweeping victory for Sheikh Mujibur Rahman's East Pakistan Awami League. Postponement of the new National Assembly, however, led to a breakdown of civil authority in the East. Sheikh Mujibur was arrested on the orders of President Yahya Khan, and in April, 1971, East Pakistan declared its independence. The overextended Pakistani army soon found itself fighting the Mukti Bahini guerrillas, and when India, prompted by the magnitude of the Bengali refugee problem, decided to support the new Republic, the military balance swung against Pakistan. Bowing to the inevitable, Pakistan's new President Bhutto released Sheikh Mujibur in January, 1972, as a prelude to recognizing Bangladesh.

Sheikh Mujibur Rahman, head of the East Pakistan Awami League and first Prime Minister of Bangladesh. His sweeping success at the polls and the subsequent postponement of the National Assembly led to the Bengali declaration of independence.

Opposite Arms turned in by members of the *Mukti Bahini* (liberation force) units at the stadium in Dacca after the independence of Bangladesh.

The RAF Comet landed at 1:30 P.M. As the rumpled, tired-looking man came out of the plane, the crowd began to heave forward, waving and cheering. An open police truck was waiting across the tarmac; he took twelve minutes to reach it, and another two hours, past thousands lining the route with homemade versions of the new flag in their hands, to make the two-mile journey to the racecourse, where an audience of more than half a million was waiting to hear him. Sheikh Mujibur Rahman had come home to Bangladesh.

It had been a long journey: from a West Pakistan prison to the rapturous crowd waiting patiently at Dacca Racecourse. Sheikh Mujibur had been arrested on the orders of Yahya Khan, President of Pakistan, and taken to a West Pakistan prison in March, 1971, following the conclusive breakdown both of constitutional talks between East and West Pakistan and of civil authority in the Eastern wing of the country.

In April, though still in jail a thousand miles away, he had become first President of the Democratic Republic of Bangladesh. The formal announcement was made in Chuadanga, only three hundred yards from the border between India and East Pakistan. The village had been nominated the provisional capital and renamed "Mujibnagar" for the occasion. The following day, when West Pakistani troops entered the village, intent on stamping out the last sparks of resistance to the central government, they could find no trace of the provisional government, the infant republic having apparently died at birth.

Nine months later, however, Pakistan's new President, Zulfikar Ali Bhutto, preferred to release Sheikh Mujibur rather than execute him, as outgoing President Yahya Khan had advised. And so, on Saturday, January 8, 1972, Sheikh Mujibur was bundled onto a plane from Karachi to London to start a roundabout journey home. In London there was scarcely time for more than a press conference at Claridges before flying on to New Delhi for a brief meeting with the Indian Prime Minister, Mrs. Indira Gandhi.

And finally, home to Dacca. At the racecourse, that first Monday afternoon, he spoke of the need to forgive. Four days later, on January 14, having stepped down from the presidency to become the Republic's first Prime Minister, he spoke of Bangladesh as a "Switzerland of the East," a neutral socialist state. Magnanimous sentiments, sober enough ambitions—but it was time for both.

Apart from the entry into neighboring India between April and November, 1971, of ten million people, all of whom would now be ready to return home, a further ten million, it was estimated, had been made homeless and destitute by the war and the monsoon floods of August; over a quarter of the population had to be fed, rehoused and employed. But the previous year's crops, rice for food, jute to earn foreign currency, had been washed away in those same August floods. As for the prospects for the new year, the area of jute under cultivation had shrunk by more than a third, and over 300,000 acres of paddy fields could not be planted because of losses in plowing cattle and equipment.

In industry the picture was as bleak: factories in ruins, production no more than twenty-five percent its normal level. One of the top U.N. men in Dacca described the devastation as more severe than that of Europe after World War II. The Bangladesh Planning Commission estimated the cost of restoring the country to its prewar standard of living at $300 million, much of which would have to come by way of foreign loans if not grants. As for local capital, the businesses with head offices in West Pakistan, which meant most of them, had repatriated their realizable assets in good time. The Chittagong office of the national airline had less than $20 left in its local account.

In this breathing space between a dreadful past and an uncertain future nothing had been settled

Young recruits for the *Mukti Bahini* receiving training in throwing hand grenades. The old East Bengal Regiment formed the nucleus of the movement, but students and leftist groups also organized resistance to West Pakistani military occupation.

After the liberation of Dacca a terrified Bihari finds himself at the mercy of armed Bengalis. A minority within East Pakistan, the Biharis had supported the Pakistani authorities.

but the country's constitutional identity. The sovereign Republic of Bangladesh was formally proclaimed the same day Sheikh Mujibur came home: January 10, 1972. The infant whose arrival had been announced to the world in such inauspicious circumstances the previous April at "Mujibnagar" had survived.

What had not survived was the quarter-century-old state of Pakistan, land of the Paks, the "spiritually pure and clean," which had itself come into being in the postwar breakup of the British Empire in the East. Ends and beginnings twine together, but August 15, 1947, is a crucial break in the thread, a place to enter the labyrinth.

August 15 was the date fixed by the British Labour government for Indian independence; it was also the date fixed for partition—the division of the subcontinent into two separate states, India and Pakistan, Hindu and Moslem. Partition was a political solution to a hideous problem, and as is commonplace in politics it was a compromise. The problem, crudely stated, bore a family resemblance to the problem of Ireland: in an undivided India the Hindu Congress Party, led by Gandhi and Nehru, would have a perpetual majority, and this the Moslem League was not prepared to tolerate. The British solution, as in Ireland over twenty years before, was to protect the interests of the minority community by physical separation from and political independence of the majority. In Ireland the Six Counties became Ulster; in India the Moslem majority areas of the northwest (North West Frontier Province, Punjab, Sind and Baluchistan) became West Pakistan, while a thousand miles to the east, the Moslem majority areas of Bengal became East Pakistan.

But a good compromise opens the door to further compromise, while partition insures that only the most violent upheaval would produce further movement. It may be argued that drawing lines

on maps requires a high degree of stringency, but on any sensible accounting it would appear that the lines drawn on the map of India were the wrong lines in the wrong places.

Partition in fact sowed dragon's teeth along the frontiers. Kashmir was the principal, most fertile battleground; for the Maharajah of Jammu and Kashmir, having chosen to disregard the fact that most of his subjects were Moslem, had adhered at the eleventh hour to India. Thus on the one side India, in possession of the disputed territory, saw nothing to negotiate about and denounced Pakistani aggression; on the other side Pakistan saw no reason to abandon a legitimate claim and suspected India of nursing ambitions to reunite the two nations by force of arms.

The border question, since it was a matter of national honor, was a potent force in domestic politics. Vows of undying hostility to India, denunciatory statements (by out-of-office politicians) on the government's lack of vigor met by strenuous declamations (by government spokesmen) on the country's military readiness all became stock items in the repertoire of the politics of West Pakistan. But the price of honor was high. In no year from 1947 to 1970 did defense expenditure amount to less than forty percent of central government revenues and in some years it rose to above sixty percent.

The British had intended partition to secure the rights of the Moslem minority. For the Moslem League, however, partition had been a way of securing their power. East Pakistan had never had a large place in the League's calculations, and for excellent reasons. Although the old Bengal state had the highest proportion of Moslems of any state in undivided India, it was geographically remote—over a thousand miles away—from what was to become West Pakistan. Its people were not even Paks, "spiritually pure and clean," in terms of the original definition of Pakistan, framed by Choudhry Rahmat Ali. Small, no bigger than England and Wales, the province was very densely populated and very poor; ninety-six percent of the people were peasants. Before 1947 Bengal's raw jute had gone south to be processed in the Calcutta mills. But Calcutta had been excluded from East Pakistan, and in any case most industry and finance was in the hands of Hindus at that time, and they were just as reluctant to be found in the wrong place and just as nimble on their feet as their West Pakistan brethren proved in December, 1970. As a result, the Eastern province stood still. In Karachi the central government made no plans for extensive modernization or investment in agriculture. Instead, the currency earned by exporting jute was used principally to finance military and industrial programs in the West. The statistics tell the story: over half the country's population of 126 million lived in the Eastern wing, but the province only received a third of development expenditure, twenty-five percent of central government expenditure, twenty-five percent of all imported goods and twenty percent of all foreign aid. In 1969 it was calculated that twenty West Pakistani families owned or controlled four-fifths of the country's banks and insurance companies and two-thirds of its industrial assets.

The kindling had been laid, and it would not need an especially adroit hand to light the fire. In effect Sheikh Mujibur's campaign during the run-up to the December, 1970, elections served exactly that purpose.

Elections were called by President Yahya Khan in response to popular demand and under pressure of a national strike, a weapon that had already been used successfully to remove his predecessor Ayub Khan in March, 1969. In January, 1970, the ban on political parties was lifted and campaigning began.

Sheikh Mujibur, leader of the East Pakistan Awami League, had been the first Eastern politician to spell out the East's demand for regional autonomy. His six-point program, which he unveiled at Lahore in January, 1966, envisaged a federal system in which the federating units would have the right to levy their own taxes, retain their own foreign earnings, and "prevent the transfer of resources and flight of capital from one region to another." The federal government would be responsible only for defense, foreign affairs and, subject to the provision about preventing the flight of capital, currency. Now Sheikh Mujibur's Awami League began to speak of Bangla Desh (land of the Bengalis) instead of East Pakistan.

On December 7, 1970, seventy million Pakistanis went to the polls to elect a National Assembly for the first time in the country's twenty-three-year existence. In the twelve months preceding the election, after President Yahya lifted the ban on political parties, forty-one parties had entered the contest for power, fourteen of which had national aspirations. When the votes were in, Sheikh Mujibur had won 167 of the 169 seats allocated to the Eastern province, giving him a clear majority in the Assembly. In the West, Zulfikar Ali Bhutto's Pakistan People's Party surprised the forecasters by taking 85 of the West's 144 seats. Both victories were significant. Sheikh Mujibur was helped by the last-minute withdrawal from the race of the candidates of Maulana Bhashani's party, a pro-Chinese faction of the National Awami Party whose election slogan was: "Peasants and workers, awake." Bhashani claimed he was withdrawing in protest at President Yahya's negligent handling of disaster relief in the Ganges delta, which had been hit by a cyclone in early November. Some commentators believed that this was a pretext and that in reality Bhashani had dropped out to avoid suffering a humiliating defeat at the polls. Either way, Sheikh Mujibur's clean sweep looked like a triumphant vindication of his strong demands for regional autonomy, which now began to sound more and more like separatism. Bhutto's victory, though not as compelling as Sheikh Mujibur's, was still substantial. He had fought his campaign on a platform of "Islamic socialism," taking a bellicose

A group of *Mukti Bahini* in Dacca celebrating the liberation of Bangladesh on December 16, 1971. The guerrilla campaign was helped by the overextension of the Pakistani army, which also had to secure West Pakistan's defenses against India.

line on India, and promising to break the power of the wealthy families. Logically enough, given that the tide was running in Bhutto's favor, particularly in the Punjab, it was Ayub Khan's old party, the Convention Moslem League, which did worst in the elections. The Convention Moslem League was the bosses' party; it symbolized the old Pakistan, the way things had been from 1947 until the present time, and it was decisively and stunningly rejected by the electorate. Of 217 candidates, 124 of whom contested seats in the Western provinces, only two were successful. The people had spoken, their representatives had been elected, but it was by no means obvious what would happen next.

Bhutto had heard ancestral voices prophesying war, but preparing for war would need a strong government at the center and plenty of money, a point on which a modern Islamic socialist and an unreconstructed Moslem Leaguer could agree. Unhappily Sheikh Mujibur was neither; as an Eastern politician he had no consuming interest in Kashmir or wars with India, and as leader of the largest single party he could presumably impose his six points on the country as soon as the Assembly met and he could bring matters to a vote. The crucial questions therefore were: when would the Assembly meet? and what would happen after the vote?

On February 13, the first question received its answer, so it seemed, when President Yahya fixed the date for the Assembly's opening as March 3, in Dacca. However, two days later, Bhutto, who had up till then been trying to persuade Sheikh Mujibur to invite the Pakistan People's Party into a grand coalition, announced that his party would boycott the Assembly. On March 1, Yahya postponed the Assembly indefinitely to give the rival politicians enough time to overcome their differences. The Assembly, like the Christian ideal, in Chesterton's phrase, had not been tried and found wanting; it had been found difficult and left untried.

Indian troops are greeted by the inhabitants of Bangladesh. India's decision actively to support the Bengali secession brought it into open conflict with Pakistan.

Opposite above Bihari refugees in Bangladesh. East Bengal's new-found freedom enabled old scores to be settled.

Opposite below Bengali refugees in India. At the outbreak of hostilities refugees started pouring over the borders into West Bengal and Assam. Their repatriation was completed in 1972; by the tripartite talks of 1973 all prisoners of war were exchanged, as well as nationals trapped abroad by the war.

There was immediate popular reaction in East Pakistan to Yahya's decision. Widespread, disorganized rioting erupted throughout the province. Dacca was paralyzed by a strike.

The direction of events was now being dictated by the quickening rhythm of the troops' response to the rioters and strikers, and their counterresponses. In the first week of March the army admitted killing 172 Bengalis while the Easterners claimed at least 500 casualties. Meanwhile, President Yahya was still desperately trying to open negotiations. On March 3, he invited Sheikh Mujibur and Bhutto to a round-table conference in Dacca the following week. Sheikh Mujibur would have none of it. The invitation, he said, was "being made at gunpoint." On March 6, Yahya tried again. In a broadcast to the nation he set March 25 as the new date for the Assembly to meet. He hoped for a "patriotic and constructive response from all our political leaders." In case the carrot was insufficiently enticing, he also announced the appointment of Lieutenant General Tikka Khan as East Pakistan's new Governor and Martial Law Administrator. In February, Bhutto had refused to attend the Assembly without a guarantee from the President that the country would remain united; now he agreed to come. And by now it was too late. The day after Yahya's broadcast, Mujibur laid down four conditions for Awami League participation in the Assembly: an end to martial law, the return of troops to their barracks, an inquiry into the previous week's killings and the transfer of power to the elected representatives.

On March 16, Yahya at last managed to get Mujibur to begin talks with him in Dacca. Bhutto joined them six days later and for the next couple of days the three men made a last attempt to find a solution.

Away from the conference room, already heavy with the smell of failure, a shadow administration was coming into being. The East Bengal Regiment and the police were pledged to the Awami League. General Tikka Khan could not find a High Court judge to swear him in, and his household staff had deserted him. It was even reported that he was reduced to eating meals prepared by the military guards.

March 23—Pakistan's Republic day—was celebrated in East Pakistan in 1971 as Resistance Day and for the first time the new flag of Bangladesh could be seen flying over schools, government offices and private houses, including Sheikh Mujibur's.

Two days later, on March 25, the day the Assembly was to have met, President Yahya Khan left Dacca and flew back to Karachi. That same day Sheikh Mujibur Rahman was arrested and taken to West Pakistan. The following day, March 26, 1971, turmoil in East Pakistan erupted into civil war. On the radio, Yahya banned the Awami League, accused Mujibur of "an act of treason," and called on the army to restore the authority of the government in the East.

The Pakistan army did exactly what it was asked to do. By April 18, with the capture of Chuadanga, the pathetic provisional capital of Bangladesh, the province had been pacified. The cost in human lives was huge and will probably never be fully known. Two British journalists evaded a military sweep designed to gather in all the foreign press correspondents in East Pakistan prior to deportation. They managed to remain at large and to escape from the country to tell the world what they had seen of the army's work. One of them spoke of troops who had occupied the university on March 26 "and were busy killing off students." He estimates the army killed 7,000 in Dacca alone. Further evidence came to light after independence: the villages of Kallayanpur and Shialbari burned to the ground and used as sites for mass executions; 300 bodies found in a trench near Dinajpur; four mass graves near Chittagong with 600 bodies in them; 1,500 dead in a mass grave in the army cantonment at Comilla.

The province had been pacified by mid-April, and yet as early as May guerrilla activity was

beginning in the hilly border areas. The East Bengal Regiment formed the nucleus, while students and leftist political groups also organized effective resistance.

By August, the army was dangerously over-extended. New divisions were needed to secure West Pakistan's defenses, and the army in the East was suffering losses at the hands of the *Mukti Fouj* (liberation forces). By mid-September ninety per-cent of all culverts and small bridges linking Dacca with Comilla, Jessore and Kushtia had been destroyed by the guerrillas. Road and rail deliveries had fallen to ten percent of their normal level. Unemployment in Dacca was reaching frightening proportions. On the other side of the border, in West Bengal and Assam, for instance, the problem was rather different. Refugees had been fleeing into India since April. Camps in the border areas had filled up, then overflowed. The problem was not simply that of providing for the refugees; there was also the problem of the host communities. Refugees had a guarantee of food and shelter, however scant; many natives of Calcutta did not. Hence refugees could underbid local labor.

From the Indian government's point of view the calculations were complex. Intervention by China was a disagreeable possibility to be carefully scrutinized. On the other hand, the political impasse in Pakistan showed no sign of resolving itself and in the absence of settlement in East Pakistan the refugees would be an ever-present and burdensome reality. After mid-September Indian troops were more and more closely involved in *Mukti Bahini* operations both on the border and inside East Pakistan. At the same time a military build-up began on both sides of the border of West Pakistan and India. War loomed ever closer.

In the early evening of December 3, the Pakistan air force hit military airfields at Srinagar, Amritsar, Pathankot, and elsewhere in the northwest. The strike was almost totally ineffective as the Indians were expecting some such action and had dispersed their aircraft round the fields in concrete bunkers. The war that everyone had expected had begun. What no one expected was that it would be over in a fortnight. General Aurora Singh, the Indian commanding officer in East Pakistan, reflecting on his victory, thought it was due not to superiority of men or matériel but simply to the failure of the Pakistani command to prepare defensive battle plans in sufficient detail and thoroughness.

Be that as it may, General Niazi, the Pakistani commander, signed the instrument of surrender, sitting beside General Aurora Singh at a table on the Dacca Racecourse at half-past four in the afternoon on December 16, 1971. Over 90,000 Pakistani troops were taken as prisoners of war, a consideration that weighed with President Bhutto when he decided to release Sheikh Mujibur rather than execute him. On December 22, the provisional government of Bangladesh—minus Sheikh Mujibur, still a captive—arrived in Dacca. Two and a half weeks later the RAF Comet touched down.

TOM RIVERS

Growing international détente

China

It was to take more than three years for Pakistan to agree to recognize Bangladesh as an independent state. No less important than the war itself was the change in international relations that it revealed. Both China and the U.S.A. had supported Bangladesh. This major shift in the relations between the two superpowers and China was largely due to an increasing Chinese desire to play a major part in world affairs.

From 1970 onward Chinese diplomacy concentrated on improving relations with other states: in 1971 diplomatic relations were established with fourteen countries and restored with many more, while China exchanged ambassadors with sixteen countries in the following year. Abandoning their previous reluctance to admit visitors from abroad, the Chinese welcomed many groups of foreigners in 1971—most notably an American table-tennis team. Later in the same year, Dr. Henry Kissinger visited Peking on President Nixon's behalf and on February 21, 1972, the President himself began a week-long visit. The improvement in Sino-American relations led to the acceptance of China as a member of the United Nations, and the Communist regime took the permanent seat on the Security Council that had previously been occupied by the Taiwan government, which claimed to be the government of China.

The American willingness to jettison the attitude of over two decades was due above all to Nixon's keenness to avoid any further political embarrassment at home by making it possible to bring the struggle in Vietnam to an end. The Chinese attitude was more complicated. The disruption that had been caused by the Cultural Revolution did not disappear quickly, and it was clear during 1971 that a power struggle still continued in the Communist Party's top leadership. This ended with the purge of Mao Tse-tung's nominated successor, Lin Piao, who was killed in an air crash during an attempt to flee from China to the U.S.S.R. With over one quarter of the Soviet army stationed along the border with China, enormous suspicion was inevitable, although armed clashes were rare, and relations between the two great Communist countries continued at a formal level. Despite China's new openness toward the outside world, it became clear during 1973 that the struggle for power was by no means over, and there were signs that a new cultural revolution might begin.

Germany

China's increasing acceptance of an important role augured well for the future of peace in the world. A development that appeared likely to be of no less significance was the *Ostpolitik* (Eastern policy) 'that was adopted by Germany's Social Democratic Chancellor, Willy Brandt. For part of the nineteenth century and the first four and a half decades of the twentieth, Germany's dominant position in Central Europe had proved disruptive and dangerous—as two world wars had shown. The end of World War II had left a defeated and divided Germany, but had not provided any permanent outcome to the German problem.

Brandt, formerly Mayor of West Berlin, a city whose divisions were a microcosm of Germany's, saw it as his main path to clear up the problems caused by the division of Germany. As Foreign Minister in the broadly based coalition with the Christian Democrats during the later 1960s, Brandt had sought to improve relations with the East European states. When he became Chancellor in 1969, after narrowly defeating the Christian Democrats, Brandt rapidly extended his Eastern contacts. By 1972, treaties had been signed with the U.S.S.R., Poland and—most significant of the three —East Germany. No less important was the four-power (U.S., U.S.S.R., Britain and France) agreement on West Berlin. After Brandt's enormous success in the 1972 elections he was able to ratify these treaties, and the way was open for both the German Federal Republic and the German Democratic Republic to enter the United Nations.

Brandt's electoral success was, however, to prove the apogee of his career. It soon became clear that the cost of the *Ostpolitik*—the recognition by West Germany of the existing frontier between East Germany and Poland—was not fully compensated for by its benefits. The Soviet government showed little willingness to improve relations at a formal level. By 1973 relations had soured and at the height of the energy crisis the Russians failed to deliver natural gas due under a trade agreement.

Along with the souring of the *Ostpolitik*, Germany was plunged into other problems. The *wirtschaftswunder*—the miracle of Germany's economic success since World War II—had become an accepted fact of life, and a slowdown in Germany's economic growth in 1973 came as a great shock to many. The end of *wirtschaftswunder* also affected relations with the other EEC countries, as Germany had grown accustomed to paying a large proportion of the community's budget: Germany's new reluctance to be the paymaster of Europe increased the problems of the Common Market at a time when they had become apparent to all.

Terrorism and hijacking

During the 1960s it had at one time seemed likely that Germany was to see a fascist revival. A National Democratic Party, with many of the characteristics of Hitler's National Socialist Party, had achieved considerable electoral success. By the 1970s, however, the National Democratic Party threat appeared to have lapsed, but no less serious was the threat posed by the appearance of urban terrorism.

President Nixon visiting the Great Wall of China.

ushers in new hopes of world peace

West Germany's President Brandt. His *Ostpolitik* opened a new era in Germany's history.

The destruction of hijacked aircraft in Jordan by Palestinian guerrillas.

The "Baader-Meinhoff gang," a group of middle-class anarchists, were arrested only in 1972 after two years of intense police activity. Other European states were also affected by the outbreak of urban guerrilla warfare; in Britain, for example, Northern Ireland proved an efficient training ground and rallying point for terrorists, whether Protestant or Roman Catholic, and non-Irish groups such as the middle-class "Angry Brigade" and Doctor Bridget Dugdale's associates found a justification for their activities in the problems of Ireland; in 1972 in Italy, Giangiacomo Feltrinelli, a well-known publishing millionaire of left-wing sympathies, was found dead near a sabotaged electricity pylon, but his death, like the bombings and street battles that disrupted Milan in the same year, was thought to have been caused by terrorists of the right rather than the left. In Spain, the campaign of violence by Basque nationalists became increasingly fierce during 1972. Part of the cause of the outbreak of urban guerrilla activity

was, perhaps, a desire to imitate American movements such as the "Weathermen." The violence was not usually directed at particular targets, but kidnap attempts became increasingly common. The example of the kidnapping of the son of the American aviator Charles Lindbergh in 1932 was less influential than the spate of kidnappings that had broken out in Latin America in the late 1960s. In the early 1970s this spread to Europe and the United States; Randolph Hearst's daughter Patty and Paul Getty's grandson were merely the most prominent victims, and an attempt had been made in 1974 to abduct the English Princess Anne from her Rolls Royce only yards from Buckingham Palace.

Such acts of violence and kidnappings were sometimes motivated by the hope of gain, but more often they were intended to publicize or benefit extremist political minorities. Palestinian Arabs in particular saw the advantage that was to be gained from such activities. The hijacking of aircraft,

whether for political or financial gain, became at one time almost a daily occurrence. The destruction of three airplanes at Dawson's Field in Jordan was merely the most publicized of hundreds of hijacks.

The damage caused by hijacking was enormous, but relatively few deaths were caused by it. Much Palestinian guerrilla activity was, however, aimed at capturing world attention by acts of indiscriminate slaughter: a group of Japanese terrorists who supported the Palestinian cause killed twenty-six and wounded seventy in an attack at Lod airport in Israel in 1972, and in the same year at the Munich

Olympics an Arab terrorist group killed eleven hostages from the Israeli team.

The Israelis responded in kind. Palestinians thought to be responsible for terrorist activity were assassinated in several European countries and the Israeli army and air force attacked villages in Lebanon from which guerrilla attacks in Israel had been launched. Nor were Arab governments favorable to the unrestrained use of force by the Palestinians.

But the attention of the world was dominated by the peace negotiations designed to end the war in Vietnam—or at least U.S. involvement there.

A Palestinian arguing with officials about the release of the hostages at Munich.

America Leaves Vietnam

Since 1954, when the Geneva convention divided Vietnam into two following the withdrawal of the French, the United States had committed itself to the maintenance of a strong, anti-Communist state in South Vietnam. For twenty years, at the cost of billions of dollars, thousands of American lives, political dissension abroad and polarization at home, the United States became more and more deeply enmeshed in its land war in Southeast Asia. In 1973, America's Henry Kissinger and North Vietnam's Le Duc Tho finally came to terms and the United States withdrew from its most bitter and costly foreign war.

January, 1973, saw the signing of a cease-fire agreement marking the end of an overt American presence in South Vietnam and of America's twenty-year struggle to suppress the influence of the Communist state of North Vietnam and its allies, the Vietcong, in the South, a struggle with roots deep in the colonial past of Indochina.

It appears absurd that, after a military effort unequaled in the story of warfare, after a cost of countless billions of dollars and thousands of lives, and at the political expense of involving almost all of East and Southeast Asia, the United States would suddenly agree to the cease-fire. Particularly as it did so at the very time when it appeared willing and able to bomb its adversaries into submission. Yet it reversed its policy, withdrew its troops and began to look benignly on the idea of a neutral zone encompassing both former enemies and former friends.

The reasons for these acts lie largely, but not entirely, in Southeast Asia itself. The antiwar movement at home, increasing international pressure to end the interminable and meaningless war, and U.S. involvement in other spheres of influence —in the Middle East and Latin America in particular—all played a role. But the central reasons lie in events in Indochina from 1970 until the actual signing of the cease-fire agreement in early 1973 (for it was not clear until the very last minute that it would be signed at all). The events of these years explain the American flexibility at the final conference table and explain why, even with the U.S. presence gone, the situation in Vietnam still appeared unresolved.

One of the keys to the control of the situation in South Vietnam has always lain outside that country, within the borders of its neighbors, Cambodia and Laos. That key is the Ho Chi Minh trail. Access to the South and the provisioning of Vietcong military units operating there passed through the Demilitarized Zone (DMZ), which separated the two

partitions of the country following the Geneva accords of 1954 when the "first" Indochinese war (with the French) technically ended. Throughout the conflict the DMZ was broached by roads and tracks (not one, as the name suggests, but many) through what was officially neutral territory. Border violations by South Vietnamese troops occurred as early as 1958 and continued with gradually increasing intensity, including the use of U.S. units to cross the border into Cambodia in "hot pursuit" of the enemy and, by 1969, U.S. bombing of targets outside Vietnam.

Until 1969, the Cambodian government was headed by Prince Norodom Sihanouk. His uneasy balancing act of sharing Cambodia's favors between the North Vietnamese and the National Liberation Front (NLF) or Vietcong on the one hand and the United States on the other ended on March 18, 1969, when he was ousted in a coup by the U.S.-backed Lon Nol, who while officially a neutralist was in practice strongly anti-Communist. The North Vietnamese and NLF embassies in Phnom Penh were sacked by crowds and the diplomats withdrawn and Lon Nol launched a "root out the Communists" campaign in both the cities and the countryside.

The United States was not slow to take advantage of this situation and on March 27, 1970, South Vietnamese troops launched a major assault against Communist sanctuaries in Cambodia with American air support. On the following day the White House announced that American troops could cross the borders. In April President Nixon made this more explicit by saying that simply to send arms to the Cambodian "loyalist" forces would not suffice. He authorized joint U.S.–South Vietnamese ventures to clean out Communist bases in Cambodia that were endangering American lives in Vietnam. The exercise was seen by Nixon as a test of "American will and character." American policy hinged on the theory that the Vietcong were planning to take over

Nguyen Van Thieu, President of South Vietnam. His refusal to compromise over the issue of coalition in the South was a major stumbling block to a negotiated settlement.

Opposite The face of war. Years of debilitating conflict in Vietnam led America to cut its losses, but left the problems of the country unresolved.

Aftermath of a U.S. bombing raid in North Vietnam. When North Vietnam escalated the war in the South after America's rapprochement with China, Nixon authorized heavy bombing raids on military and civilian targets north of the DMZ.

Cambodia and turn it into an arsenal and a refuge. On April 30, a major invasion of Cambodia began and Nixon stated to Congress that U.S. troops would withdraw in from three to seven weeks when their objectives were accomplished and would not penetrate beyond twenty-one miles from the Vietnamese border. Moreover, U.S.-financed mercenaries were flown into Phnom Penh to augment the 50,000 troops that were in Cambodia by May. NLF supply bases were found—including an enormous one that became known as "the City"—but the headquarters of the Vietcong, which was believed to be within the invasion area, was not.

In June, U.S. troops were withdrawn into South Vietnam even though the whole northeastern segment of Cambodia had fallen to Communist troops moving down from the North. It is at this point that a change in American military strategy is discernible—the withdrawal of American ground troops other than "advisers," and the leaving of the local fighting to South Vietnamese soldiers. This policy anticipated the later large-scale "Vietnamization of the War" plan that maintained the U.S. presence by way of massive air support, including the use of B-52 strategic bombers as well as tactical aircraft.

The invasion of Cambodia was thus both a high point and a turning point in U.S. involvement in Indochina. Yet in material terms little was achieved. On the ground there was military stalemate in Vietnam; in terms of progress toward a negotiated settlement it represented several steps backward, since all of Indochina was now involved; for the Americans it meant a widening of the already costly war into Cambodia and Laos, and for the anti-American forces throughout the area a stiffening of resolve and a broadening of their base among the disaffected in their various countries. The central "problem" of Vietnam, in other words, was being diluted and confused by inclusion into a far more extensive imbroglio, yet with the paradoxical result of North Vietnam remaining inviolable, except from the air. Each U.S. strategic step forward proved to be into a yet deeper quagmire, literally and metaphorically, from which the only exit could be solution of the root problem—American involve-

ment in any form and the American perception of its role in Southeast Asia.

It is at this point that another factor enters the picture—U.S. relations with China. The mutual hostility of the Peking and Washington governments had long been underscored by, if not based upon, U.S. involvement in Vietnam and its political implications. These especially included the idea of U.S. hegemony in the Asia–Pacific zone as being a buffer against Chinese expansion, whether physical or ideological. The significant development of 1971 lies in the improving relations between China and the United States, which were to play a critical role in the movement toward peace in Vietnam. It was clear that the impasse into which American strategy in Vietnam had come was not soluble by military means, but only by diplomatic ones. At the same time the scale of the conflagration and the degree of international involvement made the war no longer a dispute internal to Indochina, but a puzzle that could only be solved by a realignment of objectives on the part of the superpowers.

In February, 1972, President Nixon visited China, accompanied by, among others, Dr. Henry Kissinger, whose rise to world prominence dates from this time. Two particular results of this visit were forthcoming—a very critical and hostile reaction from the Hanoi regime which now saw its closest allies treating with the enemy, and a joint U.S.–Chinese communiqué issued on February 27, outlining an extraordinary volte-face by America. For while the Chinese reiterated their support for the Indochinese liberation movements and the NLF's peace proposals, the United States accepted publicly the principle that neither superpower should seek hegemony in the Asia-Pacific region and placated the Chinese by accepting their viewpoint on Taiwan—that there was only one China, and Taiwan was a part of it. In addition, the American government reversed its previous military policy by announcing:

The peoples of Indochina should be allowed to determine their destiny without outside intervention; its [the United States'] constant primary objective has been a negotiated solution. . . . In the absence of a negotiated settlement the U.S. envisages the ultimate withdrawal of all U.S. forces from the region consistent with the aim of self-determination for each country in Indochina.

The stalemate in Vietnam and the U.S. recognition that rapprochement with China was the first priority of American foreign policy had immense repercussions. It meant that the whole position of Vietnam in American thinking had changed—that it was worthwhile for the U.S. to abandon its South Vietnamese allies (to say nothing of Taiwan; it also meant the rapid rethinking of relations between Japan and China) and that it was worthwhile for China to alienate the North Vietnamese in the search for a multipolar rather than a bipolar power situation in Asia. (This is to leave aside the role that the impending U.S. presidential elections had on Mr. Nixon's attitude toward the war.) It also implied, in a sense, that the onus for continuing the war lay with the North Vietnamese and not with the Americans—who had shown themselves ready to talk. It should be remembered that North Vietnam had its own internal history, in the course of which it was by no means undivided as to military policy, ideological position vis-à-vis classical Marxism and the best way of organizing a tiny nation vastly overstrained by the burdens of war.

It would seem that peace should have followed rapidly on the heels of Nixon's diplomatic coup. It did not for two basic reasons. On the one hand the precise terms on which peace proposals could be discussed had never been settled between the interested parties, and this was truer now than it had been in the past; on the other, and so far as is known quite unrelated to the timing of Nixon's visit to Peking, the North Vietnamese and their allies were preparing a great offensive against the South. This was accordingly launched, after a preliminary bombardment of South Vietnamese positions below the DMZ, on March 30, 1972. On April 1, three North Vietnamese divisions supported by tanks and artillery crossed the zone and drove south rapidly overrunning all defenses. The U.S. supporting air forces were unable to do anything because of low cloud cover and their inability to distinguish fleeing allied from advancing enemy troops. On April 7 a second front was opened in the Central Highlands by Communist troops who had been grouping in the Cambodia-Laos border zone, and on April 6 two new fronts were opened by North Vietnamese troops crossing from Cambodia who advanced to within thirty-seven miles of Saigon, and by the Vietcong in the Mekong Delta. The North had clearly determined to humiliate the United States and its allies and to show Peking (and indeed Moscow) that it could win, even on the enemy's terms.

The one miscalculation in this was what America could and would do with its air might, even in the face of violent international reaction. On April 7 and 8 the United States launched heavy bombing

assaults against the advancing Northerners, and B-52s crossed the DMZ into North Vietnam itself; on April 16 (two days after Saigon's Tan Son Nhut airbase was mortared by the NLF) Haiphong, the major port of the North, and Hanoi were bombed for the first time since 1968. Bombing of non-military targets also began on a large scale. On April 18 Secretary of Defense Melvin Laird told a Senate hearing that the United States would boycott the Paris peace talks until the Northerners had withdrawn beyond the DMZ, which they showed no signs of doing. Yet at the same time, while the weakness of the South Vietnamese troops was being dramatically revealed and while the situation (from the American point of view) was deteriorating rapidly, Nixon ordered further massive withdrawals of U.S. troops to be accomplished by July 1, although the bombing was to continue. Indeed, it was at this time that commentators began to remark on the contrast between the bland Nixon of the Peking trip and the emerging director of the overwhelming forces being unleashed against a virtually undefended North and its civilian population. The bombing is equally significant for the way in which it revealed the desperation that accompanied the failure of the highly equipped Southerners to hold off an invasion of their own territory. This underlined the failure of the "Vietnamization" policy, a policy that the Americans had probably rendered unviable from the outset by destroying, with their scorched-earth tactics, such as defoliation and chemical warfare, the very foundations on which such a policy could have been built.

Thus it was that on May 8 the major ports of North Vietnam were mined on Nixon's orders and a major blockade put into effect in the China Sea, while heavy bombing continued. This went on despite vigorous protests from the U.S.S.R., which had twelve ships trapped in Haiphong harbor. In the South, President Nguyen Van Thieu declared a state of martial law, giving himself almost unlimited government powers. By June, despite continuing troop withdrawals, it appeared that the bombing was taking effect (on June 26 there had been heavy air raids against the North for seventy-

The Vietnam peace talks at St-Nom-la-Bretèche, January 13, 1973. The two chief negotiators, Henry Kissinger and Le Duc Tho, had met secretly before the official talks to settle the basic issues. The cease-fire agreement was announced on January 24.

Prince Norodom Sihanouk of Cambodia delivering a speech in 1968. Officially neutral, Cambodia was a sanctuary for North Vietnamese and Vietcong troops. Sihanouk was ousted in 1969 by a CIA-backed coup.

ARVN troops repel an attack by Vietcong and North Vietnamese in Saigon cemetery, 1968.

U.S. infantry on a search-and-destroy mission near Pleiku in South Vietnam. Ever since the 1954 Geneva conference, American military involvement in South Vietnam had steadily increased.

five consecutive days) and that the ground offensive had been slowed. In May the United States had rejected North Vietnamese requests to open another round of peace talks. Now the United States made the suggestion, only to have it brusquely rejected by Hanoi on the grounds that most of the troops and aircraft being withdrawn from South Vietnam were simply being transferred to Thailand, where they continued operating.

However, by proposing genuine concessions as well as by "bombing the North Vietnamese to the conference table," talks were resumed in Paris on July 13. These were not the only factors, though. There were two others, one being the dreadful prospect of world war, for Peking had come down heavily and unreservedly in agreement with the Moscow line. They asserted that the bombing and mining of the North was provocative aggression that involved Chinese as well as Russian individuals and property, to say nothing of the collapse of the goodwill generated by the Nixon visit in February. The other was that Dr. Kissinger had been having secret talks with Le Duc Tho of North Vietnam in May in an attempt to define the grounds on which agreement might become possible—and especially on how to resolve the stumbling block of President Thieu, whom the NLF wanted removed as a preliminary to reopening negotiations. For by this time the focus of the war had without doubt become the question of who would govern in the South in the event of, and indeed as a prerequisite for, a

cease-fire agreement. Additionally, in June Le Duc Tho and Kissinger both visited Peking, and President Nikolai Podgorny of Russia visited Hanoi. The straws of a peace deal were already in the wind.

The chief stumbling block of the July talks was that the United States wanted a cease-fire before discussing a political settlement, while the Hanoi negotiators rejected the separation of the two issues and appeared in fact to be preparing a new offensive to coincide with the build-up to the impending November American elections. Meanwhile throughout October, 1972, suggestion and countersuggestion was made at the Paris talks—the Americans sticking to their cease-fire proposal, the Communists suggesting the formation of a coalition government in Saigon with NLF representation. They also stuck to their insistence that President Thieu was the chief obstacle to agreement, especially since he would not compromise over the issue of a coalition in the South. The Americans, too, undoubtedly regarded Thieu as a severe difficulty, for the timetable for signing a treaty could not be met because of the problems of persuading the South Vietnamese to agree to the "Nine Points" broadcast by Hanoi as being the contents of the treaty. Kissinger indeed denied that there was any definite commitment to sign on October 31, the date given by the North as being settled, and from which they shifted when it became clear that the United States would not sign by then. Saigon bitterly opposed the Nine Points as they gave the North all it wanted while leaving the South unprotected from Northern aggression—a complete sellout of the South and a reversal of all previous U.S. policies.

Throughout November the negotiators returned to discussion of "linguistic difficulties" in the Vietnamese and English versions of the treaty and to the question of a reciprocal agreement by the North to remove its troops when the Americans removed theirs. Talks were suspended on November 25 while Kissinger returned to Washington for discussions with Nixon and Thieu's aide, Nguyen Puh Duc. At the end of November the North did agree to withdrawal of "all foreign troops" from Vietnam and Cambodia, but the hope of peace by Christmas passed, again because of Thieu's unwillingness to be drawn into an agreement that could undermine his own position. On December 17

Kissinger admitted that "99 percent" of the text had been agreed, and that it was merely the machinery of implementing and policing the peace that remained to be settled. Yet the next day the United States lifted restrictions on bombing North Vietnam below the 20th Parallel and escalated bombing continued until December 30 when Nixon ordered it stopped. On January 4, redrafting of the treaty began again on the basis of the North agreeing not to insist on a "one Vietnam" clause and the United States agreeing not to demand withdrawal of Northern forces from the South. President Thieu naturally still remained opposed.

Between January 8 and 13, 1973, Kissinger and Le Duc Tho met secretly in Paris and on January 23 a cease-fire agreement was announced, to take effect on January 28. The main points of the Paris agreement were: that all U.S. prisoners in Indochina would be released within sixty days; that all U.S. military personnel would be withdrawn in the same period; that the armed forces of the Vietcong and the South would remain in their positions as of January 28; that the United States pledged itself not to intervene in the internal affairs of the South; and that a control commission would be introduced to supervise the cease-fire. In addition, both the United States and North Vietnam agreed on the principle of the self-determination of the peoples of the South; the Saigon government and the Vietcong agreed to achieve national reconciliation and concord; both sides agreed to respect the neutrality of Cambodia and Laos. U.S. aid was promised for the reconstruction of North Vietnam and Indochina in general and the eventual and peaceful reunification of North and South Vietnam.

The cease-fire, which took some weeks to implement, quickly proved to be "fragile." The political struggle for power in the South continued unabated and America attempted to retain as much influence as possible in Southeast Asia. But January, 1973, was nevertheless a landmark in Asian and world history. For not since the fall of Dien Bien Phu in 1954, the event that marked the effective end of French colonial influence in Vietnam, has the stage been so dramatically reset for the next act in the unfolding of the always complex and tragic history of Vietnam—"The Little Dragon."

J. R. CLAMMER

Veterans of the Vietnam war demonstrating against American policy. By the late 1960s public opinion in the U.S. had turned against maintaining the commitment to a strong anti-Communist state in South Vietnam.

The signing of the Vietnam peace agreement in Paris. The terms of the agreement reflected a fundamental realignment of American Far Eastern policy.

Coup in Chile

In 1970 the Chilean people voted into power the predominantly Marxist coalition headed by Salvador Allende. The Allende administration's action against foreign investments, the latifundios (great estates) and the industrial monopolies, however, provoked increasing right-wing opposition both within and without the Congress. Nevertheless Allende increased his mandate in the elections of 1973. As a result, fascist elements provoked disturbances throughout the country and Allende decided to settle the crisis by means of a plebiscite. At this point right-wing military leaders put into operation a carefully prepared takeover plan, calling on the President to surrender. This he refused to do, and he perished in the bombed-out presidential palace. The military embarked upon a program of repression, returning Chile to an economic and social order rejected by the electorate. The curtailment of liberty ended a remarkable political experiment.

General Augusto Pinochet, commander in chief of the Chilean army who headed the coup that toppled the socialist regime of Salvador Allende.

Opposite The ruins of La Moneda, the presidential palace in Santiago in which Allende died rather than surrender to the military.

On September 11, 1973, the army, navy, air force and militia deposed the constitutional government of Chile by united military action. The President of the Republic, Doctor Salvador Allende, stood up to the insurrection and emphatically rejected repeated demands for his surrender; he died fighting in La Moneda, the Chilean seat of government.

The government of the Popular Front (*Gobierno de la Unidad Popular*) had grown from a powerful social movement. Its main support came from middle-class public officials and small to medium industrialists and businessmen, almost all the working class, a high proportion of country people and most of the indefinable community of the poor. All had suffered from the failure of the social and economic reform program of the Christian Democrat government of President Eduardo Frei, which had not prevented stagnation in production, growth in unemployment, rising foreign debts and the ever spiraling process of endemic inflation. They found political expression in a coalition of parties, the Unidad Popular, which consisted of the two largest Marxist organizations, the Socialist and Communist Parties, the essentially reformist-humanitarian Radical Party and some Christian parties. The presidential candidate was Salvador Allende, a militant of the Socialist Party and a political leader with a long record of serving the lower classes.

The program of the Unidad Popular had as its main objective the replacement of the economic and social structure that had always existed in Chile, by ending the power of the monopolistic domestic and foreign capital and the *latifundios* (enormous estates), and building a socialist state. This last goal was to be achieved gradually through the progressive construction of a new power structure. The constitution and existing laws were to be respected. Within this framework, a democratic opposition would be allowed to continue, as democracy and liberty were a living heritage of

Chile's history. There was, therefore, a clear contrast between the "dictatorship of the proletariat" and the so-called "Chilean way toward socialism" by pluralistic and democratic means. Although such a national path to socialism had already under certain circumstances been seen as possible by the classical thinkers of the Marxist doctrine, until then it had never been carried into practice. It was hoped that the traditional political institutions would be flexible enough to adapt themselves to create a new political, social and economic structure constitutionally.

While the violent establishment of socialism historically had always taken place in countries either facing an insoluble social crisis, or recently involved in a cruel war, Chile in 1970 was not faced with either situation. There did, however, appear to be favorable conditions of a different sort for achieving socialism without destroying the existing social order. Chile had the strongest democratic-liberal regime in Latin America. Its civil tradition had accustomed people to accept electoral decision and respect both the constitution and the laws. The political-legal system was not rigid or authoritarian but was sufficiently elastic to take new political currents into account. The constitution allowed for powers independent of the state and provided for a powerful Executive which had various means of carrying forward anti-oligarchical and anti-monopolistic initiatives. In 1970 most of the basic means of production were controlled by the state to a far greater degree than in any other Latin American state. The distribution in sectors of the labor force showed a clear predominance of industrial workers, miners, construction and transport workers (34 percent) and workers engaged in services and commerce (41 percent) as against agricultural workers (25 percent). The Chilean proletariat had long been engaged in social and political struggle. The people were organized into powerful unions and in general found a natural and disciplined political expression

President Allende addressing the press after the elections of 1970. Subsequent elections increased the mandate of the Popular Front—a trend that alarmed the right-wing opposition.

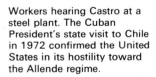

Workers hearing Castro at a steel plant. The Cuban President's state visit to Chile in 1972 confirmed the United States in its hostility toward the Allende regime.

within two parties, the Socialist and Communist, which went forward hand-in-hand to complete their program. The country people were well on the way toward acceptance of unions. This is shown by the rapid creation of unions from 1967. The middle class, for its part, had by 1970 separated itself from the old oligarchic class that had traditionally been dominant. It had in fact taken its own stand with a presidential candidate, Radmiro Tomic, a supporter of vast social and economic reforms. Finally, the international scene was favorable. The Soviet Union was no longer a fortress under siege but was advancing at the head of a major group of socialist countries who would be definitely well disposed toward helping the new regime in Chile. The Cuban Revolution had shown the Latin American peoples that if they were decisive, they could determine their destiny. Recent political developments in the neighboring countries, Argentina, Bolivia and Peru, were also in Chile's favor.

In the elections of September 4, 1970, the Popular Front obtained 36.3 percent of the votes cast, Tomic about 28 percent and Alessandri, the right-wing candidate, the rest. This meant that about 65 percent of Chileans wanted major changes in their lives. The elections were followed by obscure machinations and conspiracies to prevent Allende from taking power. One of the victims was the constitutionalist general, Rene Schneider, the commander in chief of the army, who was assassinated. When Allende was proclaimed President of the Republic in Congress, the Christian Democrat members threw their votes behind him, and the new President took power on November 4.

Even though the new government did not have a majority in Congress, it immediately set about carrying out its program. It commenced action against certain foreign investments, the *latifundios* and the industrial monopolies. It recognized that in these factors lay the main obstacles to harmonious and just development and to true independence.

A constitutional amendment proposed to Congress by the Executive suggesting that the major U.S.-owned copper companies—Anaconda, Kennecott and Andina—should be nationalized received unanimous support. The text recognized the right of the parent companies to compensation. At the same time it instituted a procedure by which the Comptroller General of the Republic, an official independent of the Executive, would establish the amount of compensation to be paid while the President of the Republic had powers to determine how much the state should be indemnified for excessive profits made by the companies. It soon became clear that the Chilean state was owed far more by the companies than it owed to them. Within the first nine months of Allende's rule, Chile's most important natural resource, from which it obtains more than 70 percent of its total foreign earnings, had been nationalized. In the next few months coal, nitrate and iron were also nationalized.

Action against the *latifundios* was based on the agricultural reform law promulgated in 1967 by the Frei government. Estates with a surface area of 1,000 hectares or more represented some 72.7 percent of the total agricultural surface area, whereas they made up only 1.3 percent of the total agricultural production. A few large agricultural estates had already been expropriated under the 1967 law. Although inadequate and too rigid, the Popular Front government decided to use the same law to eradicate these gigantic estates. Its application was

so drastic, speedy and far-reaching that before Allende had been in power for two years, more than two-thirds of the *latifundios* had been expropriated and by the middle of 1973 almost all had been abolished.

It is interesting to note that this reform was carried out within the existing framework of the law with a minimum of disorder and violence and that it brought about an increase in total agricultural production. Non-revolutionary agricultural reform carried out in such countries as Colombia, Ecuador and Italy have only affected some 10 percent of agricultural land. Where there is anything comparable to the magnitude of the Chilean venture, such changes followed violent revolutions (Soviet Union, China, Cuba, Bolivia, Mexico) or devastating wars (Japan, South Korea, Eastern Europe). In Latin America, only the Peruvian agricultural reform process could be compared with Chile's.

Left-wing political posters in Santiago.

Left Revolutionary mural in Santiago. The poster in the background reads: "Neruda, glory of the country." In 1971, the Marxist poet Pablo Neruda was awarded the Nobel Prize for literature. He died in hospital a few days after the coup.

The third field of action by the government was against industrial monopolies. An attempt was made to transfer to state ownership only ninety-one companies from a total of thirty-five thousand. However, these ninety-one companies manufactured 60 percent of total gross industrial production. Once more the government used existing legislation that allowed the intervention, inspection and in some cases the expropriation of industries. In many of the expropriated industries, the transfer to state ownership led to the replacement of the board by workers' boards.

At the same time the government bought shares in private banks. These were organized in Chile as limited companies. It was, therefore, sufficient for the state to purchase more than half the shares to become the majority shareholder and to control the bank. So, by the use of capitalist means, the government was quickly able to transfer banks to state ownership.

Nationalization and agricultural reform formed an essential part of the long-term plan for transforming the Chilean economic and social structure. But the government had at the same time begun a short-term plan running along parallel lines for increasing demand by redistributing income and stimulating production by special programs based on the immediate utilization of unused capacity in the economy. The redistribution of income was achieved through an increase in wages and salaries and a reduction of unemployment by building and forestry programs. At the same time prices were frozen, which reduced company profits. Companies were obliged to absorb increases in salaries into their normal profit margin and could only compensate themselves by increasing production and sales. By means of such measures, the government hoped to increase production and to bring about full employment and the better use of underutilized industrial capacity.

At first the plan operated successfully. Demand increased sharply; there was a noticeable increase in production; unemployment levels fell drastically; and inflation dropped substantially. But those who saw their interests damaged by the government's long-term plans had already begun to operate openly against the government.

Despite the need for investment to meet growing demand, industrialists decided not to reinvest their profits in any expansion of their industrial production apparatus. Something similar happened in the agricultural sector, where farmers, influenced by adverse propaganda against the government, held back sowing. This caused an increasingly serious imbalance between demand and supply. And a consequent surge in inflation, which by the

Troops loyal to the Allende government guarding government house during the abortive coup of June 29, 1973.

middle of 1972 had become difficult to halt. Problems started to multiply. Foreign commercial credit was suddenly and drastically cut, especially that coming from the United States, Chile's major trading partner. The same occurred with certain international credit organizations. The North American copper companies that had been nationalized brought legal action in consumer countries in an attempt to halt shipments. The government found it increasingly difficult to re-negotiate Chile's huge overseas debts, almost all of which had been contracted before Allende assumed power.

At home, the Christian Democrat parliamentary majority persistently refused the Executive the right to impose taxes to meet the budget. The opposition became more critical and used the very laws which, although built around a capitalist economy, had included legal mechanisms legitimizing government moves toward state ownership. Thus in 1972 Congress approved a draft constitutional reform that virtually brought back the situation of nationalized companies to what it had been in 1970, and tied the government's hands almost completely from undertaking any further initiative without the approval of Congress. The President vetoed the draft reform, and the opposition then began claiming that the government was illegal, although the veto was constitutional.

From the beginning of 1972, accusations were laid against ministers, although impeachment and political trial by Congress had been abolished under the Constitution of 1925, which only permitted constitutional accusation when the penal responsibility of ministers for specific crimes mentioned in the basic code was established.

The economic situation became daily more difficult; shortages of goods were exacerbated by a systematic monopolization of products and, from October, 1972, a political strike by truck owners. In a country whose geography makes a complete railway communications system impossible, the effect of such a stoppage was disastrous. During the crisis the government survived by its own discipline and wide popular support. After the transport problem had been overcome, some military ministers were added to the cabinet. It was with this cabinet that the government prepared for the general parliamentary elections at the beginning of March, 1973.

These elections had enormous political importance. Months before, the opposition had been counting on obtaining two-thirds of the seats in Congress, the only constitutional way of removing the President. After seeing the popular support given to the government during the transport strike in October, the opposition declared that if the government were defeated substantially in the election it should withdraw its program. Despite the serious state of the country, however, the government obtained more than 44 percent of the votes cast; that is to say, it obtained greater electoral support than it had had when carried into power in 1970. It was obvious that the Executive was gaining popular support. The government's electoral success destroyed the opposition's hopes of removing the President constitutionally. But senior army officers had already resolved to use force to overthrow the government. The election results merely heightened their determination and provided them with support from other opponents of the government.

All types of goods, however essential, finally disappeared from the markets. A black market, with prices well beyond the reach of the average man's pocket, flourished. A shortage of fuel made both local and long-distance transport for people and goods very difficult. Attacks on means of communications, bridges, electricity supply systems and private houses, increased daily. Militants of the National Party (*Partido Nacional*) from the extreme right and groups from the fascist organization Fatherland and Liberty (*Patria y Liberdad*) provoked disturbances in the streets, denouncing the ineptitude and lack of authority of the government, calling brazenly for the rejection of the President and carrying out terrorist activity throughout the country. All the major traditional papers, most of the radio stations and some television stations were involved in the campaign to denigrate the authorities. When those responsible for these acts were taken before the courts, in general they were acquitted.

The leaders of the Christian Democrat Party, now allied with the right, prevented any attempt by the government to reach a political understanding with moderate sectors of their ranks. They voted in the Chamber of Deputies for a resolution listing specific illegal acts carried out by the Executive, without, however, going so far as a general declaration of illegality on the part of the Executive as was later claimed. They incited and supported strikes.

The armed forces had been ordered by law in April to exercise control of arms. They had the authority to carry out checks and searches of any suspected place without first obtaining a warrant. A great deal of effort was put into this work. During these months, attention was drawn to the fact that the search was always directed toward finding illegal arms among government supporters but not among the fascist groups that were daily defying authority.

At the end of June, with the loyal support of the then commander in chief of the army, General Carlos Prats Gonzalez, the government put down an uprising by an armored unit in Santiago. One month later the President's aide-de-camp was assassinated. In June there had been a strike provoked by some of the trade-union leaders at the nationalized *El Teniente* copper company near Rancagua. This was followed by a strike by shopkeepers and then a second total stoppage by truck owners, who refused to go back to work even when almost all their demands were met.

On Monday, September 10, the President informed some members of the government and General Augusto Pinochet, the new commander in chief of the army, of his decision to seek a solution to the grave national crisis by means of a plebiscite, which he was authorized to convoke under the constitution. The military leaders decided to act immediately.

Early the next morning they put into operation a carefully prepared plan. They overcame those units and officers who refused to go back on their oath of loyalty to the civil authority. They took over military control of the country, quickly taking charge of radio stations and for several hours during the morning called, to no avail, on the head of state to surrender. Allende had declared his firm decision to resist to the bitter end in La Moneda. The palace was repeatedly bombed from the air and then heavily fired upon by tanks. Finally the building was invaded by the army and the President of the Republic died fighting, with a machine gun in his hands. Some hours before he had addressed his people for the last time: "Fellow workers: I have faith in Chile and its destiny. Other men will overcome these gray and bitter times when treason seeks to prevail. You know that sooner rather than later avenues will open up along which free men will pass to construct a better society."

The whole world witnessed the events that followed. The armed forces rapidly reduced the weak pockets of spontaneous reaction, shooting guerrillas where they captured them, imposing a rigid curfew and embarking on a period of repression. In the months that followed almost 20,000 people were killed and many thousands more tortured, mutilated, raped, wounded, jailed and degraded. Hundreds of thousands of people lost their jobs. Almost 10,000 people sought diplomatic asylum abroad and many more left the country to avoid future difficulties. The National Congress was dissolved and a military junta governed by decree. Political activity was forbidden. The parties that had formed the Unidad Popular were declared illegal and their leaders and many of the militants who had not been able to obtain asylum in foreign embassies were assassinated, imprisoned or persecuted. Even the parties in opposition to Allende's government were suspended. Freedom of expression disappeared. Union organizations were dissolved. The universities were controlled by the military. Several thousand teachers and students were expelled for no other reason than the ideas they held. Literature thought to be subversive was burned on great pyres in the streets. The repression of the first few weeks, directed toward massive intimidation, was followed by more subtle and selective means as the military intelligence services coordinated and integrated files and records.

Systematic repression was inherent in the form of power installed by the armed forces in Chile. With its support, the forces hoped to reestablish, reinforce and perpetuate an economic and social order that could not be restored by the will of the people. Thus violence seemed indispensible for the annihilation of the democratic political movement that was taking Chile in the opposite direction. All the articles that had been absent from the shop windows quickly reappeared after the coup. Foreign investors again filled the elegant hotels of Santiago. Many of the nationalized companies and expropriated estates were returned to private hands. The freezing of prices and raising of salaries carried out by the previous governments were followed by the so-called social economy of the market, that is to say, the absolute dominance of private initiative which calls for a freezing of wages and an increase in prices. As a result inflation again reduced the real value of wages.

For how long? Can the deepest and most prominent wishes, strengthened through long years of struggle on the part of the people, be undermined and spurned by a repressive order? History will tell whether "sooner rather than later avenues will open up along which free men will pass to construct a better society."

ALVARO BUNSTER

General Carlos Prats Gonzalez, the commander in chief who suppressed the June coup. He was subsequently exiled by Pinochet's right-wing junta.

Chilean soldiers burning Marxist literature: part of General Pinochet's ruthless campaign to remove the "malignant tumor of Marxism."

War in the Middle East

October 6 of 1973 was Yom Kippur, the most solemn day in the Jewish calendar. It was the day chosen by Egypt and Syria to launch an attack on the territories held by Israel since the war of 1967. Taking the Israeli army completely by surprise, their invasion achieved stunning initial successes. The end of hostilities saw Israel once more on the way to military victory but nearing political defeat, and plainly dependent on continued American support. The war had shattered the status quo, and raised again the Palestinian issue. Moreover, the Arabs had proved the effectiveness of their oil weapon and radically changed their relationship with Western Europe. Superpower détente was seen to have strict limits, but the concept held, and the United States was able to act resolutely towards a disengagement of forces and win new respect in the Arab world, temporarily eclipsing the Soviet Union.

Israeli Minister of Defense Moshe Dayan touring the Golan front on October 11, 1973.

Opposite Suez after the cease-fire. The guns of this Egyptian antiaircraft battery are still pointing at the sky.

On October 6, 1973, the armies of Egypt and Syria simultaneously attacked the territories held by Israel since the war of June, 1967, and the kaleidoscope of the Middle East was violently shaken. In Sinai, the seemingly impregnable Israeli defensive Bar-Lev Line along the east bank of the Suez Canal proved as illusory as the Maginot Line, while in the north around 700 Syrian tanks crashed through the 1967 cease-fire lines, backed by MIG fighters and artillery fire, and rolled inexorably across the Golan plain toward less than 100 Israeli tanks. For the next sixteen days the war continued, and the two fronts, tiny areas in global terms, were the scene of tank battles comparable with those fought in World War II; and both sides fought with the most sophisticated weapons yet made available by the superpowers.

In a meticulously planned operation, Egyptian forces burst the Israeli defenses along the Suez Canal within twenty-four hours. Under cover of massive artillery fire from the west bank of the Canal and MIG attacks from the air, which took the 600 reservists manning the Bar-Lev Line completely by surprise, 8,000 Egyptian soldiers launched rubber dinghies and crossed the Canal. The previous night, Egyptian commandos had sabotaged the Bar-Lev Line's secret weapon by blocking the pipes that would have allowed oil to be spread over the water's surface and then set alight, thus turning the Canal into a raging inferno. Armed with Russian-built bazookas and anti-tank guided missiles, the first Egyptian assault force sped past the bunkers, intent on destroying the Israeli tanks and artillery entrenched behind the Bar-Lev Line. Driving holes into the sand barrier of the Canal's steep banks using heavy pressure jets of water, and using new Russian bridges that could be assembled with greater speed than had previously been thought possible, at nightfall Egyptian tanks and missiles streamed across the Canal. Meanwhile, in the Golan, a far more fragile border, the Syrian forces advanced southward.

The first few days of the fourth Arab–Israeli war saw the shattering of myths that had grown up after twenty-five years, and especially since 1967. An astonished outside world saw a kind of mirror image of the previous war; this time the stunned prisoners were Israelis and the victorious advance was Arab. Clearly it was no longer possible to believe that the Arabs were poor military material. Were the famed fighting capacities of the Israeli soldier to prove equally mythical?

Since 1948, it had been a matter of doctrine in Israel that the country could only afford short, decisive wars that would demonstrate to the Arabs that Israel could not be destroyed by military might. A country with a small population, relying mainly on a reservist army, could not wage a protracted battle and the best hope of success lay in a preemptive strike. This lesson was not lost on the Arabs, who were determined that this time the first blow would be theirs. There is no doubt that in the fall of 1973 both Israeli and American Intelligence were aware of the build-up of Arab forces on the two fronts, but they both initially discounted the possibility of war. Syrian armor took up offensive positions on the Friday morning, and the Israeli army was alerted to some extent, but the reserves were not called up. In spite of subsequent enquiries, and vociferous, contradictory comment, the reasons for the Israeli government's delay remained unclear. When mobilization did begin it was chaotic. Reservists were horrified to find that their army had grown fat on success, that equipment and ammunition were in poor order and short supply.

Although the actual outbreak of hostilities was unexpected, the reasons for renewed belligerency were endemic in the state of affairs then in existence. The third Arab–Israeli war, of June, 1967, had left Israel in control of large tracts of Arab territory. Soon after the war, a conference of heads of Arab states affirmed at Khartoum: no recognition of Israel; no negotiations; no peace. Attempting to

Moment of joy for Egyptian troops on first crossing over to Sinai. Having knocked out Israel's burning-oil device and destroyed the Bar-Lev sand barrier, Egyptian forces bridged the Canal in under half an hour, using the new Russian PMB pontoon.

create some measure of agreement, Security Council Resolution 242 was drafted, and all the parties except Syria concurred. Unfortunately, the resolution was ambiguous, probably intentionally so. During all U.N. special representative Gunnar Jarring's efforts to find a peace formula, one stumbling block was never removed: Israel insisted on direct negotiations between the parties; the Arabs refused, considering that such negotiations constituted a *de facto* recognition of Israel. The next six years saw the costly war of attrition on the Suez Canal; an enormous increase in Russian military aid to Egypt; growing Russian involvement in Syria and Iraq; and increasingly violent acts by Palestine guerrilla groups. The Israeli government's failure to look hard for a peace formula was understandable, but regrettable. Not only the Arabs watched with dismay as Israel literally dug herself in in the occupied territories.

Preparations for war probably began in April, 1973, with a meeting of Arab chiefs of staff in Cairo. Syria and Egypt drew closer together, Syria agreeing reluctantly that war aims should be limited to the recovery of territory lost in 1967. Diplomatic gestures were made toward King Hussein of Jordan, with whom relations had been severed as it was feared that he was prepared to enter into separate

negotiations with Israel. At a meeting with President Assad of Syria and Hussein in Cairo on September 10, President Sadat of Egypt confirmed that Israel was to be attacked on two fronts: Hussein was to remain simply a potential threat. Superpower intervention to try to force a cease-fire was of course envisaged, but a surprise massive attack would obviously leave the Arabs in a far better bargaining position in any subsequent talks.

During the first week of bitter fighting and heavy losses, while Egypt consolidated her position on the Canal but Israel began to make some gains in the north, there was intense diplomatic activity to promote a cease-fire. A Russian airlift of supplies to Egypt and Syria had begun on October 9, but the U.S. hung fire on fresh supplies to Israel. U.S. Secretary of State Henry Kissinger, anxious to preserve as much as possible of his policy of détente with the U.S.S.R., appears to have been holding back in an effort to force the Israelis to agree to a cease-fire based on the current battle lines. In the event, it was President Sadat who rejected any such moves, insisting firmly that Egypt would only agree to a long-term settlement based on the Arab reading of U.N. Resolution 242. The American airlift proper began on October 14 (though some supplies had been slipped through earlier).

After eight days the Syrian assault was largely broken and Syrian troops were forced to fall back toward their capital, which was being attacked from the air. The Egyptians settled in on the east bank, securely protected by a curtain of missiles. The Israelis continued their advance into Syria, defeating Iraqi and Jordanian divisions that had been sent to help their northern ally. In Cairo, Sadat proclaimed that Egypt's aim was to liberate land held by Israel since 1967 and to restore "the legitimate rights of the Palestinians." He would accept a cease-fire when Israel returned to the pre-1967 lines, and would attend a conference under the auspices of the U.N. to seek a peace "based on the legitimate rights of all the people in the area." In her speech in Jerusalem a few hours later, however, Premier Golda Meir reiterated her belief that the Arabs' ultimate aim was the destruction of Israel, that events had proved how right Israel had been to hold on to the occupied territories, and that anyway a task force of the Israeli army was now in operation on the west bank of the Suez Canal.

Led by General Arik Sharon, two Israeli brigades attempted, under cover of a diversionary attack, to cross the Canal through a gap between the Egyptian Second and Third Armies. By midnight, October 15, 200 men had reached the other side. Unobserved, they were able to put out of action four SAM missile sites, thus enabling increasing numbers of Israeli forces to cross in safety through this gap. After some delay, almost certainly resulting from their cumbersome hierarchical chain of command, the Egyptians acted, but the delay had given the Israelis time to build up their forces. The ensuing battle was protracted, with the Israelis slowly gaining control.

But the Arabs were not prepared to rely on

Israel's General Yariv (*left*) and Egypt's General El Gamasy (*right*) shake hands at the third round of disengagement talks at Kilometer 101 on the Suez–Cairo road.

fighting power alone. As the war continued they determined to use their most powerful weapon—oil. To an increasing degree, oil has become the essential lubricant of modern industrial society. Far and away the bulk of oil imports of Western Europe and Japan come from the Arab world and Iran, while the U.S. imports about eleven percent of its needs from the area. The international oil companies, however, are a very important sector of U.S. business and their continued operation depends on the goodwill of Middle Eastern states. Previous Arab cuts in oil supplies for political purposes made in 1956 and 1967 had been little more than a severe inconvenience; in 1973 Western Europe and Japan reeled under the blow.

When the Gulf States section of OPEC (Organization of Petroleum Exporting Countries) met in Kuwait on October 17, 1973, it had two objectives. One was the raising of the price by seventy percent to all consumer countries demanded by the Iranian minister. The other was the determination of the Arab producers to cut production so that Western industrial nations would be forced to put pressure on the U.S. to change its policy toward Israel. Saudi Arabia, whose absolute monarch was previously a firm supporter of the United States against Communism, declared a *jihad* (Moslem holy war) and suspended all oil supplies to the U.S., King Faisal having finally decided that the defense of Moslem interests (particularly the recovery of Jerusalem, Islam's third holy city) took precedence over friendship with the United States. Holland, which had been strictly neutral during the war, was included in the total ban. Production was to be cut by five percent until Israel withdrew from all the

occupied territories and the rights of the Palestinians were restored (and not simply, as Resolution 242 states, until there was "a just settlement of the refugee problem"). Any friendly state "which has extended or shall extend effective material assistance to the Arabs" would be exempted.

In an undignified scramble to demonstrate their "friendship," the countries of Western Europe scurried in all directions, desperately seeking to become "favored nations," yet hypocritically insisting that they were not giving in to blackmail. As a result of secret undertakings France and Britain improved their status. Japan severed relations with Israel. Sensible efforts by a justifiably irritated United States to foster some measure of cooperation among consumer countries, and to work out countermeasures, were disregarded. The rift between the U.S. and Europe deepened. Israel was confirmed in her deepest-held fear, that gentiles would always sacrifice Jews if their interests were threatened.

Spurred on by the effects of the oil weapon on European economies, U.S. efforts to arrange a cease-fire increased. Israeli successes on the west bank of the Suez Canal provided stronger goads than the U.S.S.R. Resolution 338, accepted by the U.N. Security Council on the evening of October 21, called for: an end to the fighting twelve hours after acceptance of the resolution, the immediate implementation of Resolution 242, and the start of negotiations between all parties concerned. It was little less ambiguous than 242, but at least it held out hopes of gains to both sides. Sadat accepted the cease-fire, Assad remained silent, and Golda Meir indicated grudging acceptance. Within the next forty-eight hours, Israeli forces had surrounded the Egyptian Third Army, cutting it off entirely from supplies of food, ammunition and water, and decidedly strengthening Israel's bargaining position. Hard-pressed by Russia, Assad indicated that he might accept the non-operative cease-fire.

At a meeting of the Security Council on October 24, the Soviet ambassador vehemently supported the Egyptian call for a joint U.S.–U.S.S.R. peacekeeping force. The Americans demurred. A few hours later, Brezhnev informed Kissinger in a harshly

Middle Eastern Conflict, 1973

— De facto frontiers of Israel from June 11, 1967 to October 6, 1973

⬤ Deepest penetration of Arab forces, October 6-8

⬤ Farthest limits of Israeli counterattacks, October 8-24

• Towns and ports bombed by Israeli forces

First use of the oil weapon. By cutting back production in general—and boycotting the U.S.A. and Holland—the Arab oil producers plunged Western Europe into considerable disarray, but were unable to exert pressure on Israel's chief supplier, America.

Top Presidents Sadat of Egypt and Assad of Syria with King Hussein of Jordan at the summit of September 10, during which differences were settled and war objectives determined.

The war in the north. A line of Israeli armored personnel carriers (foreground) rolls out of the contested Syrian village of Mashara, as Iraqi artillery (smoke puffs, background) begins to pour in on the village, October 17, 1973.

worded note that in the absence of U.S. involvement, the U.S.S.R. might well act alone. As U.S. Intelligence had just passed on the news that a number of Soviet ships in the eastern Mediterranean and airborne divisions were on stand-by alert, the Americans reacted by putting the U.S. military throughout the world on alert. The upshot was acceptance of the idea of a U.N. peace-keeping force.

Finally, on November 11, 1973, representatives of Israel and Egypt met at Kilometer 101 on the Cairo–Suez road and signed a six-point disengagement agreement. Israel withdrew to passes in the Sinai well east of the Suez Canal. A U.N. force took up its buffer position. The stage was set for a peace conference in Geneva in December, attended by Egypt, Jordan and Israel, but boycotted by Syria. After 100 days of fierce fighting in the spring of 1974, Syria and Israel signed a similar disengagement agreement in Geneva on May 31. To a very large extent, these settlements were the work of one man—U.S. Secretary of State Henry Kissinger, who displayed apparently indefatigable energy and patience as he sped from one Middle Eastern capital to another patching up an accord. While his efforts were widely applauded, some disquiet was felt at settlements that depended so much on one man, known for his tendency toward secret agreements and under increasing attack at home.

During the war the Palestinian organizations, which in the intervening six years had insured that their cause was not forgotten by indulging in desperate acts of terrorism that made international headlines, were powerless. But it did become apparent that any settlement acceptable to the actual inhabitants of the area had to include two factors: Arab, and Palestinian, acceptance of the Jewish state, and Israeli, and Jordanian, acceptance of Palestinian national ideals. Moves toward settling for, in the first instance, a "mini-Palestine" established in the West Bank and the Gaza Strip were in the air for a year or two. Just after the war, there were hints that the PLO (Palestine Liberation Organization), the umbrella for the various guerrilla groups, might be willing to negotiate some such agreement. At a meeting of heads of state in Rabat in October, 1974, the entire Arab world (including Hussein) recognized the PLO as the sole, legitimate voice of the Palestinians. This received worldwide ratification when PLO leader Yassir Arafat was invited in November to address the U.N. debate on the Palestine problem. While small but not insignificant numbers of Israelis were prepared to negotiate with the PLO at the prospective Geneva peace conference, the majority of the country and both government and opposition—the right-wing Likud Party had made important gains in the post-war Israeli elections—were radically opposed to this. Brutal terrorist attacks within Israel in 1974 bore out the general view.

The PLO seemed prepared to accept a state in a reasonable part of Palestine without forgoing the historic right to the whole of it. The PLO's insistence that the West Bank–Gaza state must be an "independent, fighting national authority," and that they would "struggle against any Palestinian entity whose price was the recognition of Israel," plus their determination to escalate terrorist operations within Israel and the occupied territories, obviously precluded its gaining any Israeli support. Hussein of

Jordan, under whose rule almost a million Palestinians lived, effectively withdrew his claim to the West Bank in 1974 at Rabat, thus stiffening local support for the PLO within the occupied territories. It became fairly clear that some Palestinian leaders hoped that a peace agreement would prove impossible. Over-sanguine in the view of most observers, they looked forward to the imminent demise of the Zionist state.

The end of the fourth round saw Israel once more on the way to military victory, but nearing political defeat. It had been made brutally clear that she was almost totally dependent on the United States, and that expediency might curb U.S. support in the future. Israel's manifold critics were triumphant. A great deal of sanctimonious nonsense was talked about "hubris," suggesting that Israel had been justly punished for her arrogance—nonsense that ignored the fact that in the eyes of Western leaders Israel could have been as arrogant as she liked had the Middle Eastern oil lain under the sands of the Negev. Painful reassessments became necessary within Israel. It was recognized on many sides that the 1967–73 stability was no more than insubstantial self-deception and that Israel's only hope was some accommodation with her Arab neighbors. The population felt cheated by its old leaders, but no convincing new ones were at hand.

Egypt and Syria emerged from the war with honor restored, a military defeat that could be hidden behind the brilliant initial successes, and at least with the knowledge that they had broken the status quo. They had probably hoped for little more. Both could look forward to the economic benefits of cooperation with the U.S. that would follow a settlement. For Sadat himself the war was a triumph: his leadership of his country was secured and he established a remarkable personal rapprochement with Kissinger. The Arab unity that had been forged by the war soon crumbled. Those who had contributed least complained loudest about its outcome.

About Western Europe the less said the better. The concept of a united Europe as a third power was revealed as a pathetic myth. The leaders of the former colonial masters of the belligerent parties showed themselves to be petty, self-seeking men with a dangerously narrow view of self-interest. By their folly in reacting in panic to blackmail, they revealed that much of their future lay in the hands of those who ruled the oil fields. The Soviet Union could hardly have overlooked this. What else the U.S.S.R. gained from the war is difficult to assess. Coming to the aid of clients they always considered unreliable, they secured at least the prospective reopening of the Suez Canal, more important to the Soviet Union than to the West. Since the long-term Soviet aim of control over the Middle East appeared to be unchanged, it was hard to see what stake she had in established peace. The United States, with reluctance too in some quarters, also bailed out her protegée. In spite of this, she was able to act resolutely toward disengagement and won new respect in the Arab world, enabling her to play

a part in the "recycling" of the vast Arab oil revenues. Superpower détente was seen to have strict limits, but the concept held.

The conflict between the Arab states and Israel has always been a political struggle based on the realities of their own existence. Their capacity to wage ever costlier and bloodier wars has not. Time alone will show whether they are prepared to accept that their very deep differences should remain the potential testing-ground for the ambitions and weapons of the superpowers, or whether they can begin the painful adjustment process involved on both sides in the search for a true peace.

MOIRA PATERSON

The Israeli causeway across the Canal, looking from West to East. General Sharon's breakthrough to Egypt proper left Israel in a much improved bargaining position at the disengagement talks.

Top Troops of the encircled Egyptian Third Army loading an amphibious craft to ferry supplies across the Suez Canal from the east bank.

In the wake of the Arab-Israeli war

World recession

Events such as the Arab-Israeli war and the coup in Chile raised serious questions about the future prosperity of the advanced industrial countries. While poorer countries battled with the problems of natural disaster and military dictatorship, the developed world faced the no less intractable problems of inflation, shortage of raw materials and world recession. The vast price rises in oil in the wake of the Arab-Israeli war affected industrial countries very seriously, as oil had become the world's most important fuel source. The rise in oil prices coincided with a boom in other commodity prices, such as gold and silver, the base metals, wheat and coffee and sugar. In part, the price inflation had been caused by genuine world shortages and rising demand. Distrust of money in an inflationary age itself added to inflation and the reduction in the value of money. It was not merely the price of raw materials that rose: antique furniture and picture prices escalated wildly and even modern works of art fetched prices previously unheard of at auctions.

The combination of the end of American involvement in the Vietnam war and the vast rise in commodity prices brought a new fear—world recession. This became particularly acute as a result of the rise in oil prices. Although America was relatively little affected directly, most of the major European economies and that of Japan, the

industrial wonder of the postwar world, were seriously threatened by a drop in gross national product and by huge balance of payments deficits. Neither in the United States, affected as it was by the crisis of national confidence that followed Watergate, nor in Europe were governments in any position to take strong steps to avoid the problem of recession.

During 1974, throughout the world, governments appeared to have lost the will to survive. In Canada, Pierre Trudeau's Liberal government lacked a parliamentary majority, and anti-government feeling in Australia ran so high that the federal Prime Minister was attacked by rioters. Most of the governments of Europe lacked parliamentary majorities; even Britain with its tradition of strong parliamentary majorities, was ruled by the minority government of Harold Wilson after the failure of Edward Heath's Conservative administration to secure reelection, and in France Gaulism found itself finally on its deathbed as a result of the illness and death of President Georges Pompidou. The death of Pompidou brought with it the possibility of the election of François Mitterand as a Socialist president and of a government that would include Communists; the election of Valéry Giscard d'Estaing narrowly averted this, but it was clear that the massive left-wing vote could no longer be ignored as it had been by previous presidents and governments. In Germany, President Brandt, whose government had already been weakened by electoral losses and disillusion

Athenians celebrating the end of the Greek military dictatorship in 1974.

with the *Ostpolitik*, resigned after it was shown that a Communist spy had infiltrated his private office. European governments were so weak that their ability to deal effectively with economic problems had virtually disappeared, as became clear in Italy, which was in effect bankrupt. Serious doubts about the future of the E.E.C. were inevitable, and Common Market institutions found themselves under attack. The only consolation for Europe's democracies was that the situation was no better in authoritarian states.

Greece

Although in some countries, most notably Brazil, military governments were able to claim some economic improvement as a justification for their continued existence, more often they argued that military rule was better than Communism. The main problem that faced most military regimes was the lack of popular support. In Greece, for example, where the army had taken over the country in 1967, there was almost continual political tension. Student rioting became commonplace, despite the draconian measures taken by the police and courts to suppress opposition. Under pressure from the other members of NATO, President Papadopoulos was forced to make some political concessions and even to promise elections. The measures of liberalization were unpopular among many senior army officers

and on the morning of November 25, 1973, after a particularly violent student demonstration, army officer rose against army officer and Papadopoulos was placed under house arrest. The new government attacked the "electoral adventure" into which its predecessor had been pushed, but it was not clear that it would be able to ignore foreign pressure more effectively, nor that it would be able to overcome the economic difficulties that faced it.

Cyprus

The overthrowing of Archbishop Makarios' government in Cyprus was an attempt by the colonels to gain popular support. But the failure of the adventure in Cyprus gave the regime's critics within the army their chance. They demanded the junta's dismissal. Amid scenes of wild jubilation, similar to those in Portugal a few months before, the conservative politician Constantine Karamanlis was recalled from exile to form a new administration. As in Portugal the full story of torture and repression was released.

Spain

In Spain, too, there were increasing signs of discontent with the government. Disagreements between the ultraconservative Falangists and the slightly more liberal Opus Dei members of the government led to the fall of the latter in 1973, after

Giscard d'Estaing at his inauguration as President of France.

the world fears economic recession

General Franco with Prince Juan Carlos, his successor as Spain's head of state.

The deposed Emperor Haile Selassie.

an industrial scandal. General Franco, now aged 81, resigned the premiership and was replaced by Admiral Luis Carrero Blanco. But there were many disruptive pressures, as the assassination of Carrero Blanco in December, 1973, was to show. Basque separatists—responsible for the assassination—proved to be a growing problem for the Franco regime, but there were other troubles too. The dispute between the Falange and Opus Dei represented a fundamental disagreement about Spain's future style of government. In addition, as in Portugal, the Roman Catholic Church found itself increasingly in dispute with the government. The change of government in Portugal brought with it further pressure for Franco's government, so similar in its attitudes to that of Salazar, to change.

Africa

Partly as a result of the pressure brought to bear by the Middle Eastern oil producers and partly because of the weariness of Israel and Egypt and their arms suppliers, the prospects of a lasting peace settlement in the Middle East seemed far better after the war in 1973 than at any time since World War II. With the end of American military involvement in Southeast Asia and the hope of peace in the Middle East, other areas began to assume increasing importance, although a Chinese territorial dispute with South Vietnam threatened to disrupt peace negotiations. Nixon had hailed 1973 as "the year of Europe," but by the beginning of 1974 it was clear that relations between the United States and

Europe had reached a new low and that all Kissinger's talents would be required to heal the breach that had been exacerbated by the oil boycott. Africa, too, began to assume a new importance. During 1973 a vast strip of Africa was devastated by drought and it was clear that 1974 was going to bring even more hardship; international organizations poured relief funds into Africa but could not prevent whole villages from starving to death, while, as water levels fell, prosperous fishing towns that had been on the shores of Lake Chad found themselves anything up to seventy miles inland.

While nature was proving more than usually hostile, the tender growth of institutionalized democracy granted by the former colonial powers showed little ability to survive the traumas of independence. In country after country during the later 1960s military dictatorship replaced conservative monarchies—as in Burundi (1966), Libya (1969) and the Sudan (1969) —and more democratic regimes— as in Algeria (1965), Zaïre (1965), the Central African Republic (1966), Congo (1966), Nigeria (1966), Upper Volta (1966), Togo (1967), Mali (1968), Dahomey (1969) and Somalia (1969). In other states, such as Lesotho, the government was forced to rely on the security forces to control disorder. Even in Ethiopia, in most respects Africa's most conservative state, the army began to flex its political muscles in 1974, gradually taking over the government, deposing the Emperor, the ageing Haile Selassie, who had been accustomed to ruling as an autocrat. Revolution in Ethiopia seemed

likely at first to follow a peaceful course, but in November, 1974, after a change of leadership in the military junta, over sixty prominent politicians and officers were executed, and even Haile Selassie's life was threatened.

The trend toward military government continued after 1970. In 1971 the Ugandan army, led by Idi Amin Dada, overthrew the government while the President, Dr. Milton Obote, was at the Commonwealth Prime Ministers' Conference. Edward Heath's English Conservative government immediately recognized Amin's authority, and in this there was a certain irony, as Amin's subsequent volatile behavior was far more anti-British than that of Obote. Amin's failure to build up an effective power base left him entirely dependent on military support, and his hold over the country was purchased at the cost of many thousands of lives. In 1972 the Ghanaian army overthrew the government of Dr. Kofi Busia, and in the same year the Malagasy chief of staff took over power. In 1973 the high command of the Rwanda army dissolved the National Assembly and took over control and in 1974 the army seized power in Niger. In many

other states a one-party political system was introduced.

In southern Africa guerrilla groups continued to struggle against white rule and both in Rhodesia, where a number of white farmers were killed, and in the Portuguese colonies they had considerable effect. Even in the great bulwark of white rule, South Africa, attitudes were beginning to change as the polarization of opinion in the 1974 elections showed. It was, however, to be in Portuguese Africa that the pressure for change became overwhelming.

General Amin, Uganda's volatile President.

A New Era for Portugal

From 1932, when he came to power, Portugal had been ruled according to the autocratic ideas of its dictator, António de Oliveira Salazar—even after his death in 1970. His government was founded on an economically repressive corporate state, distrust of parliamentary democracy, fear of Communism and maintenance of Portugal's overseas colonies, supported by a virtually unrestrained secret police. Then a group of army officers, disillusioned with the seemingly endless African wars, overthrew the government, opening the way for free and democratic institutions. The repercussions would be felt as far away as southern Africa and the coast of China.

At half past five on the morning of April 25, 1974, the Radio Clube Português, a commercial radio station, broadcast a surprise message, announcing that a "Movement of the Armed Forces" had taken over the country and that troops should await orders at their barracks. The broadcast was an exaggeration—rebel troops had scarcely begun to move against the government—but by mid-afternoon it was clear that there had indeed been a coup and that it had succeeded; the rebels had seized all the main strategic centers in the country and Prime Minister Marcello Caetano and President Américo Tomás had handed over power to a newly appointed seven-man military junta, lest it "fall into the hands of the man in the street."

The background to the coup was the forty-year regime of Dr. António de Oliveira Salazar, who had remained Prime Minister until he had suffered a stroke in 1968. Salazar's fundamental attitudes—his belief that Portugal's future should remain closely bound up with Africa, his insistence that the corporate state he had created was the ideal structure for the Portuguese economy, his distrust of parliamentary democracy and his fear of Communism as an anti-Christian phenomenon—had not disappeared with his replacement as Prime Minister by Caetano. Salazar had successfully destroyed all organized electoral opposition, but the Communist Party, which favored violent revolution, had managed to retain its organization despite the activities of the Policia Internacional e de Defesa do Estado (PIDE), later officially renamed Direcção General de Segurança—the secret police. The only democratic politician who could really stand up to Salazar, General Humberto Delgado, had been murdered in 1965 by PIDE agents and the Socialist, Liberal and Monarchist parties were in total disorder. Salazar had approved not only the creation of the PIDE as a force that was entirely independent of the judicial police—and to some extent of the courts—but also laws against strikes

and the increasingly unpopular involvement of the army in wars to suppress independence movements in Portugal's African colonies. President Tomás saw himself as the guardian of Salazarist orthodoxy and was reluctant to allow far-reaching change.

Caetano had resigned from the rectorship of Lisbon University in 1962 after a disagreement with the government, and was regarded as being very much on the liberal wing of the ruling National Union. He was not, however, a strong politician and he found himself faced by the establishment in the form of Tomás, the army and the party, and also by the whole legacy of Salazar's rule. Caetano did attempt to make some changes. He sought to improve relations with the rest of Europe, from which Portugal had been largely isolated, and began negotiating with the European Economic Community. Had these negotiations succeeded, a change in Portugal's colonial policy would have been inevitable, but the National Union distrusted close links with the more liberal governments in Western Europe. During his first few years as Prime Minister, Caetano was able to moderate the zeal of the PIDE and the Ministry of the Interior. The number of political prisoners in metropolitan Portugal fell to 124 in 1969, compared with 353 in 1963. But the increasing opposition to the regime that was caused by the African wars and by economic problems beginning about 1970 gave the secret police a new freedom of action, and the Prime Minister's control over them was progressively weakened.

The main problem that led to this change was the government's inability to control guerrilla movements in the African provinces. In Guinea-Bissau the rebels of the Partido Africano da Independência da Guiné e do Cabo Verde (PAIGC) could rely on the assistance of President Sékou Touré of neighboring Guinea, whose attitude was that "if these people don't want to be liberated we—being free and conscious—have a duty to liberate them." The assassination of PAIGC secretary general Amilcar

Portuguese soldier with a carnation, symbol of the revolution, in the barrel of his rifle.

Opposite Troops and demonstrator in the streets of Lisbon. The Armed Forces Movement that overthrew the government, restored civil liberties and opened the way for democracy.

In the fortress of Caxias, members of the hated secret police are frisked for arms, before being locked in the cells from which General Spínola's government had released all political prisoners.

There were also rumors that Portuguese soldiers, many of whom were black, had on occasion massacred those whom they suspected of harboring terrorists. One such incident, at the village of Wirryamu in Téte Province, came to light early in 1974. The authorities in Mozambique denied that there had been a massacre and denied the very existence of the village. The weight of the evidence, most of it supplied by missionary priests and nuns, was, however, overwhelming. As a result, Church–State relations, already weakened by ecclesiastical disapproval of Portugal's colonial policy, deteriorated further. This was a serious blow to Caetano's government, which saw the Church as one of its main power bases. Disaffection in the army was to be still more serious.

The relative lack of success of the military campaign against the guerrillas in Africa brought with it increasing discontent in the armed forces. A few senior officers, of whom Kaulza de Arriaga was the most powerful, felt that by escalating the war the rebels would be beaten. Other, mostly younger, officers—influenced by the failure of the Americans in Vietnam—were convinced that they were fighting a war that could not be won. Another reason for disapproval of the war was its immense cost. In 1967 nearly 37 percent of the Portuguese budget was spent on defense and in 1973 this figure had risen to over 40 percent. These younger officers looked to General Antonio Ribiero de Spínola, the newly appointed Deputy Chief of Staff of the armed forces, for support. They were not disappointed. In February, 1974, Spínola, a sixty-four-year-old monocled former cavalry officer who had made his reputation fighting the guerrillas in Guinea-Bissau, published *Portugal and the Future*. He believed that because of Portugal's relatively limited resources, "there can be no military solution to Portugal's overseas question." Instead, he proposed that Portugal should acknowledge the standards that were accepted by the rest of the world. The overseas provinces should be allowed self-determination and encouraged to join with Portugal in a Lusitanian federation. This was not the first time that Spínola had made his views known. Three years before, Cabral had taunted him, saying:

Spínola is now claiming not only that he will lead our people forward to independence under the Portuguese flag but also that he will create a social revolution. That is very strange because in Portugal itself it is illegal to talk about social revolution. We suggest that Spínola goes back to his own country and creates a social revolution there.

The words were to prove prophetic.

The popularity of Spínola's views in military circles placed Caetano's government in an embarrassing position. Caetano was believed personally to favor Spínola's approach. Others, however, did not. The weakness of Caetano's position had been apparent for some time, and it was thought that Kaulza de Arriaga had been plotting with the President to remove him from power. Caetano's

Cabral in 1971 did not end rebel pressure. By 1973, PAIGC claimed control over much of the country. Although Portuguese troops were able to control the coastal strip and the main towns, this was only possible by keeping one Portuguese soldier for every fifteen civilians. In Angola, the government was better able to control the situation, although by 1972 it needed 60,000 troops to do so. The rebels in Mozambique presented a threat almost as great as those in Guinea-Bissau, but Mozambique was a far more important province than Guinea both strategically and in its natural resources. There, the rebel movement, Frente de Libertação de Moçambique (FRELIMO), claimed control over much of the Cabo Delgado, Niassa and Téte districts. Although the Portuguese were able to operate in all parts of the country, they kept permanent garrisons only in a few large towns. During 1973, FRELIMO's claims grew, and raids on the railroad between Rhodesia and the port of Beira showed that they had begun operating in Manica—Sofala. They also posed a threat to the huge Cabora Bassa Dam.

Under General Kaulza Oliveira de Arriaga, the Commander in Chief in Mozambique, the army used increasingly desperate measures to control the guerrilla threat. Increasing use was made of large, well-fortified villages, into which the black population from the surrounding countryside was moved. Road traffic in FRELIMO-controlled or -threatened areas was sent in convoys, protected by the army and police. The rail link with Rhodesia, so useful for Portugal's balance of payments, was guarded, and a huge defense operation was mounted to prevent the guerrillas from approaching Cabora Bassa. In some areas Rhodesian troops assisted the Portuguese, and the armies worked closely with the South African and Rhodesian military authorities.

weakness was now emphasized by Tomás who, on March 13, summoned senior officers to swear an oath of loyalty to Portugal's overseas ambitions. Spínola and his immediate superior, Francisco da Costa Gomes, were dismissed when they refused to attend the ceremony. In addition, the government made its disapproval of *Portugal and the Future* clear by forcing the book's publisher, Dr. Paradela de Abreu of Arcadia Press, to resign.

The army's discontent at the dismissal of its hero soon showed itself. On the night of March 15, 200 men at a barracks north of Lisbon arrested their senior officers and drove toward the capital. Although they were forced by a larger force to return to their barracks, it was widely suspected that a more general rising had been called off at the last moment.

The failure of the hastily organized rising of March 15 did not end the military discontent. Over the next five weeks the group of about ninety officers who called themselves the Movement of the Armed Forces planned a new attack on the government. These officers, mostly youngish captains, had begun to agitate in 1973 for better conditions in the army. Now their aims were wider: they sought the complete overthrow of the government. On April 25 they acted. The coup was carried out quickly and with great efficiency and at the cost of only ten lives. By evening the whole country was quiet. Only in the Lisbon headquarters of the PIDE did resistance last, and within twenty-four hours the secret police, too, surrendered.

At first the aims of the rebels were unclear, but in the evening of April 25 the Movement of the Armed Forces issued a statement announcing the restitution of civil liberties and the setting up of a

"junta of national salvation," composed of generals and admirals, including Spínola and Costa Gomes. On the following day the junta released prisoners— about 180 in Portugal and over 1,500 in the overseas provinces—held on political charges. It also announced that a civilian provisional government would soon be appointed and that a general election would be held within a year. The secret police in metropolitan Portugal was abolished—and 800 of its members were arrested, taking the place of the freed political prisoners; trade unions and political parties (with the exception of the National Union, which was abolished) were permitted; and censorship was abolished. What had started as a coup had become a revolution.

As it became clear that the coup was organized by opponents of the system of repression rather than by those who wanted to strengthen it, popular enthusiasm grew. For years Portugal's basic economic and social problems—low educational standards, a large, depressed peasantry and lack of industrial investment—had been exacerbated by a political system that silenced opposition. There had been an emigration of 900,000 people between 1960 and 1971—up to 20 percent of the population in some areas. The international inflation that occurred in 1972–73 hit Portugal more than most countries, and the government, totally out of touch with popular opinion, did little to insulate the public from the effects of price rises. Fear of the PIDE made people wary about complaining openly.

Tens of thousands took to the streets of Lisbon on May Day to celebrate the end of the Salazar system: slogans appeared on walls; political parties —mostly of the left—mushroomed; and, instead of bullets, soldiers carried red carnations—the symbol of the revolution—in the barrels of their guns. Popular enthusiasm seemed to know no bounds. As the political prisoners were released and the exiles—such as Dr. Mario Soares, leader of the Socialist Party, and Alvaro Cunhal, Secretary General of the Communist Party—returned they were met with a tumultuous welcome.

In Portugal's overseas territories, the revolution was greeted with little less enthusiasm. The army gave its backing to the junta without reservation and mass meetings were held in many towns to celebrate the end of the old regime. But the enthusiasm was not universal. The liberation movements all refused to abandon fighting. Although they declared themselves willing to meet members of the new provisional government when it was appointed, they would not discuss the principle of Portugal's withdrawal but only its timetable. In Mozambique, where many white settlers feared that they would find themselves ruled by a black government, an anti-liberation movement, FICO ("I stay"), sought in September to overthrow the government in an attempt to maintain white rule.

In Portugal there were substantial changes in the weeks after the coup. Newspaper editors and government officials who had favored the Caetano regime were ousted by their staffs. The full truth about

Mario Soares, Secretary General of the Socialist Party, on his return from France. As Foreign Minister in the new provisional government he was to negotiate the independence of Portugal's African territories.

Top Marcello Caetano, the Premier whose failure to reform Portugal's forty-year-old autocratic regime and end the wasteful African wars led to the coup of the armed forces.

Left Gates of the Carmo barracks of the Republican Guard. Caetano sheltered here with his cabinet and President Tomás before surrendering to General Spínola.

Mozambique: a Portuguese army search-and-destroy operation. Under General Kaulza de Arriaga increasingly desperate measures were used to control the guerrilla threat.

Opposite above As Lisbon embraces liberty a demonstrator on a car roof gives the victory sign.

Opposite below May Day, 1974, and tens of thousands of Portuguese throng the streets of Lisbon in a spontaneous demonstration for the Revolution.

General Antonio de Spínola, the army's hero, with members of the "junta of national salvation." What had begun as a coup had become a revolution.

PIDE's use of torture—which had often been dismissed as nonexistent by apologists at home and abroad—was published. A number of senior army officers including Kaulza de Arriaga were dismissed and it was announced that several highly placed ministers would be brought to trial. But, in what was certainly its most unpopular action, the junta allowed Caetano and Tomás to leave Portugal for political asylum in Brazil. This was the first sign of the fundamental split that soon became apparent between the centrist and leftist supporters of the coup.

The junta was conscious that the heady atmosphere of freedom brought dangers with it; for example, unregulated wage bargaining would have an inflationary effect on prices, so left-wing parties were encouraged to prevent strikes. There was also a danger of violence from extremists of the right and left, and the junta made clear that the army and police would step in to prevent this. In the months that followed as unions demanded wage increases and political parties looked for advantages restrictions became necessary to prevent uncontrolled inflation and anarchy.

On May 16, the junta handed over power to a fifteen-man provisional government. Many of the ministers were not associated with any political party, but there were three members of the Socialist Party, including Dr. Soares as Foreign Minister, two members each of the Communist and Popular Democratic parties (center), and one of the left-wing Portuguese Democratic Movement. So, after Salazar's determined opposition to Communism, Portugal became the first country in Western Europe since 1947 with Communists in the government.

In the following months the main problems facing the government were the economy and the future of the overseas provinces. Negotiations between Soares and the main guerrilla movements in the provinces began almost at once. It rapidly became clear that all the main parties in Portugal favored giving the provinces independence as quickly as possible. This reduced Spínola's hopes of a Lusitanian federation, but he still insisted that independence should only be given to the provinces after a referendum.

There were, however, serious problems in handing over the provinces to the independence movements. Only PAIGC could claim to have had any sort of mandate, as it had held elections in Guinea-Bissau; the other movements were largely run by self-appointed expatriates, and the Portuguese government itself had been appointed by the junta rather than elected by the people. But negotiations over Guinea-Bissau presented the further problem that PAIGC demanded the Cape Verde Islands, 300 miles from the African mainland; the population of the islands appeared in general to be hostile to association with Guinea-Bissau, and in addition the islands were of strategic importance to NATO. The situation in Angola was complicated by the mutual hostility of the three main independence movements, which appeared to be even greater than their hostility to the continuance of Portuguese rule. Despite all the difficulties, however, it became clear that as a result of Soares' diplomacy, the Portuguese government's determination to grant independence to Guinea-Bissau in 1974 and to Mozambique and perhaps Angola in 1975 would not allow any interruption. This was one of the underlying causes that led to Spínola's resignation after only six months.

The changes made in April and May, 1974, had enormous importance for Portugal and her overseas territories, but the real significance of the coup was the effect that it had on other countries and in particular on the future of white rule in South Africa and Rhodesia. Since the imposition of sanctions against the illegal Rhodesian National Front government by the United Nations, the Rhodesian economy had largely been dependent on Portugal's goodwill. Essential imports came through Mozambique, and exports were sent through the ports of Beira and Lourenço Marques with false documents claiming that they came from Mozambique rather than Rhodesia. The provisional government and FRELIMO made clear that they were going to observe the United Nations sanctions. The danger to Rhodesia was not merely economic: with FRELIMO in control of Mozambique, guerrillas would be able to operate along the whole distance of the border between Rhodesia and Mozambique. As a result the pressure on the Smith government to reach a settlement with the Rhodesian African National Congress (ANC) was much increased. At the same time the ANC's attitude hardened; settlement terms that had been agreed between Prime Minister Ian Smith and Bishop Abel Muzorewa, the ANC president, were rejected by the Congress.

For South Africa the prospects were less serious, but the threat of a militant black government was a blow to Prime Minister Vorster's policy of surrounding the country with friendly client states south of the Zambesi. Quite apart from the danger that guerrillas might cross the South African border from Mozambique, there was also a labor problem. The South African economy depended to an extent on the 100,000 black workers who came each year from Mozambique, and FRELIMO threatened to withdraw them, thus exacerbating South Africa's shortage of labor. The threat to South Africa's policies helped further to emphasize the polarization of opinion that had already shown itself in the 1974 South African general election, which had been disastrous for the main opposition United Party.

The effects of the Portuguese revolution were felt widely outside southern Africa. For example, General Franco's government in Spain, so similar in attitude to Salazar's, also found itself under pressure to make liberal and democratic reforms. Unwilling to make any concessions, the government reacted harshly by violent attacks on peaceful student demonstrations, by tightening the country's already draconian press censorship, and—an ominous gesture in view of Portugal's recent experience —by dismissing the Chief of Staff, because of his

moderate views. Even in far distant Hong Kong the repercussions of the Portuguese events would be felt if the Portuguese government, in its determination to get rid of all traces of colonialism, handed Macao back to China.

On the face of it a military coup in Western Europe's most backward and underdeveloped country had little significance, yet in reality the events of April 25 were of great importance. Portugal—Europe's first and last great colonial power—had finally recognized the need to abandon the heady dreams and more sordid realities of empire and to turn, as the other former colonial powers had already done, to a European future. The balance of power in southern Africa, the last bastion of white supremacy in the "Dark Continent," was shifted; and—as was to happen shortly after in Greece—an old-fashioned police state had been toppled by the armed forces in the name of democracy and civil rights.

ADRIAN BRINK

The Watergate Affair

In August, 1974, after a two-year-long struggle with Congress and the courts, Richard Milhous Nixon finally admitted defeat and resigned the presidency of the United States. What had begun as a "third-rate burglary attempt" at the Watergate offices of the Democratic Party had escalated into a constitutional crisis unequaled since the Civil War. The separation of powers, presidential ability to override the law, the political influence of big business, campaign funding and the power of the CIA were all brought into question. While the world looked on, the United States drifted policyless as judges, politicians and journalists sought to restore confidence in the American system of government.

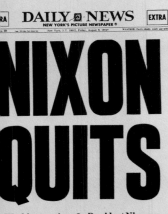

DAILY NEWS
NEW YORK'S PICTURE NEWSPAPER

NIXON QUITS

Washington, Aug. 8—President Nixon announced his resignation tonight in a TV address to the nation. Vice President Gerald R. Ford will become 38th President tomorrow.

Special 8-Page Pullout; Stories Start on Page 2

New York's *Daily News* announcing President Nixon's resignation.

Opposite above President Nixon speaking to the nation. Reading from a prepared script Nixon admitted that he lied about his knowledge of Watergate and asked for mercy—to be allowed to continue his term of office. But within days of his speech the President was to resign.

Opposite below Richard Nixon, confetti falling around him, giving the "V" for victory in Philadelphia, after his narrow victory in the national election (November, 1968).

On Thursday evening, August 8, 1974, Richard Milhous Nixon, thirty-seventh President of the United States, announced his resignation from office. On the following day, President Nixon's one-sentence letter of resignation was delivered to the Secretary of State, thus legally terminating his five-and-one-half years as occupant of what is often described as the world's most powerful office.

The announcement came in the form of a sixteen-minute television address to the nation that climaxed a chaotic week in which the world witnessed the presidency slide away from the sixty-one-year-old Republican leader.

The resignation of the President—the first in the history of the Republic—came a little more than two years after a group of five men, including the security coordinator for the Committee for the Reelection of the President (CRP), was arrested at 2:00 A.M., June 17, 1972, in the act of breaking into and installing wiretaps in the offices of the Democratic National Committee in the Watergate office-apartment complex in Washington, D.C. During the subsequent two years the so-called Watergate Affair—the conspiracy, break-in, and obstruction of justice or cover-up—was to mushroom into the most far-flung and sordid political scandal in American history. In the end it was to bring President Nixon disgrace and resignation.

At the time of the President's resignation a total of seventeen of the top men who worked for Mr. Nixon had faced criminal charges growing out of the Watergate cover-up or other scandals. Among these were four Nixon cabinet members, the President's chief of staff, and his chief domestic adviser. In addition, two dozen lower-level figures, several of them on the White House staff, had been convicted or were awaiting trial. Also, three grand juries and the office of a Special Prosecutor were still investigating Watergate-related crimes as well as other scandals, including criminal fraud in the preparation of the President's income-tax returns;

bribery involving a former Secretary of the Treasury; illegal wiretaps; illegal solicitation and receipt of campaign funds from corporations and business executives; use of government agencies for political purposes; expenditure of public money on the President's private estates at Key Biscayne, Florida, and San Clemente, California; the sale of ambassadorships in return for campaign contributions; and allegations of shady dealings by the President's close friend and adviser, banker Charles G. "Bebe" Rebozo.

This catalog of crimes and wrongdoings did not begin with the attempted burglary of the Democratic Party headquarters, but were it not for the bungled Watergate break-in and its unsuccessful cover-up, most or all of the crimes might have gone undetected and unpunished.

The seeds of the President's downfall obviously lay in the nature of the man, but this had best be left to psychohistorians. The hard facts of Watergate's genesis can be traced to the night of September 3, 1971, when a team of burglars led by E. Howard Hunt, former employee of the Central Intelligence Agency (CIA), broke into the office of the psychiatrist who had treated Dr. Daniel Ellsberg. Ellsberg had acknowledged turning over the classified documents known as the Pentagon Papers to newspapers. Hunt, then on the payroll of the White House, was part of a group called the "plumbers," because their job was to stop security leaks. Another covert and illegal unit was headed by Donald H. Segretti, who had organized a campaign of espionage and "dirty tricks" to upset the Democrats in the 1972 election.

The pre-dawn Watergate break-in appeared at first to have been a routine burglary but with some admittedly bizarre twists; indeed, for a while the burglary was referred to as the "Watergate Caper," stressing the frivolousness of the enterprise. Two days after the break-in the White House Press Secretary, Ronald L. Ziegler, dismissed it as "a third-rate burglary attempt." However, even while

The Senate Investigating Committee, set up in the wake of Watergate to discover if there had been any breaches of electoral law and if amendments were necessary.

Top Senators Howard Baker (left) and Sam J. Ervin (center) and Majority Counsel Samuel Dash (right) of the Senate Committee.

of the Watergate burglars. On that same day, Haldeman with the President's chief domestic aide, John D. Ehrlichman, met with CIA Director Richard Helms and Deputy Director Vernon Walters. By shutting off the FBI probe the President hoped to conceal White House and CRP involvement in the break-in. The actions of the first week, particularly Mr. Nixon's June 23 meeting with Haldeman, set the White House pattern for dealing with Watergate. The overall strategy called for containment and concealment. Moreover, the power and mystique of the presidency would be used to counter periodic public outcries.

The case of the five burglars did not go to trial until the following January. However, in the intervening months the country was involved in a presidential election campaign, and questions were increasingly raised about the break-in. The President felt compelled on several occasions in 1972 to state that no one in the Administration was involved in the Watergate Affair. Though the charges against the Administration persisted, President Nixon was reelected by the largest landslide in history in the November election. For a while it appeared that Watergate would not become a great national issue.

This muting of the scandal was short-lived, however, as events in the late winter and spring of 1973 took shape. That the Watergate cover-up began to come apart early in 1973 was due largely to the unrelenting probing of a few journalists, the tough and astute tactics of Federal District Court Judge John J. Sirica, and the decision by a few of the conspirators to reveal what they knew.

The trial of the Watergate defendants opened on January 8, 1973, before Judge Sirica. In addition to the five men arrested in the break-in, two others were indicted as co-conspirators: Howard Hunt and G. Gordon Liddy, former counsel to CRP. Five of the defendants pleaded guilty to all charges. Sirica, who had stated that he was not satisfied that all the facts in the case were revealed, provisionally set sentences of up to forty-five years. Later, the Cubans petitioned to change their pleas to innocent, claiming they had been duped into guilty pleas. Liddy and McCord refused guilty pleas and were convicted of conspiracy, burglary and wiretapping. Liddy was sentenced to a maximum of twenty years. McCord's sentencing was postponed after he told Judge Sirica that perjury was committed in the trial, that the defendants were under pressure to remain silent to protect people higher up who were involved and that McCord had been offered executive clemency in exchange for silence.

The Watergate case was now a major scandal. The White House policy of containment and cover-up was becoming unglued. In February, 1973, the United States Senate, spurred on by new reports of campaign irregularities and espionage, established a Select Investigating Committee of seven Senators to be headed by Senator Sam J. Ervin Jr.; their deliberations began in May.

In the meantime, Federal prosecutors were busy listening to the testimony of three persons who had

these words were being uttered, the cover-up was in progress in the White House offices and in the office of CRP. There was a rush to destroy incriminating evidence, to obstruct the investigation and to pay the Watergate burglars to keep them from revealing their ultimate connection with the highest officials in the White House. For the President and his staff, Watergate represented the potential exposure of the crimes of the Nixon Administration, "the White House horrors," as John N. Mitchell, former Attorney General and later director of CRP, would call them.

After first giving false names, the five arrested men identified themselves as James W. McCord Jr., a retired official of the CIA, and four Cuban-Americans. The arresting police officers, who had been alerted by a private security guard, confiscated wiretapping equipment and thirty-two sequentially numbered $100 bills.

Within hours of the arrests the Federal Bureau of Investigation (FBI) entered the case. Six days later, on June 23, the President took a definite and what was to prove to be a crucial step when he ordered his chief of staff, H. R. Haldeman, to have the CIA block the FBI investigation into the financing passed beyond the control of Mr. Nixon. They were John W. Dean III, counsel to the President; Jeb Stuart Magruder of CRP; and James McCord. Dean, on March 21, had warned the President that there was "a cancer on your presidency."

On April 15, prosecutors told the President that Haldeman, Ehrlichman, Dean and other White House officials were implicated in the cover-up. Two days later the President announced on national television that he had received new information on March 21, that there had been an effort to conceal from him the facts of the Watergate case, and that as a result he had launched an investigation of his own. He denied any personal knowledge of the cover-up, accepted responsibility for Watergate but maintained his innocence in the case. He also announced that he had authorized the setting up of a Special Prosecutor's office independent of the Justice Department. This office was set up on May 18 with the appointment of Harvard law professor Archibald Cox as Special Prosecutor.

Thirteen days later, on April 30, the President again went on national television, this time to announce that he regretfully accepted the resignations of Haldeman and Ehrlichman. He also announced the dismissal of John Dean, and pledged "no whitewash at the White House."

Throughout the late spring and summer of 1973 the Senate Watergate Committee and the Special Prosecutor collected massive amounts of evidence. Faced with a flood of new and embarrassing disclosures, Nixon said that he had restricted certain aspects of the investigation because of "national security."

For five days, June 25–29, 1973, the Senate Committee and the nation heard the nationally televised testimony of John Dean, who emerged as the President's chief accuser. Dean stated that Nixon knew about the cover-up as early as September 15, 1972, not March 21, 1973, as the President maintained. Dean's charges were still a matter of his word against the President's and his supporters', Haldeman, Ehrlichman and Mitchell.

In the meantime, a truly devastating blow to the cause of the President came on July 16 when Alexander P. Butterfield, a former White House aide, revealed to the Ervin Committee that an automatic recording system had been taping most of the President's office conversations and telephone calls, "for historic purposes."

This revelation spurred moves by both the Committee and the Special Prosecutor for access to the tapes that could show what Mr. Nixon knew and when he knew it. The President declined the requests for the tapes on the grounds that compliance would violate the principle of executive privilege and the doctrine of separation of powers. The rejection brought subpoenas from Cox's grand jury and the Ervin Committee for nine tapes of the President's conversations. It was the first subpoena served on a president in 166 years. On October 12, the same day that Nixon nominated Gerald R. Ford to succeed to the vice-presidency vacated by Spiro

Transcripts of Nixon's tapes. Nixon's decision to tape his office and telephone conversations played a vital role in forcing his resignation.

Agnew, the U.S. Court of Appeals ruled that Nixon must honor the Cox subpoena on the tapes. Instead of taking his appeal to the Supreme Court, the President offered a compromise plan for making the tapes available in summary form. Cox rejected the plan. What followed became known as the "Saturday Night Massacre." Nixon first ordered Attorney General Elliot Richardson to fire Cox; instead Richardson declined and resigned. Then his former deputy, William Ruckelshaus, was ordered to fire Cox. Ruckelshaus too declined and was discharged, leaving a new Acting Attorney General, Robert H. Bork, to dismiss Cox. Three days later, in the wake of a thunderous public outcry and with many public officials calling for the President's impeachment or resignation, Nixon changed his policy on the tapes and offered them in their entirety to Judge Sirica's court; he also promised to appoint a new Special Prosecutor.

In the mind of the public, the firing of Cox demonstrated two things: first, that the President had violated the promise made on April 17 that the Special Prosecutor would be independent, and second, the President appeared to act as if he was above the law. The result of the removal of Cox was that the President was put on the defensive.

On November 1, 1973, the new Special Prosecutor, Leon Jaworski, a former President of the American Bar Association, set to work and soon was eliciting guilty pleas and producing indictments.

The President, whose tactics had failed repeatedly, was to commence a new one in mid-November, 1973. It was dubbed Operation Candor. As it turned out, it amounted to a series of meetings ("stroking sessions") with Republican Congressmen in which Mr. Nixon promised full disclosure of the facts of Watergate. The new tactic, it was hoped, would forestall possible defections in the House of Representatives, where the Judiciary Committee under Congressman Peter J. Rodino was examining the possibility of impeachment proceedings. When the candor was forthcoming it was not to be about Watergate. Before a group of editors meeting in Florida, the President was to reveal that he paid only "nominal" income tax in 1970 and 1971, but that he had not been enriched by public office.

Opposite below John Wesley Dean III with his wife Maureen. Having played a major role in the White House cover-up of Watergate, Dean later gave crucial damaging testimony about Nixon's involvement in it.

1969

May 9 *New York Times* reveals that Administration is secretly bombing Cambodia. White House demands wiretaps on officials and newsmen.

1970

April 30 U.S. invades Cambodia. Many Americans demonstrate in protest.
July 23 Nixon approves "Domestic intelligence plan" despite its self-admitted illegalities.
July 28 Plan withdrawn on opposition of FBI Director J. Edgar Hoover.

1971

March 22 Dairy lobby gives $10,000 to Republican committees.
March 23 Dairy lobby leaders invited to meet Nixon at White House.
March 24 Another dairy lobby pays $25,000 to Republicans.
March 25 Administration reverses milk policy and increases milk price supports.
June 13 *New York Times* begins to publish Pentagon Papers.
June 13-20 Nixon sets up "plumbers."
July 31 Settlement of antitrust suit against ITT announced.
September 3 "Plumbers" burgle office of Ellsberg's psychiatrist.

1972

January 27, February 4, March 30 John Mitchell hears G. Gordon Liddy's plans for campaign surveillance, including bugging Democrat headquarters.
June 17 Break-in and arrests at Watergate.
June 20 Ronald L. Ziegler, Nixon's press secretary, dismisses break-in as "a third-rate burglary attempt."
July 1 Mitchell resigns as campaign manager.
August 29 Nixon says: "I can state categorically that his [John Dean's] investigation indicates that no one on the White House staff, no one in this Administration, presently employed, was involved in this very bizarre incident."
September 15 Liddy, Hunt, McCord and four Cubans indicted for break-in; Nixon sees John Dean for first time over Watergate.
November 7 Nixon reelected with 61% of votes cast.

1973

January 8 Trial of Watergate Seven begins. All but Liddy and McCord subsequently plead guilty.
January 30 Liddy and McCord convicted.
February 2 Judge Sirica says he is "not satisfied" whole truth was told at trial.
February 28 Dean talks to Nixon about way in which to handle Senate Watergate Committee.
March 15 McCord writes to Sirica that perjury was committed at the trial and suggests his own life could now be in danger.
March 21 Nixon and Dean discuss hush money and executive clemency for the burglars.
March 28-April 15 John Dean and Jeb Magruder begin to negotiate with prosecutors.
April 17 Nixon announces "major new developments": Ziegler says all previous Watergate statements are "inoperative."
April 27 Prosecution reveals at Ellsberg trial that "plumbers" burgled his psychiatrist's office.
April 30 Haldeman, Ehrlichman, Kleindienst resign, Dean is dismissed; Nixon promises "no whitewash at the White House."
May 11 Ellsberg case dismissed.

Watergate Chronology

May 17 Senate Watergate hearings begin.
May 18 Archibald Cox appointed Special Watergate Prosecutor.
May 22 Nixon admits 1969 buggings and 1970 surveillance plan and creation of "plumbers"; justifies all in terms of "national security."
June 25 John Dean begins his crucial damaging testimony before Senate Watergate Committee about Nixon's involvement in Watergate cover-up.
July 10 John Mitchell begins his testimony.
July 16 Alexander Butterfield reveals existence of Nixon's secret taping system.
July 17 Senate Committee asks Nixon for access to the tapes.
July 23 Nixon rejects request. Special Prosecutor Cox announces he will subpoena them.
July 24 Ehrlichman begins testimony.
July 26 White House says Nixon will abide by a "definitive" ruling on the tapes by the Supreme Court.
July 30 Haldeman begins testimony.
August 6 *Wall Street Journal* reports Vice-President Agnew is being investigated on suspicion of corruption in Baltimore, Md.
August 29 Sirica orders Nixon to hand him tapes to decide whether they should be given to Grand Jury. Nixon refuses.
October 10 Spiro Agnew resigns the vice-presidency.
October 12 Appeals Court upholds Sirica.
October 19 Nixon says he will not comply but will allow Senator Stennis to listen to tapes and will give prosecutors a transcript.
October 20 Prosecutor Cox refuses offer. Nixon orders his dismissal. Attorney General Richardson resigns and Deputy Attorney General Ruckelshaus is fired as both refuse to dismiss Cox.
October 23 White House, faced with public uproar, agrees to turn over tapes after all.
October 24 Peter Rodino, Chairman of House Judiciary Committee, says Committee will proceed "full steam ahead" with investigating impeachment.
October 31 White House says two of nine tapes subpoenaed do not exist.
November 5 Leon Jaworski sworn in as new Watergate Special Prosecutor.
November 21 White House announces $18\frac{1}{4}$ minute hum obscures crucial portion of June 20, 1972, tape.
December 6 Gerald Ford sworn in to succeed Agnew as Vice-President.
December 8 Nixon publishes tax returns 1969–73; asks Congress to audit them.
December 21 Sirica gives Jaworski Watergate-related tapes and documents.

1974

January 2 IRS announces it will reexamine Nixon's tax returns.
January 15 Tape experts report $18\frac{1}{4}$ minute gap in June 20, 1972, tape was result of 5 erasures.
January 30 Nixon says he has "no intention whatsoever" of resigning. Says he has given prosecutors everything requested.
February 1 Ziegler says he will answer no more Watergate questions unless he or Nixon's

lawyers think it necessary.
February 3 Prosecutor Jaworski denies Nixon has handed over all requested evidence.
February 25 Nixon—"I do not expect to be impeached."
February 28 Trial of John Mitchell and Maurice Stans on charges of obstruction of justice, conspiracy and perjury begins in New York.
March 1 Watergate Grand Jury indicts Nixon aides Mitchell, Haldeman, Ehrlichman, Colson, Mardian, Strachan and Parkinson on Watergate break-in charges. Grand Jury give Sirica secret report naming Nixon as "unindicted co-conspirator."
March 6 President decides to give Impeachment Committee all material given prosecutor.
March 7 Grand Jury indicts Ehrlichman, Colson, Liddy, Bernard Barker, Eugenio Martinez, Felipe de Diego on Ellsberg break-in.
March 11 Judiciary Committee requests another 42 tapes.
March 25 Grand Jury's secret report on Nixon given to Judiciary Committee.
April 4 Judiciary Committee agrees to give Nixon until April 9 to meet Committee's request for 42 tapes.
April 11 Committee votes 33–3 to subpoena tapes.
April 18 Jaworski subpoenas another 64 tapes.
April 28 Mitchell and Stans acquitted.
April 29 Nixon announces he will publish selected, edited tape transcripts and hand them to Committee.
May 1 Nixon refuses Sirica's request for more tapes.
May 3 Vice-President Ford "a little disappointed" by transcripts.
May 24 Jaworski appeals to Supreme Court for ruling on 64 subpoenaed tapes.
May 30 House Judiciary Committee warns Nixon that his refusal to supply the tapes might "constitute grounds for impeachment."
June 7 Former Attorney General Richard Kleindienst receives a one-month suspended sentence for his part in the ITT affair.
June 10 Nixon leaves for Middle East and then Moscow on trips which some regard as diversionary.
July 8 U.S. Supreme Court hears arguments from Special Prosecutor Leon Jaworski and Nixon counsel James St. Clair on tapes.
July 11 Judiciary Committee releases 8,000 pages of impeachment evidence against Nixon.
July 12 U.S. District Court finds Ehrlichman guilty of perjury and conspiracy on Ellsberg break-in.
July 16 Nixon tells supporter Rabbi Baruch Korff that Watergate will be remembered as "the broadest but thinnest scandal in American history."
July 22 The Supreme Court rules 8–0 that Nixon must turn over the 64 tapes requested by Jaworski. After hesitation, Nixon agrees to comply.
July 27-30 The House Judiciary Committee votes three articles of impeachment charging Nixon with obstruction of justice, abuse of presidential power and contempt of Congress.
July 31 Ehrlichman sentenced to 20 months to 5 years for his part in Ellsberg break-in.
August 2 Dean sentenced to 1–4 years prison for his role in the Watergate cover-up.
August 5 Nixon releases transcripts of 3 conversations with Haldeman in June, 1973: they show that he approved the cover-up. Impeachment demands from Congress intensify.
August 8 Nixon resigns presidency.
August 9 Gerald Ford sworn in as President.
September 8 President Ford grants Nixon a "full, free and absolute pardon" for all crimes he may have committed in office.

In January, 1974, a year and a half after the Watergate burglars were apprehended, the President still had plenty of fight left, and briefly he went on the offensive. The theme in the White House was "One year of Watergate is enough." Meanwhile, the Rodino Committee seemed to be bogged down in procedural and partisan squabbling. The President and his supporters were counting on an eventual acceptance by the public that the President could bring peace abroad and prosperity at home if only the Watergate issue was somehow gotten rid of ("Let others wallow in Watergate" and "Dragging out Watergate drags down America," the President said). Nixon's strategy called for handling the President's case as a purely political matter. Members of the House were importuned to ignore evidence of the President's wrongdoings and to consider rather that the best interests of the nation lay in giving greater weight to his acknowledged record in foreign affairs. This, the last strategy for polarizing and distracting the Judiciary Committee, failed almost totally.

Events were inexorably entering a final though protracted stage. For some months, the Judiciary Committee and the Special Prosecutor had been issuing subpoenas to no avail for a number of the tapes of the President's conversations. Finally, in one grand gesture, on April 29, 1974, the President decided to satisfy the Committee by publishing a thick book containing 1,254 edited pages of some of the subpoenaed conversations, with the President proclaiming on television: "These actions will, at last, once and for all, show that what I knew and what I did with regard to the Watergate break-in and cover-up were just as I described them to you from the beginning."

But the transcripts backfired devastatingly. There was disgust and disapproval from supporters and detractors alike, for, despite being heavily censored, in language and outlook, the President's private conversations were replete with evidence of what the Senate Republican minority leader, Hugh Scott, called "deplorable, disgusting, shabby and immoral performances." Moreover, these "sanitized" transcripts, which were seriously at variance with the original tapes, still seemed to uphold at least two of John Dean's most serious allegations: that the President knew about some aspects of the cover-up before March 21, 1973, and that the hush money for Howard Hunt seemed to have been approved by the President.

With the release of these transcripts the President's base began to erode alarmingly. There was an avalanche of calls for resignation.

The Judiciary Committee, which had successfully withstood charges that its progress was too slow and too partisan, was in fact building an overwhelming case against the President. Beginning on May 9, and continuing for two months, the Committee inquired into the President's conduct in office. In all, some nineteen volumes of evidence were compiled.

During that period several aides of the President either pleaded guilty or were convicted of Watergate-related offenses or crimes. They were Richard G. Kleindienst, former Attorney General; Charles W. Colson, former Special Counsel; and Ehrlichman.

Special Prosecutor Jaworski meanwhile went to court to gain possession of the sixty-four unedited tapes he required for the prosecution of cases involving principally Mitchell, Ehrlichman and Haldeman. The President had rejected Jaworski's subpoena on the grounds of executive privilege. (While the case was on appeal, the country learned that the nineteen-man grand jury had named President Nixon an unindicted co-conspirator in the cover-up. The jurors were instructed by Jaworski to let the matter of the President's guilt or innocence rest with the Congress.)

The Jaworski appeal for tapes reached the Supreme Court, and on July 24 it ruled in an eight to nil decision that the President's claim of absolute executive privilege did not apply in this case, and it ordered that the tapes be turned over to Judge Sirica. The scene was set for the final judgment as to the President's guilt or innocence.

The Judiciary Committee on July 27 voted twenty-seven to eleven to recommend impeachment for obstruction of justice. Two more articles—abuse of power and failure to obey lawful subpoenas—were passed during the next three days. Among the "ayes" were seven Republicans and three Southern Democrats. Impeachment was not only possible but probable. The solemnity and fairness with which the House Judiciary Committee conducted itself impressed a large majority of the American people; even some Nixon supporters admitted that the proceedings were conducted with dignity and equitableness.

The principal evidentiary materials, the tapes, were now to provide the biggest bombshell of the entire two years of Watergate. On August 5, the President, with the knowledge that the tapes could not be kept from Congress for long, released three conversations he had with Haldeman on June 23, 1972, which contained incontrovertible proof of the President's complicity in the cover-up six days after the Watergate break-in. With this final revelation virtually all support for the President vanished overnight.

Faced with what was now absolute certainty of impeachment by the House and conviction by the Senate, the President, on August 8, 1974, went before a national television audience of some 130 million and said: "I would say only that if some of my decisions were wrong—and some were wrong—they were made in what I believed to be the best interests of the nation." The following day, with Mr. Nixon airborne en route to his California home, Gerald R. Ford was sworn in as the thirty-eighth President of the United States. One month later, the new President issued a blanket pardon for any acts committed by his predecessor while in office. The decision was greeted by instant and intense public outrage, evidence that the Watergate Affair was not yet over.   HERBERT A. GILBERT

Signpost to the Watergate building, Washington, where the Democratic Campaign Committee had their offices.

Gerald Ford, Richard Nixon's successor to the presidency. President Ford's pardon of Nixon met with widespread opposition. Congress expressed its disapproval by cutting the former President's removal and other expenses by two-thirds.

Georges Clemenceau 1841–1929
French statesman

Douglas Haig 1861–1928
British soldier

Frank Lloyd Wright 1869–1959
U.S. architect

Alb
Germ

Paul von Hindenburg 1847–1934
German general, statesman

Franz Ferdinand 1863–1914
Archduke of Austria

Rosa Luxemburg 1870–1919
German socialist

Fra
Gern

Paul Gauguin 1848–1903
French painter

Gabriele d'Annunzio 1863–1938
Italian writer and soldier

Nikolai Lenin (V.I. Ulyanov) 1870–1924
Russian revolutionary leader

Ivan Pavlov 1849–1936
Russian physiologist

Edvard Munch 1863–1944
Norwegian painter

Marcel Proust 1871–1922
French writer

Horatio Herbert Kitchener 1850–1916
British soldier

David Lloyd George 1863–1945
British statesman

Ernest Rutherford 1871–1937
British physicist

Henry Cabot Lodge 1850–1924
U.S. statesman

Henry Ford 1863–1947
U.S. industrialist

Orville Wright 1871–1948
U.S. aircraft inventor

Ferdinand Foch 1851–1929
French general

Erich Ludendorff 1865–1937
German general

Grigori Rasputin 1872–1916
Russian monk

Joseph Joffre 1852–1931
French general

Jean Sibelius 1865–1957
Finnish composer

Roald Amundsen 1872–1928
Norwegian polar explorer

Vincent van Gogh 1853–90
Dutch painter

Sun Yat-sen 1866–1925
Chinese statesman

Bertrand Russell 1872–1970
English philosopher, mathematician

James Keir Hardie 1856–1915
British socialist statesman

J. Ramsay MacDonald 1866–1937
British statesman

Guglielmo Marconi 1874–1937
Italian inventor

Theobald von Bethmann-Hollweg 1856–1921
German statesman

Wilbur Wright 1867–1912
U.S. aircraft inventor

Arnold Schoenberg 1874–1951
Austrian composer

Woodrow Wilson 1856–1924
U.S. President

Marie Curie 1867–1934
French physical chemist

Chaim Weizmann 1874–1952
Russian-British Zionist leader

Hussein ibn Ali 1856–1931
Grand Sharif of Mecca

Stanley Baldwin 1867–1947
British statesman

Herbert Clark Hoover 1874–1964
U.S. president

Sigmund Freud 1856–1939
Austrian psychoanalyst

Robert Falcon Scott 1868–1912
British Antarctic explorer

Winston Churchill 1874–1965
British statesman

George Bernard Shaw 1856–1950
British writer

Nicholas II 1868–1918
Tsar of Russia

Carl Gustav Jung 1875–196
Swiss psychiatrist

Theodore Roosevelt 1858–1919
U.S. President

Maxim Gorky 1868–1936
Russian writer

Albert Schweitzer 1875–196
Alsatian philosopher, mission

Max Planck 1858–1947
German physicist

Neville Chamberlain 1869–1940
British statesman

Mohammed Ali Jinna
Pakistani statesman

Wilhelm II 1859–1941
German Kaiser

Victor Emmanuel III 1869–1947
King of Italy

Konrad Adenauer 187
German statesman

Raymond Poincaré 1860–1934
French statesman

Mohandas Gandhi 1869–1948
Indian leader

Leon Trotsky (L. D. Bronste
Russian revolutionary leade

Vittorio Emanuele Orlando 1860–1952
Italian statesman

Henri Matisse 1869–1954
French painter

Joseph Stalin (I. V. Dzhugash
Russian statesman

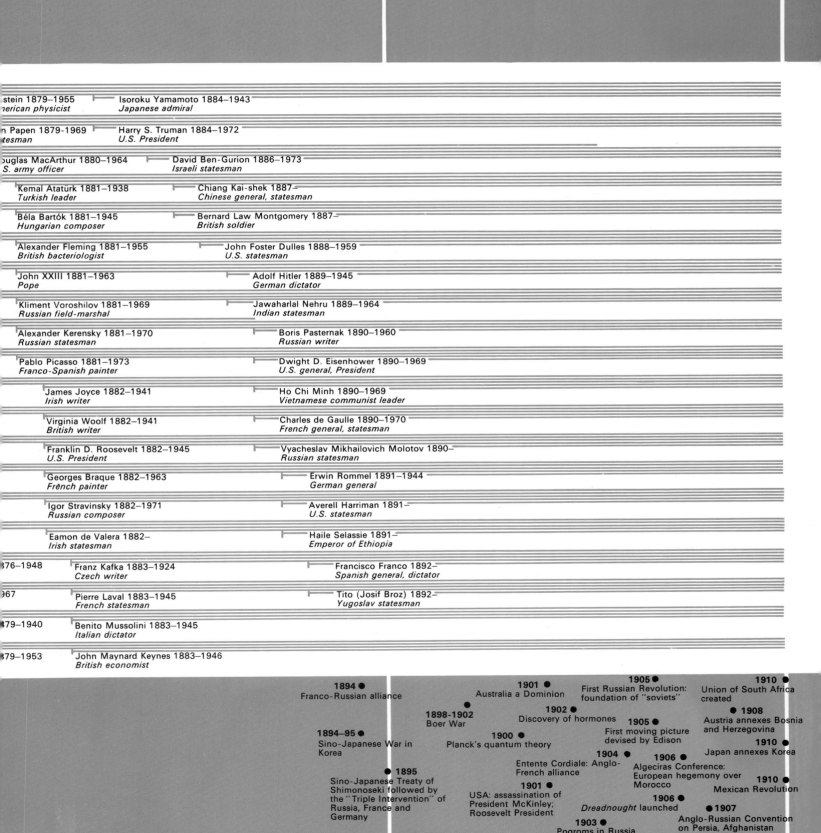

stein 1879–1955
merican physicist

Isoroku Yamamoto 1884–1943
Japanese admiral

n Papen 1879-1969
tesman

Harry S. Truman 1884–1972
U.S. President

uglas MacArthur 1880–1964
S. army officer

David Ben-Gurion 1886–1973
Israeli statesman

Kemal Atatürk 1881–1938
Turkish leader

Chiang Kai-shek 1887–
Chinese general, statesman

Béla Bartók 1881–1945
Hungarian composer

Bernard Law Montgomery 1887–
British soldier

Alexander Fleming 1881–1955
British bacteriologist

John Foster Dulles 1888–1959
U.S. statesman

John XXIII 1881–1963
Pope

Adolf Hitler 1889–1945
German dictator

Kliment Voroshilov 1881–1969
Russian field-marshal

Jawaharlal Nehru 1889–1964
Indian statesman

Alexander Kerensky 1881–1970
Russian statesman

Boris Pasternak 1890–1960
Russian writer

Pablo Picasso 1881–1973
Franco-Spanish painter

Dwight D. Eisenhower 1890–1969
U.S. general, President

James Joyce 1882–1941
Irish writer

Ho Chi Minh 1890–1969
Vietnamese communist leader

Virginia Woolf 1882–1941
British writer

Charles de Gaulle 1890–1970
French general, statesman

Franklin D. Roosevelt 1882–1945
U.S. President

Vyacheslav Mikhailovich Molotov 1890–
Russian statesman

Georges Braque 1882–1963
French painter

Erwin Rommel 1891–1944
German general

Igor Stravinsky 1882–1971
Russian composer

Averell Harriman 1891–
U.S. statesman

Eamon de Valera 1882–
Irish statesman

Haile Selassie 1891–
Emperor of Ethiopia

876–1948

Franz Kafka 1883–1924
Czech writer

Francisco Franco 1892–
Spanish general, dictator

967

Pierre Laval 1883–1945
French statesman

Tito (Josif Broz) 1892–
Yugoslav statesman

879–1940

Benito Mussolini 1883–1945
Italian dictator

879–1953

John Maynard Keynes 1883–1946
British economist

1894 ● Franco-Russian alliance

1894–95 ● Sino-Japanese War in Korea

● **1895** Sino-Japanese Treaty of Shimonoseki followed by the "Triple Intervention" of Russia, France and Germany

● **1896** Russo-Chinese defensive alliance; railway concession in Manchuria

1898-1902 ● Boer War

1901 ● Australia a Dominion

1900 ● Planck's quantum theory

1901 ● USA: assassination of President McKinley; Roosevelt President

1902 ● Discovery of hormones

1904 ● Entente Cordiale: Anglo-French alliance

1903 ● Pogroms in Russia

1904 ● Building of Panama Canal under US protection

1905 ● First Russian Revolution: foundation of "soviets"

1905 ● First moving picture devised by Edison

1906 ● Algeciras Conference: European hegemony over Morocco

1906 ● *Dreadnought* launched

● **1907** Anglo-Russian Convention on Persia, Afghanistan and Tibet; Anglo-French Entente expanded to Triple Entente (Britain, Russia, France)

1910 ● Union of South Africa created

● **1908** Austria annexes Bosnia and Herzegovina

1910 ● Japan annexes Korea

1910 ● Mexican Revolution

Hermann Göring 1893–1946
German Nazi leader

J. Robert Oppenheimer 1904–67
U.S. physicist

Jonas Edward Salk 1914–
U.S. physician

Mao Tse-tung 1893–
Chinese statesman

Dag Hammarskjöld 1905–61
U.N. Secretary-General

Moshe Dayan 1915–
Israeli general, statesman

Jomo Kenyatta 1893–
Kenyan statesman

Jean Paul Sartre 1905–
French writer, philosopher

Francis Crick 1916–
British scientist

Nikita Khrushchev 1894–1971
Russian statesman

Samuel Beckett 1906–
Irish-French writer

Harold Wilson 1916–
British statesman

Harold Macmillan 1894–
British statesman

Leonid I. Brezhnev 1906–
Russian statesman

John F. Kennedy 1917–63
U.S. President

Georgi Zhukov 1895–1974
Russian general

Frank Whittle 1907–
British aeronautical expert

Gamal Abdel Nasser 1918–70
Egyptian statesman

Juan Perón 1895–
Argentinian statesman

Joseph McCarthy 1908–1957
U.S. Senator

Pierre Trudeau 1919–
Canadian statesman

F. Scott Fitzgerald 1896–1940
U.S. writer

Lin Piao 1908–71
Chinese statesman

Alexander Dubček 1921–
Czech statesman

Imre Nagy 1896–1958
Hungarian statesman

Salvador Allende 1908–73
Chilean statesman

Henry Kissinger 1923–
U.S. statesman

Trygve Lie 1896–1968
U.N. Secretary-General

Lyndon B. Johnson 1908–73
U.S. President

Robert F. Kennedy 1925–68
U.S. statesman

Bertold Brecht 1898–1956
German writer

John K. Galbraith 1908–
U.S. economist

Fidel Castro 1927–
Cuban revolutionary leader

René Magritte 1898–1967
French painter

Kwame Nkrumah 1909–72
Ghanaian statesman

Ernesto "Che" Guevara 1928–67
Argentinian revolutionary

Chou En-lai 1898–
Chinese statesman

Dean Rusk 1909–
U.S. statesman

Martin Luther King, Jr 1929–6
U.S. civil rights leader

Henry Moore 1898–
British sculptor

Andrei Gromyko 1909–
Russian diplomat

Hus

Ernest Hemingway 1899–1961
U.S. writer

U. Thant 1909–
U.N. Secretary-General

Heinrich Himmler 1900–45
German Nazi leader

Georges Pompidou 1911–74
French statesman

Louis Mountbatten 1900–
British admiral

Jackson Pollock 1912–56
U.S. painter

Enrico Fermi 1901–54
Italian physicist

Willy Brandt 1913–
West German statesman

Hirohito 1901–
Emperor of Japan

Richard M. Nixon 1913–
U.S. President

Georgi Malenkov 1902–
Russian statesman

Benjamin Britten 1913–
British composer

1911● German gunboat at Agadir creates international tension

1911● *Lusitania* Revolution in China; imperial rule overthrown and republic proclaimed

Votes for women in 1918● Britain

1915● First U-boat (submarine) attacks: sinking of the

1916● Battle of Jutland; Gallipoli and Salonika campaigns

Battles of Passchendaele 1917● and Cambrai

1915● Battles of Neuve Chapelle, Ypres, Aubers Ridge, Loos

1914● League of Nations, World Court, International Labor Organization established

Battles of Tannenberg and Masurian Lakes: Germany defeats Russia

USA enters World War 1917●

1921● Russia: Kronstadt mutiny; ban on opposition in Party; New Economic Policy 1919●

Gandhi's civil disobedience campaign in India: troops fire on Indians at Amritsar

Ireland: South gets a ● 1922 republican constitution; Ulster remains British

1920● Votes for women in USA; prohibition of alcohol (until 1933)

1919● Trotsky asserts opposition to Stalin's "Communism in One Country": exiled 1929

1923-25● French troops occupy the Ruhr

General strike in Britain 1926●

1925● Sun Yat-sen dies; Chiang Kai-shek takes over Kuomintang leadership

1925● Locarno Pact guarantees Germany's western borders and allows her entry to League of Nations 1926●

First television transmission

Washington Naval 1927 Disarmament Conference

1925● Sino-Japanese War: Japan withdraws from League of Nations

1927● China: massacre of Nationalists by Communists by Nationalists in Shanghai begins civil war 1926●

1929● Lateran Treaty: papal recognition of Italy

●1928 A. Fleming discovers penicillin

1929● The Young Plan on German reparations

1930● The Allies withdraw troops from the Rhineland

1931● Financial crisis reaches climax in Europe

1935-36● Italy conquers Ethio League of Nations powerless

●1933 Hitler Chancellor of Germany; Germany lea Geneva Disarmament Conference and Leagu Nations 1935●

The Saar is restore Germany

●1934

1931● Nazi *putsch* in Au

1935● First practical ra equipment

1932● Geneva Disarmament Conference

●1934

1931● China: "Long Mar north of Commun guerrillas under M Tse-tung

1950 The Korean War

1953 Death of a Tyrant

1953 Conquest of Polio

1956 Crisis at the Canal

1956 The Hungarians' Revolt

1957 Earth's First Space Satellite

1964 "We Shall Overcome!"

1958 De Gaulle Returns to Power

1962 The Cuban Missile Crisis

1962 Pope John's Vatican Council

1967 Strife in Black Africa

1967 China's Cultural Revolution

1969 Man on the Moon

1971 Birth of Bangladesh

1973 America Leaves Vietnam

1973 Coup in Chile

1973 War in the Middle East

1974 A New Era for Portugal

1974 The Watergate Affair

935—
f Jordan

resley 1935—
ock and roll singer

1936 Coup by
military in Japan

1937
taly withdraws from
he League of Nations

1936
Rome-Berlin
Axis: military pact

1937
Sino-Japanese War: fall
of Peking, Shanghai and
Nanking

1936
German troops enter the
Rhineland

1936-39
The great purges in Russia

1941
Lend-Lease allows
Britain to buy war supplies
from US on credit

1939 Molotov-Ribbentrop pact
of non-aggression between
Russia and Germany

1941
Beginning of the
"Manhattan Project"
for atomic research

1938 Hitler effects Anschluss
(union) with Austria

1938 Munich Agreement —
Czech Sudetenland ceded
to Germany: height of
appeasement policy

1944 Bretton Woods Conference
(44 nations) sets up
International Monetary Fund

1949
North Atlantic Treaty
Organization established

1949
USSR demonstrates
possession of nuclear
weapons

1947
Independence for India
and Pakistan; 1948 —
for Burma and Ceylon

1955
Warsaw Pact for mutual
defense of East European
countries

1958
Cuban Revolution;
Castro Premier (1959)

1952
Hydrogen bomb developed

1957
Treaty of Rome establishes
European Economic
Community

Krushchev falls from 1964
power: Leonid Brezhnev
First Secretary, Alexei
Kosygin Prime Minister

1961
Berlin wall erected

Assassination of Martin 1968
Luther King, Jr., and of
Robert F. Kennedy

1965
US troops authorized to
engage in offensive
operations in Vietnam

1963
Assassination of John F.
Kennedy; Johnson
President

Hijacking becomes an 1969
international problem

Overthrow of Prince 1970
Sihanouk in Cambodia;
combined US-South
Vietnamese attacks on
Communist bases there

Officers rebellion in Libya 1969
topples King Idris;
Col. Gaddafi Premier

1970
Chancellor Brandt's
Ostpolitik, leading to
treaties with Soviet
Union, Poland and
East Germany

Jordan: Royal army 1970
defeats Palestine guerrillas

1973
EEC: Britain, Denmark
and Ireland admitted

1972
Rising violence in Ulster:
direct British rule
introduced

1971
China admitted to the
United Nations

1973
Arab-Israeli "Yom
Kippur" War

1972
President Nixon visits
Peking and Moscow

1973
Peace treaty in Vietnam:
US troops withdrawn

Acknowledgments

The authors and publishers wish to thank the following museums and collections by whose kind permission the illustrations are reproduced. Page numbers appear in bold, photographic sources in italics.

12 *Photo Research International*
13 *Camera Press*
14 (1) *Soldier Magazine*
(2) *Camera Press*
15 (1, 2) *Camera Press*
16 *Photo Research International*
17 *Camera Press*
18 *Photo Research International*
19 (1, 2) *Photo Research International*
20 (1) *Keystone Press Agency*
(2) *Popperfoto*
21 (1) *Popperfoto* (2) United States Information Service (3) *Associated Press*
22 The National Foundation—March of Dimes
23 The National Foundation—March of Dimes
24 *Diane Wyllie Filmstrip*
25 (1, 2) The National Foundation—March of Dimes
26 The National Foundation—March of Dimes
27 (1, 2) St. Bartholomew's Hospital, London: *Raymond Heath*
28 *Diane Wyllie Filmstrip*
29 *Diane Wyllie Filmstrip*
30 *EUPRA GmbH*
31 *Syndication International*
32 (1) *EUPRA GmbH* (2) *Popperfoto*
33 *Syndication International*
34 (1) *Radio Times Hulton Picture Library* (2) *Deutsche Presse-Agentur* (3) *Weidenfeld and Nicolson Archive*
35 *Pictorial Press*
36 (1) *Keystone Press Agency* (2) National Iranian Oil Company
37 (1) *Camera Press* (2) *Camera Press/V. Blye* (3) *Keystone Press Agency*
38 *Keystone Press Agency*
39 *Central Press Photos*
40 Imperial War Museum, London
41 *Keystone Press Agency*
42 (1, 2) *Keystone Press Agency*
43 *Keystone Press Agency*
44 *Radio Times Hulton Picture Library*
45 *Suddeutscher Verlag*

46 (1) *Keystone Press Agency* (2) *Radio Times Hulton Picture Library*
47 (1) *Radio Times Hulton Picture Library* (2) *Suddeutscher Verlag*
48 *Suddeutscher Verlag*
49 (1, 2) *Suddeutscher Verlag*
50 (1) *Radio Times Hulton Picture Library* (2) *Keystone Press Agency* (3) *David Low: Weidenfeld and Nicolson Archive*
51 (1) *Camera Press/B. Hamilton*
(2) *Camera Press*
52 *Novosti Press Agency*
53 *Novosti Press Agency*
54 (1) British Aircraft Corporation
(2) *Camera Press*
55 (1, 2) *Novosti Press Agency*
56 *Popperfoto*
57 (1) *Popperfoto* (2) *Novosti Press Agency*
58 (1) *Popperfoto*
(2) *Keystone Press Agency*
59 (1, 2, 3) *Keystone Press Agency*
60 *Camera Press*
61 *Camera Press*
62 (1) Imperial War Museum
(2) *Camera Press*
63 (1) *Keystone Press Agency*
(2) *Popperfoto* (3) *Camera Press*
64 (1) *Phoebus Picture Library*
(2) *Popperfoto*
65 (1) *Popperfoto* (2) *Keystone Press Agency*
66 (1) *Popperfoto* (2) *Camera Press* (3) *Keystone Press Agency*
67 (1) *Keystone Press Agency*
(2) *Associated Press* (3) *Camera Press/I. Berry*
68 United States Information Service
69 *Camera Press*
70 (1, 2) *Popperfoto* (3) *Transworld Feature Syndicate*
72 (1, 2) United States Information Service
73 (1) Department of Defense, Washington D.C. (2) *Novosti Press Agency*
74 *Keystone Press Agency*
75 *Keystone Press Agency*
76 (1) *Keystone Press Agency*
(2) *Popperfoto* (3, 4) *Keystone Press Agency*
77 (1, 2) *Keystone Press Agency*

(3) *Felici*
78 (1, 2) *Keystone Press Agency*
79 (1) *Felici* (2, 3) *Keystone Press Agency*
80 (1) *Associated Press* (2) *Keystone Press Agency* (3) *Camera Press*
81 (1) *Keystone Press Agency*
(2) *Camera Press* (3) *Associated Press*
82 *Transworld Feature Syndicate*
83 *Associated Press*
84 (1) *Transworld Feature Syndicate*
(2) *Popperfoto*
85 (1) *Camera Press* (2) *Transworld Feature Syndicate*
86 *Popperfoto*
87 (1) *Keystone Press Agency*
(2) *Camera Press*
88 (1) *Camera Press* (2) *Keystone Press Agency*
89 (1) *Fox Photos* (2) *Camera Press/C. Doyle*
90 *Popperfoto*
91 *Camera Press*
92 *Camera Press*
93 *Popperfoto*
94 (1, 2) *Transworld Feature Syndicate*
95 (1, 2, 3) *Camera Press*
96 *Camera Press*
97 *Camera Press*
98 *Camera Press/D. Robinson*
99 *Popperfoto*
100 *Associated Press*
101 (1, 2) *Keystone Press Agency*
102 (1) *Associated Press* (2) *Camera Press/D. Lomax*
103 (1, 2) *Camera Press/D. Lomax*
104 (1) *Weidenfeld and Nicolson Archive*
(2) *Popperfoto*
105 (1) *Popperfoto* (2) *Keystone Press Agency* (3) *Popperfoto*
106 United States Information Service
107 United States Information Service
109 (1) *Novosti Press Agency*
(2) United States Information Service
110 (1) *Newsweek* (2) *Popperfoto*
111 (1, 2, 3) United States Information Service
112 (1) British Broadcasting Corporation (2) *Camera Press*
113 (1, 2, 3) *Camera Press*
114 Government of Bangladesh
115 *Camera Press*
116 (1) Government of Bangladesh

(2) *Camera Press/P. Tweedy*
117 Government of Bangladesh
118 *Camera Press*
119 (1, 2) *Keystone Press Agency*
120 *Keystone Press Agency*
121 (1) *Camera Press* (2) *Associated Press* (3) *Keystone Press Agency*
122 *Transworld Feature Syndicate*
123 *Camera Press*
124 *Transworld Feature Syndicate*
125 (1, 2) *Camera Press*
126 (1, 2) *Photo Research International*
127 (1) *Keystone Press Agency*
(2) *Camera Press*
128 *Camera Press*
129 *Keystone Press Agency*
130 (1) *Camera Press* (2) *Camera Press/D. Goldberg*
131 (1) *Camera Press/D. Goldberg*
(2) *Camera Press/E. Manewal*
132 *Keystone Press Agency*
133 (1) *Camera Press* (2) *Camera Press/M. Piquemal*
134 *Popperfoto*
135 *Camera Press*
136 (1) *Camera Press* (2) *United Nations/T. Nagata*
137 (1) *Camera Press* (2) *Barnaby's Picture Library*
138 *Popperfoto*
139 (1) *Keystone Press Agency*
(2) *Camera Press/W. Braun*
140 (1) *Central Press Photos*
(2) *Associated Press*
141 (1) *Associated Press* (2) *Camera Press/M. Kaplan* (3) Gala Film Distributors
142 *Camera Press*
143 *Camera Press*
144 *Camera Press/M. Murias*
145 (1) *Camera Press/M. Murias*
(2) *Camera Press* (3) *Popperfoto*
146 (1, 2) *Camera Press*
147 (1, 2) *Camera Press*
148 *John Frost World Wide Newspaper Collectors' Club*
149 (1) *Camera Press* (2) *Popperfoto*
150 (1, 2) *Black Star/D. Brack*
(3) *Black Star/F. Ward*
151 *Camera Press/O. Atkins*
153 (1) *Black Star/D. Brack* (2) *Camera Press*

Managing Editor *Adrian Brink*
Assistant Editors *Geoffrey Chesler, Francesca Ronan*
Picture Editor *Julia Brown*
Consultant Designer *Tim Higgins*
Art Director *Anthony Cohen*

Index